MW00583410

CLINICAL PEARLS OF WISDOM

TORONTO
PUBLIC
LIBRARY
Sale of this book
supports literacy programs

A Norton Professional Book

●●●●●●●●

Clinical Pearls of Wisdom
21 Leading Therapists Offer Their Key Insights

Michael Kerman, editor

W. W. Norton & Co.

New York • London

Copyright © 2010 by Michael Kerman
"Reconstructing Life Out of Loss: Reorganizing the Continuing Bond" copyright ©
2010 by Robert A. Neimeyer
"Riding Up and Down The Worry Hill: Engaging Children in OCD Treatment" copyright
© 2010 by Aureen Wagner

All rights reserved
Printed in the United States of America
First Edition

For information about permission to reproduce selections from this book, write to
Permissions, W. W. Norton & Company, Inc., 500 Fifth Avenue, New York, NY 10110

For information about special discounts for bulk purchases, please contact W. W. Norton
Special Sales at specialsales@wwnorton.com or 800-233-4830

Manufacturing by Courier Westford
Book design by Paradigm Graphics
Production manager: Leeann Graham

Library of Congress Cataloging-in-Publication Data

Clinical pearls of wisdom : 21 leading therapists offer their key insights / Michael
Kerman, editor. -- 1st ed.
     p. cm.
"A Norton professional book."
Includes bibliographical references and index.
ISBN 978-0-393-70587-4 (pbk.)
1. Psychotherapy. 2. Clinical psychology. I. Kerman, Michael.
RC480.C556 2010
616.89'14--dc22
                              2009028478

ISBN: 978-0-393-70587-4 (pbk.)

W. W. Norton & Company, Inc., 500 Fifth Avenue, New York, N.Y. 10110
                    www.wwnorton.com
W. W. Norton & Company Ltd., Castle House, 75/76 Wells Street, London W1T 3QT

1 2 3 4 5 6 7 8 9 0

CONTENTS

●●●●●●●

INTRODUCTION

This book offers insights from some of today's most respected therapists about what really works in therapy. These therapists reveal their methods of helping people change their habitual patterns of behavior, thoughts, and emotions.

In the 21 chapters that follow, you will find the interventions they most trust, drawn from a diversity of approaches including:

- Attachment-focused therapy
- Mindfulness and contemplative practices
- Cognitive-behavioral therapies
- Mind-body therapies
- Relational therapies
- Brief therapies
- Eclectic therapies.

These chapters are a testimony to the rich range of perspectives influencing psychotherapists today. They are a powerful reminder that there can be no "one size fits all" approach to helping people.

As founder of Toronto's Leading Edge Seminars, I've had the privilege of presenting over 400 workshops by many of the leading therapists of our times, including many of the contributors to this book. It has been an incredible opportunity to witness these top therapists in action as they share the wisdom they have accumulated over many years.

On these pages, they share pearls of their clinical wisdom, based on their experiences as clinicians, authors, teachers, and workshop presenters. I asked each writer to choose the three insights or techniques that have had the greatest impact on their work with their clients and the clinicians they have trained. These pearls have been honed through observation and direct experience via clinical practice, research studies, "aha" moments, and feedback from colleagues, students, and workshop participants. They include specific guidelines, meaningful insights, imaginative questions, and creative interventions.

HOW THIS BOOK IS ORGANIZED

The book is divided into seven "theme" areas. The first six represent the most common presenting problems of those who seek help:

- Depression
- Trauma
- Anxiety
- Grief
- Couple-relationship issues
- Issues related to children and adolescents

The concluding chapter considers the therapist's attachment patterns and their relationship to the therapeutic process.

Each chapter includes a detailed explanation of the contributor's pearls and demonstrates the use of the pearls through a case example.

OUR CONTRIBUTORS

Though our contributors come from diverse backgrounds and theoretical orientations, they have several crucial attributes in common. Each of them displays ingenuity, inventiveness, and curiosity toward his or her work. They are adept at integrating what they have learned through their own practice with the best of current thinking and research.

Furthermore, regardless of clinical orientation, every one of these therapists possesses an excellent ability to connect with people. Both as lecturers and clinicians, they can stay present in the moment, listening without judgment or rushing for solutions.

Their amalgamation of presence, experience, knowledge, and technique is central to the art of psychotherapy.

THE ART AND TECHNIQUE OF PSYCHOTHERAPY

Confronted with enormous pressure to produce predictable and successful outcomes, and faced with a scarcity of resources, clinicians are sometimes seduced into seeking a universal treatment procedure or protocol. They long for the assurance that a precise set of techniques might offer.

But as the case examples in this book demonstrate, psychotherapy is not only a set of techniques but also an art. They imply that the most important factor contributing to therapeutic success is a quality that goes by many names: emotional intelligence, joining or empathy skills, attentiveness, unconditional positive regard, the therapeutic alliance, staying present, compassionate listening. Although the list is long, each of these descriptions points to the very basic human need for connection.

The ability to be spontaneous and yet still keep an overall focus on therapeutic goals, having the flexibility and the confidence to react in the moment to the current situation in the therapy setting—these are the hallmarks of a successful therapeutic alliance, regardless of how this is defined. However, the cultivation of a strong therapist-client relationship alone is not sufficient. Mutual alliance is therapeutically beneficial only when it is combined with effective techniques, approaches, or tools. The wide survey of pearls offered in this book, with all their differences, will enlarge your therapeutic repertoire and complement your existing knowledge base. These pearls will enhance your ability to plan for treatment and to improvise in the moment-to-moment contact with your client.

As your repertoire grows, so will your instinctive ability to perceive and understand your clients. With increasing subtlety, you will know when to comment or remain silent, offer direction or not, attend to subtle cues about a client's readiness to change, stay on track with planned interventions, or modify and change your plans.

THE ONLY THERAPIST YOU WILL EVER BE

Although you may achieve great success as a therapist with an allegiance to, or deep interest in, a particular therapeutic modality, ultimately you can be accurately identified only as a "[insert your name here] therapist." Your therapeutic approach will always have the flavor of you. It can never be replicated by anyone else except you. Your style, your temperament, your sense of humor, and your way of being present with others are the indispensable and unique elements of your therapeutic alliances.

I invite you to read these chapters in whatever order makes most sense to you. Balance what you learn from their many insights with ongoing curiosity about the "you" who performs this meaningful and interesting work. My hope is that the following chapters will inform and inspire you to continually evolve as a "[insert your name here] therapist" . . . the *only* therapist ever to work in the unique way you do.

ACKNOWLEDGMENTS

A book like this is collaborative by nature, made possible only by enlisting the interest and support of many people. I would like to thank the many contributors for their dedicated effort and supportive cooperation.

Thank you to Deborah Malmud, who initially conceived of the concept, and Kristen Holt-Browning, of Norton Professionals Books; to my colleague Dr. Rob Guerrette, who proposed my involvement in this project; to Vicki Fraser for her suggestions and perspectives on the field of psychotherapy; to Timothy Bentley for his sustaining friendship and his way with words; to Kim Koyama for his ongoing commitment to Leading Edge Seminars.

A note of profound gratitude to Angelo Szeto, my colleague at Leading Edge who devoted countless hours, as well as focus and dedication through every stage of this project. Finally, love and appreciation to wife Janet, Emily, daughter and occasional staff member, and son Max. Each inspires me and helps me to remember what's important.

Michael Kerman
Leading Edge Seminars
Toronto, Ontario

Section One:
Depression

Chapter 1
Modulation, Mindfulness, and Movement in the Treatment of Trauma-Related Depression

Pat Ogden, PhD

So many clients with depression in their history complain of feeling sad, disinterested in life, unable to enjoy themselves, and challenged by normal daily activities. Sustained by a debilitating cycle of interaction between body and mind, trauma-related depression often manifests as a perpetual physiological state of low arousal, which is characterized by a lack of motivation and movement. These symptoms of depression prove difficult to treat, and therapists and clients alike may feel discouraged, perplexed, or defeated when therapeutic interventions fail to achieve the desired results again and again. In a sensorimotor approach, the use of mindfulness and movement to modulate low arousal levels may help to uplift the spirit and assist clients in fully reengaging in life.

PEARLS

Pearl #1. Keep arousal in a window of tolerance.

The "window of tolerance" (Siegel, 1999) refers to a zone of autonomic and emotional arousal that is optimal for well-being and effective functioning. Falling between the extremes of hyper- and hypoarousal, this is a zone within which "various intensities of emotional and physiological arousal can be processed without disrupting the functioning of the system" (Siegel, 1999, p. 253). When arousal falls within this window, information received from both internal and external environments can be integrated (Figure 1.1).

Figure 1.1

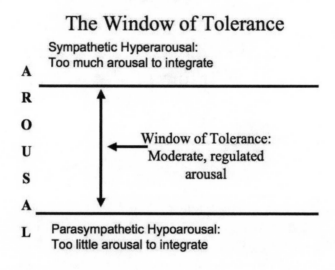

The Window of Tolerance

Sympathetic Hyperarousal:
Too much arousal to integrate

A

R

O

U   Window of Tolerance:
          Moderate, regulated
S   arousal

A

L   **Parasympathetic Hypoarousal:**
     Too little arousal to integrate

Most traumatized clients experience "too much" arousal (hyperarousal), or "too little" arousal (hypoarousal), and often oscillate between these two extremes (Ogden, Minton, & Pain, 2006; Post, Weiss, Smith, Li, & McCann, 1997; van der Hart, Nijenhuis, & Steele, 2006; van der Kolk, van der Hart, & Marmar, 1996). Hyperaroused clients are typically hypervigilant and anxious, suffering from intrusive images and dysregulated emotions. Hypoaroused clients endure another kind of torment, stemming from a dearth of emotion and sensation—a numbing, a sense of deadness or emptiness, passivity, and immobilization (Bremner & Brett, 1997; Ogden, Minton, & Pain 2006; Spiegel, 1997; van der Hart, Nijenhuis, Steele, & Brown, 2004). Prolonged states of hypoarousal are thought to contribute to depressive states.

In treatment, clients must first learn to modulate dysregulated arousal so that it returns to a window of tolerance. Once arousal is thus stabilized, clients can expand their window of tolerance by working with painful traumatic memories, repressed or dissociated emotions, and new physical actions. Bromberg (2006) stated that therapy must address such difficult issues in an atmosphere that is "safe but not too safe" in order to expand the window of tolerance. If their emotional and physiological arousal consistently remains in the middle of the window of tolerance (for example, at levels typical of low fear and anxiety states), clients will not be able to expand their capacities because they are not in contact with disturbing traumatic or affect-laden attachment issues in the here-and-now of the therapy hour. However, if arousal greatly exceeds the regulatory boundaries of the window of tolerance, experience cannot be integrated (Figure 1.2).

Figure 1.2

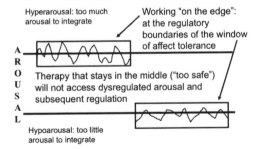

The therapist and client must continuously evaluate the client's capacity to process at the regulatory boundaries of the window of tolerance to assure that arousal is high enough to expand the window but not so high as to sacrifice integration. Once arousal is at the regulatory boundary, it is imperative to avoid stimulating additional emotional or physiological arousal, or execute physical actions that cause further dysregulation at the expense of integration. Addressing traumatic memories and expressing painful emotions, along with implementing new, empowering physical actions, might provide an antidote to depression and serve to expand affect array and even increase the client's capacity for positive affect (Figure 1.3).

Figure 1.3

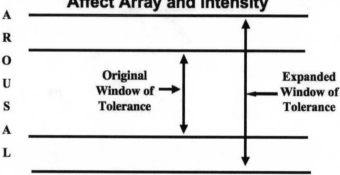

Expand the Regulatory Boundaries of the Window of Tolerance to Integrate Previously Dissociated Emotions, Expand Affect Array and Intensity

Pearl #2. Challenge procedural memories.

Most human behavior is driven by procedural memory, the memory for physical *processes*—the "how" rather than the "what" or "why." Negative early attachment experiences and unresolved trauma both leave their imprint on the body's procedural memory system, shaping the posture, gestures, and movements of the body. These physical tendencies, such as a sunken chest, limp arms, and shallow breath, reinforce chronic negative emotions and cognitive distortions and constrict affect array. Powerful determinants of current behavior, procedural tendencies are formed by repeated iterations of physical movements.

Long after environmental conditions have changed, we remain in a state of readiness to perform the procedurally learned actions that were adaptive in the past. Procedural learning is characterized by automatic, reflexive performance, becoming an even more potent influence because of its relative lack of verbal articulation, thus rendering most procedural behavior unavailable for thoughtful reflection.

In therapy, clients learn to execute new physical actions that challenge their maladaptive procedural tendencies. Replacing a slumped posture and shallow breath with an aligned, erect but relaxed posture, full breathing, and supple tonicity tends to support a positive sense of self and can alleviate depression. Learning actions of boundaries and defense, such as pushing away, can mitigate the immobilizing defenses of freezing and submission that often accompany trauma-related depression. Clients can also learn a variety of actions that engage a wide range of emotions, including positive affect. For example, adaptive anger is supported by increased alignment of the spine, a degree of physical tension, and the capacity to push away or strike out; joy by an uplifting of the spine and expansive movement; empathy by a softening of the face and chest and perhaps a gentle reaching out; play by a tilt of the head and spontaneous, rapid changes in movement. Executing these movements and experiencing the accompanying emotions can help to expand the regulatory boundaries of the window of tolerance.

Pearl #3. Use directed mindfulness.

In therapy, clients are taught to mindfully observe their procedural tendencies—their movements, sensations, impulses, posture, and gestures—and to notice the interplay of these tendencies with cognitions, emotions, and perceptions. Therapist and client together "study what is going on, not as disease or something to be rid of, but in an effort to help the patient become conscious of how experience is managed and how the capacity for experience can be expanded" (Kurtz, 1990, p. 111). Through mindfulness, clients shift from being caught up in the story and upset about their reactions to becoming curious and interested in their experience. They discover the difference between "having" an experience and exploring their procedural tendencies in the here and now, days or weeks or years after the event itself.

Mindfulness is generally thought of as a state of awareness that is receptive to whatever elements of experience arise in the mind's eye. However, when mindfulness is open-ended, clients may find themselves at the mercy of dysregulated arousal and internal experiences that appear most vividly in the forefront of consciousness. Instead of allowing clients' attention to drift randomly toward whatever emotions, memories, or thoughts might emerge, "directed mindfulness" (Ogden 2007) interventions guide the client's awareness toward particular elements of present-moment experience that are thought to support therapeutic goals. Directing mindfulness toward the movements, sensations, and gestures of the body makes it possible to utilize precise interventions targeted at procedural memory.

CASE EXAMPLE: TINA

A single woman in her late 30s, Tina sought therapy for a variety of reasons. She reported feeling depressed, haunted by the memories of sexual and physical abuse in her childhood, and complained that she was unable to enjoy herself. Although Tina maintained a high level of functioning in her profession as an associate professor, she stated that she felt awkward in groups, had few "real" friends, and was "not a social person." She yearned for meaningful friendships as well as a mate.

Tina appeared depressed. Her posture was slumped, she walked into my office with a heavy and plodding gait, and she sat quite still on the sofa, head down. She was an attractive woman, with short, curly, dark hair, and a lovely peaches-and-cream complexion. Slightly overweight and dressed in baggy jeans, T-shirt, and sneakers, Tina wore no jewelry or makeup, and her general presentation was a bit unkempt. There was visible tension across her hunched shoulders and a lack of movement throughout her body. Her speech was flat, punctuated by sighs, and lacked vitality and enthusiasm.

Tina and I determined that we would begin with physical interventions targeted at her slumped posture (*pearl #2: Challenge procedural memories*). I suggested that positioning her legs and feet squarely under her body and aligning her spine so that her head could sit centered over her shoulders would support an ergonomic posture and might also lead to more vitality and confidence. First, I asked Tina to explore her lack of alignment by standing and slightly exaggerating her head jutting forward, tail tucked under, shoulders hunched, and spine curved. As she mindfully observed the emotions and thoughts that spontaneously emerged when she exaggerated her habitual posture, she discovered that her posture went hand in hand with feelings of inferiority, helplessness, and passivity.

I guided her to imagine being lifted upward by the crown of her head while sensing her feet firmly planted on the ground and allowing her spine to straighten and her chest to lift, thus enhancing her breathing and permitting her head to rest squarely on her shoulders. Tina reported that indeed, this new posture helped her "feel better" and raised her arousal level. Her thoughts correspondingly started to become less negative, her emotions more buoyant.

Although this "somatic resource" did not resolve Tina's underlying depression, it did alleviate her tendency to slump and taught her a tangible skill (she called it "standing tall") that she could use to make herself feel better. This countered her usual feeling that she was a victim of her moods. Although the new posture felt awkward initially, Tina agreed to practice it daily, and gradually it became increasingly comfortable. Tina learned to sense the physical support of her spine, taking deep, regular breaths, sensing her feet firmly on the ground, and perhaps most importantly, differentiating her experience as a dependent child (exemplified by her old posture) from her experience as a competent adult who could take positive action to modulate her excessively low arousal.

After a few months of treatment with a primary focus on developing somatic resources like the alignment described above, Tina began to discuss her desire for more ease in social situations. Abused by her father throughout childhood, Tina said her body was always tense in childhood, and she shunned play dates with other kids. As an adult, the muscular tension remained, and although Tina desperately longed for a mate and meaningful friendships, her tension and accompanying fear were exacerbated at the thought of social contact. She said that when she thought of being with others, her first impulse was to withdraw.

I suggested that we explore what happened as Tina decreased the physical distance between us. We stood at opposite ends of the office, and Tina slowly walked toward me while mindfully noticing her physical reactions. This exercise was intended to stimulate Tina's procedural tendencies about social contact, and, indeed, she reported that the tension in her body increased as she reached a distance of about 6 feet from me. She felt a constriction of her breath and tension in her viscera, and she expressed feeling uncomfortable as the distance between us decreased. The tension, the ensuing emotional numbing, and a physical preparedness to move away from me felt "familiar." Tina said she was afraid of what I would want from her if she sought to be close to me, and she talked about being forced to submit to more contact than she wanted in relation to her father. These realizations were accompanied by a reexperiencing of the pain and despair she had felt as a child.

Tina's window of tolerance expanded through practicing new actions and processing these painful early experiences over many therapy sessions (*pearl #1*). She eventually learned to consciously refrain from tightening her body when in social situations, remind herself to take a deep breath, and sense her spine. She also tried new mental actions—such as repeating to herself that she was no longer a child and that she did not have to do anything she did not want to do.

Eventually, Tina was ready to directly address memories of early sexual abuse by her father. When traumatized clients first turn their attention to traumatic memories, they typically become aware of disempowering, immobilizing defenses rather than triumphant actions, and Tina was no exception. As she first talked about the abuse, she became aware of increased physical tension, but then reported that she was spacing out, feeling "nothing." **I directed her to be mindful of her body and see if there was anything that came to her attention** (*pearl #3: Use directed mindfulness*). She noticed a slight tightening in her jaw and throat. As she stayed with the constriction, she said she wanted to shout "stop!"—an impulse she may have had during her childhood but wisely refrained from expressing because such assertive action probably would have made her father angry. We decided that on the count of 3 we would both shout the word *stop*. Tina enjoyed this intervention, saying she felt empowered and more energetic.

In a sensorimotor approach, clients are helped to rediscover their truncated physical defensive impulses to push away, strike out, or run—actions that were not executed during the abuse. As Tina remembered a particularly disturbing abusive event, she reported a small movement of her fists, a curling that seemed indicative of a larger aggressive movement. I asked her to see what her body "wanted" to do, and Tina became aware of an impulse to strike out, and she slowly executed this motion against a pillow that I held. Being able to be mindful of how her body wanted to respond, she became aware of the previously aborted physical urge to not only punch her father but also run away, reflected in a tightening and feeling of energy in her legs. These physical impulses that she did not—could not—act upon at the time of the abuse appeared spontaneously as she directed mindful attention toward her physical sensations and impulses as she recalled the abuse. Tina again reported feeling empowered and said that her body was "coming alive."

Later in therapy, Tina's hands came up in a protective gesture as she remembered her father coming into her bedroom. When I asked her to notice this movement, Tina expressed being ashamed and said she wanted to curl up and hide. As she followed the impulse to curl up, she tearfully said that as a child she thought she deserved this abuse. As we processed the shame, Tina began to believe that the abuse was not her fault—she was only a little girl when it happened. With that realization, she reported a tension in her arms and a feeling of anger—contrary to her usual pattern of helplessness, shame, and fear.

In previous therapy, Tina had repeatedly expressed shame and help-lessness, but her propensity to dissolve into tears contributed to her depression and feelings of being victimized and unable to take action, which prevented more adaptive emotional and physical responses such as anger and assertive action. Once she discovered her anger at what had happened and was able to execute protective physical actions such as pushing away, she reported a core feeling of empower-ment and strength, reflected in an upright posture and deeper breath. The future looked promising, Tina said. Together, we shared our deep appreciation for these gains, and Tina began to softly cry. She expressed a depth of grief at the loss of the innocent trust in her father that she had treasured as a young girl. These very powerful emotions were accompanied by another surge of arousal, challenging the regu-latory boundaries of her window of tolerance. Afterward, Tina reported that that she felt a new sense of movement and overall soft-ening in her body. The depression was beginning to lift.

Over time, Tina's wish for a mate came to the fore. I encouraged her to be mindful of her body as she felt her need for a partner, and she experienced a softening in her entire body. She said that she felt less defensive and more vulnerable as her body softened, and then said she could also feel the desire for connection in her heart. We explored sensing the desire in her heart and initiating a reaching-out movement from the core of her body through her arms. Tina first said that the thought of reaching out made her uncomfortable. When she did, her arm was stiff, the movement was awkward, and her body tightened again. Tina said the gesture felt unfamiliar, and that she felt more vulnerable, again afraid of having to meet the other's needs. She became sad, and her old belief emerged again as she said: "Others will use me if I reach out." Giving way once again to strong feelings of anger and hurt about the past helped to soften Tina's aversion to intimacy as well as to relax her body.

Tina first practiced actions of reaching out merely as a physical exercise, attending only to integrating the core and periphery of her body, with no psychological content until that task was accomplished. She then practiced reaching out to me, which brought up the long-forgotten childhood longing for her mother's protection from her abusive father, and Tina again wept with grief. Naturally, these new motor actions were accompanied by new meanings: Tina began to express the conviction that perhaps it would be safe to reach out in her current life, that she knew everyone was not like her father. Eventually, she found herself spontaneously reaching out to others instead of isolating herself, which had been her tendency for so long.

Tina also verbalized her desire to be more playful. Her history of abuse precluded playfulness, which cannot develop in the shadow of threat and danger, a fact that carries debilitating and far-ranging consequences characteristic of the plight of traumatized individuals. During the course of therapy, Tina and I practiced other movements that facilitated playfulness and lightness of spirit, such as exchanging her plodding gait for a bouncy, "head up" walk, and her hunched shoulders and rounded spine for an upright, shoulders-down posture that encouraged eye contact and engagement with others. We giggled as we together exaggerated the "bounce" and talked about what her life would be like if she sustained this playful bounce in her step. Over time, with continued practice, Tina's new upright posture and movements became more natural, and her enjoyment of social interactions increased.

CONCLUDING COMMENTS

We cannot change what happened in the past, but we can help clients change the procedural tendencies that they formed in response. I believe that therapeutic change occurs not only by formulating a narrative but also by mindfully challenging and changing procedural tendencies that sustain trauma-related dysregulation and depression. If traumatic memories largely consist of reactivated nonverbal implicit-type memories and habitual procedural responses with limited explicit-memory components, then such memories may not be transformed adequately by insight alone.

Sensorimotor interventions that directly address the movement of the body can work to process implicit-type memories, challenge procedural memory, help to regulate dysregulated autonomic arousal, and expand modulation capacities. The clients' cognition can be engaged in mindful observation of the interplay of their perceptions, emotions, movements, sensations, impulses, and thoughts to discover procedural tendencies, and then to change them. Innate somatic regulatory capacities, or "somatic resources," become spontaneously available or can be evoked by the therapist—resources such as taking a breath, adjusting the spine, making a movement, and orienting perceptually and physically to the environment. Through mindful attention to the body, clients become aware of the previously aborted physical impulses that they did not—could not—act upon in childhood because they would not have been effective. Clients can be helped to discover truncated movements—from defensive actions, such as pushing, kicking, or running, to actions that support relationships, such as reaching out, opening up, or letting go.

Although words are indispensable in the treatment of trauma, they cannot substitute for the meticulous observation of how clients attempted to defend themselves and the exploration of how such physical defenses were thwarted during the original traumatic event.

Nor can words take the place of the thoughtful therapeutic facilitation of the client's actual experience of empowering, adaptive physical actions. I propose that the satisfaction and pleasure of finally being able to know and perform direct physical actions such as those described earlier alter the somatic sense of self in a way that talking alone does not. Knowing, feeling, and doing—and thus experiencing—these physical actions helps to reorganize the way in which clients consciously and unconsciously hold and organize their understanding of past traumas, and this may prove effective in the treatment of depression. Changing these procedural tendencies through movement changes the way clients respond in their current life and the way they envision the future.

BIBLIOGRAPHY

Bremner, J. D., & Brett, E. (1997). Trauma-related dissociative states and long-term psychopathology in posttraumatic stress disorder. *Journal of Trauma Stress, 10*, 37–49.

Bromberg, P. M. (2006). *Awakening the dreamer: Clinical journeys.* Mahwah, NJ: The Analytic Press.

Kurtz, R. (1990). *Body-centered psychotherapy: The Hakomi method.* Mendocino, CA: LifeRhythm.

Ogden, P. (2007). *Beneath the words: A clinical map for using mindfulness of the body and the organization of experience in trauma treatment.* Paper presented at Mindfulness and Psychotherapy Conference, Los Angeles, CA: UCLA/Lifespan Learning Institute.

Ogden, P., Minton, K., & Pain, C. (2006). *Trauma and the body: A sensorimotor approach to psychotherapy.* New York: Norton.

Post, R., Weiss, S., Smith, M., Li, H., & McCann, U. (1997). Kindling versus quenching: Implications for the evolution and treatment of posttraumatic stress disorder. In R. Yehuda & A. C. McFarlane (Eds.), *Psychobiology of posttraumatic stress disorder* (pp. 285–295). New York: New York Academy of Sciences.

Siegel, D. (1999). *The developing mind.* New York: Guilford.

Spiegel, D. (1997). Trauma, dissociation, and memory. *Annals of the New York Academy of Sciences, 821*, 225–237.

van der Hart, O., Nijenhuis, E., & Steele, K. (2006). *The haunted self.* New York: Norton.

van der Hart, O., Nijenhuis, E., Steele, K., & Brown, D. (2004). Trauma-related dissociation: Conceptual clarity lost and found. *The Australian and New Zealand Journal of Psychiatry, 38,* 906–914.

van der Kolk, B., van der Hart, O., & Marmar, C. (1996). Dissociation and information processing in posttraumatic stress disorder. In B. van der Kolk, A. McFarlane, & L. Weisaeth (Eds.), *Traumatic stress: The effects of overwhelming experience on mind, body and society* (pp. 303–327). New York: Guilford.

BIOGRAPHY

Pat Ogden, PhD, is a pioneer in somatic psychology and the founder and director of the Sensorimotor Psychotherapy Institute, an internationally recognized school specializing in somatic-cognitive approaches for the treatment of posttraumatic stress disorder and attachment disturbances. She is a clinician, consultant, international lecturer and trainer, cofounder of the Hakomi Institute, and faculty member at the Naropa University. Ogden is the first author of the groundbreaking book *Trauma and the Body: A Sensorimotor Approach to Psychotherapy* (W. W. Norton, 2006). She is currently working on her second book, *The Body as Resource: Sensorimotor Interventions for the Treatment of Trauma.*

Chapter 2
Escape From Depresso-Land

Bill O'Hanlon, MS, LMFT

Having been a therapist for over 30 years, I have learned that therapy is always "learned on the job" with an N of 1, as the researchers like to say. Each person is different. Each clinical situation is different.

In my early years, it was a tradition to videotape many sessions. When I began teaching workshops, I showed participants excerpts of some of these sessions. I would often watch them 50 to 100 times over the course of several years. I, like many therapists, considered myself a pretty good listener. But after watching those sessions again and again, I was amazed at how often my clients were telling me the answers to their problems several times before I actually registered this fact.

This leads to my three pearls.

PEARLS

I guess the essence of my message, as exemplified in these three pearls, is to trust yourself as a therapist and to trust your clients; you don't have to be such a clever expert and you don't have to work so hard.

Pearl #1. The client is the expert on the details and experience of his or her problem.

I sometimes joke that I do "cab driver" therapy. I don't go anywhere in the therapy process until I get direction from my client. This is based in part on not having any prejudice about what is "normal" or "healthy," aside from the general proviso that it is not okay to hurt others.

Therapy starts when the client (or someone else in the client's life) complains that something is not right. That gives me the initial direction for therapy assessment and intervention.

This lines up with the notion that clients are experts: They know more about their problem situation than I do. They know what their experience of suffering is, certainly. But they also know details about how the problem happens, when it happens, when it doesn't happen, what makes it better, and what worsens it.

Some therapy approaches consider the therapist the expert on the problem. The therapist's special knowledge or theory gives the therapist primacy in the problem-defining and problem-solving process. But in my view, clients are the primary experts in this area. I have few, if any, theories before I begin to speak to the client. Often I never develop any theories as the process goes on, but only rely on the client's theories and insights.

This is not to say that I as the therapist don't have any expertise. I have trained and acquired expert knowledge about how to interview people and how to elicit from them the reports necessary to find a focus for the therapy. I am an expert in evoking solutions from people. I am trained and expert in making rapid connections with people who are frightened, upset, and anxious.

Pearl #2. Clients often have useful ideas and experience about solutions or partial solutions to their problems.

The thing that most distinguishes the "solution-based" therapies (solution-oriented; solution-focused; narrative; and collaborative, competency-based, and strength-based approaches) is that they all consider the client to have solutions (or at least the seeds of solutions) to their problems much of the time.

I remember being on a panel with a prominent proponent of the Mental Research Institute (MRI) interactional approach to therapy many years ago and introducing this notion into the conversation. Because the MRI approach holds that "the problem is the attempted solution," this man became livid at the suggestion that clients had solutions. "If clients had solutions, they wouldn't need to come to therapy!" This attitude is less common these days, but it still pervades many approaches to change.

Clients don't always recognize the solutions they have. One of my teachers, the late psychiatrist Milton Erickson, used to say, "You know a lot of things you don't know that you know." The process of therapy, then, sometimes involves eliciting these solutions and highlighting them to help people recognize them as solutions.

Of course, sometimes the solutions are only partial and need some fine-tuning before they are workable.

Pearl #3. *The human connection between client and therapist is the medium for change.*

When I was trained as a therapist, there was a general sense that the therapist should be a good listener but, aside from conveying a sense of compassion and understanding, should not really relate anything personal to the client. Sharing anything personal was considered a boundary violation and would only serve to distract the client from the change process.

But as I have gotten further and further from graduate school, I have gradually loosened myself from this restraint. I regularly tell stories from my own life and the lives of my clients, friends, and family; I respond as a person and generally bring as much of my overall humanity as I can muster into the therapeutic encounter. Strangely, it takes a lot of work to be yourself in a seamless way in a professional context. Invitations to distance and not be authentic are ubiquitous in the therapy context and in our training. Mastering being appropriate and not using clients as friends (or doing your own personal therapy on their time or dime) is a delicate balancing act, but one that I find becomes more effortless as time goes by.

The response from most clients is unambiguously positive, especially from those clients who have been in a previous course of treatment. Comments like "I didn't feel like a bug under a microscope—I felt like we were equals working together" or "I felt you got what was going on with me right away" are common.

It turns out that the human connection that can form in the therapy process may be the most significant thing that enables what the therapist offers to be effective, according to recent research (see Bertolino and O'Hanlon, 2001). But I didn't need research studies to tell me that: Clients have been teaching me that for decades.

All the clever theories and methods don't have much of an impact if the human connection, the sense of two human beings understanding and caring for one another, is missing.

CASE EXAMPLE: ELLEN

Some years back, I set up a series of videotaped interviews to show how I work in therapy. I went to a distant city and put out a call to therapists and other people I knew in the area to send along people who would like to have a one-time consultation to change something they felt stuck about.

One of my friends in the area told a therapist she knew about the offer, and that therapist said she had just the person in mind who would be good for this situation. Ellen had sought help from this therapist for major depression. She had had several rounds of psychotherapy before and they had always ended badly, with the therapist nearly driven crazy by the dependency and frequent crises Ellen developed. Ellen would call her therapist regularly, sometimes nightly, seeking help for dealing with her overwhelming feelings of depression and hopelessness during her depressive episodes. The depressive episodes would typically last for 2 months, during which time Ellen would quit the job she had (usually as a secretary or receptionist). Gradually, she would pick up the pieces, get another job, and dread the coming of the next depression.

Her current therapist was happy to arrange a consultation for Ellen, as she was desperate for some ideas about how to help her client. She had diagnosed Ellen as having dependent personality disorder as well as major depression. Because Ellen was in the midst of a depressive episode, the therapist felt that she was "sucking the marrow out of her bones"— she was incredibly "needy" and calling on an emergency basis often.

When Ellen and I met, she explained that she would go in and out of depression. **This was exciting for me to hear, as it meant that she had a lot of experience with both the onset as well as the subsiding of** depression. I asked her to compare and contrast her experiences and habits when she was experiencing depression and when she wasn't (*pearl #1: The client is the expert on the details and experience of his or her problem*).

I also told her that I had "majored" in depression when I was first in college. I had spent a lot of time alone, reading self-help books on depression and dwelling on the past and mistakes I had made. Since becoming a therapist, I had also treated many people who had experienced severe depression, so I had a formula for creating a good depression. Here was my formula: Spend a lot of time isolated and alone; compare yourself to other people and lose by the comparison; don't move around physically (exercise could seriously endanger one's depression); limit one's access to new ideas and information; decide one had always been depressed and always would be depressed in the future. That's how I would do a good depression, I told Ellen. How did she do hers? She laughed at this notion of "doing" depression, but soon launched into a comparison of the "doing" of depression versus the doing of "not depression."

This going back and forth in reporting the experiences of both served two purposes. It gave me a pretty good idea of the kind of suffering and isolation Ellen experienced during the depressive episodes and a way to join with and validate her. And it gave me a chance to elicit and highlight the kinds of solutions and helpful habits that were associated with not being depressed.

I soon learned that during the depressive episodes, Ellen would stay home all day (having quit her job), spend time alone, stay in bed until noon, stay in her bedclothes until about 6 or 7 in the evening before taking a shower, stop doing the artwork she often did when she was not depressed, and find herself dreading a future in which she was even less functional and might have to move in with her father and stepmother or, even more worrisome, be placed in a psychiatric hospital. The only people she would talk to during these times were her friend Paul, who was also depressed, and her therapist.

I began to refer to this constellation of experiences and actions as "depresso-land." She chuckled a little at the first few mentions of this name, but soon used it herself when she was referring to depressed episodes (*pearl #3: The human connection between client and therapist is the medium for change*).

In describing what was different during the times she wasn't living in depresso-land, she reported that she would often meet a friend for lunch, she would typically get out of bed earlier in the morning, even on weekends when she didn't have to be at work, and she would get out of the house during the day and some evenings. She would do some artwork most days. She would also think of something she had done in the recent past and feel good about having done it.

During this discussion, it became clear to both Ellen and me that there were two aspects of life outside of depresso-land that were both helpful and were under Ellen's influence (*pearl #2: Clients often have useful ideas and experience about solutions*). After some back and forth, we mutually decided that she would experiment with trying to bring these aspects of the non-depresso-land patterns into the depression to discover whether or not they could help her escape from depresso-land.

Ellen decided to arrange to bring two cups of coffee to her therapist's office every morning and sit and chat for 5 minutes or so with the therapist between the therapist's 8 A.M. and 9 A.M. clients. This would give her motivation to be up, dressed, and out of the apartment before 9 A.M. Then she would arrange to meet a friend for lunch for the next few weeks (she had a number of friends and would rotate among them for these lunch dates).

After about a week and a half with this plan, Ellen and the therapist reported that she had been able to "walk" herself out of depresso-land. Ellen was especially happy that she had been able to do this by dint of her own efforts, as prior to this time she had felt powerless to make any dent in the depressive feelings. She now had a sense that she could either avoid or lessen the severity or duration of future depressive episodes using this or similar strategies. And the therapist was relieved not to have the emergency phones calls coming in.

CONCLUDING COMMENTS

My teacher, Dr. Erickson, used to say that troubles are "the roughage of life." I took this to mean that we could use troubles, including problems that are brought to therapy, as possibilities both to learn about ourselves and life and to move forward.

Ellen had many opportunities to learn about herself and move forward each time that she became depressed, but until this time, the lessons had not been learned or used. She solved her own problem, using only the knowledge she had accumulated from past experience (of depression and not being depressed). I couldn't have done it without her and she couldn't have done it without me. The therapist and client coming together and drawing on both the client's and the therapist's expertise creates a unique setting in which to move forward and gain insights into the client's resources, strengths, and solutions.

Ellen told me later that she didn't feel the need to tell me everything about her depression because I "had been there and knew how it was." That human connection and sharing of my previous experience of depression, so devalued and discouraged in my professional training, had been a crucial element in the success of the intervention in this case. I also genuinely liked Ellen and she could tell this. I joked with her during the session and, despite being depressed when she arrived, she laughed several times during the session. This lightened her up in the moment, making her non-depressive memories and resources more available. It also communicated that she was not a "fragile mental patient." We were both competent partners in the change process.

BIBLIOGRAPHY

Bertolino, B., & O'Hanlon, B. (2001). *Collaborative, competency-based counseling and therapy*. Needham, MA: Allyn & Bacon.

O'Hanlon, B. (2003). *A guide to inclusive therapy: 26 techniques for respectful, resistance-dissolving therapy*. New York: Norton.

O'Hanlon, B. (2006). *Pathways to spirituality: Connection, wholeness, and possibility for therapist and client*. New York: Norton.

BIOGRAPHY

Bill O'Hanlon, MS, LMFT, has authored or coauthored 29 books, the most recent being *A Guide to Trance Land* (W. W. Norton, 2009), *Write* is a Verb, Pathways to Spirituality (W. W. Norton, 2006), Change 101: A Practical Guide to Creating Change (W. W. Norton, 2006), and Thriving Through Crisis (winner of the Books for a Better Life Award). He has published 54 articles or book chapters. His books have been translated into 15 languages, and he has appeared on Oprah (with his book Do One Thing Different), The Today Show, and a variety of other television and radio programs. Since 1977, O'Hanlon has given over 2000 talks around the world. He has been a top-rated presenter at many national conferences and was awarded the Outstanding Mental Health Educator of the Year in 2001 by the New England Educational Institute. O'Hanlon is a licensed mental health professional, certified professional counselor, and a licensed marriage and family therapist. He is a clinical member of AAMFT (and winner of the 2003 New Mexico AMFT Distinguished Service Award), certified by the National Board of Certified Clinical Hypnotherapists, and a fellow and board member of the American Psychotherapy Association. O'Hanlon is known for his storytelling, irreverent humor, clear and accessible style, and boundless enthusiasm for whatever he is doing. His website is www.billohanlon.com.

●○●●●●●○

Chapter 3
Depression Blues: Three Pearls of Wisdom for Turning *Toward* Depression

Michael Stone, MA

> The way through the world
> is more difficult to find than the way beyond it.
> — Wallace Stevens, "Reply to Papini"

Depression is characterized by turning *away* from life through withdrawal and inwardness, whereas psychotherapy and mindfulness meditation orient us *toward* whatever it is that we are experiencing. Entering into the dark blue of depression is more difficult than getting caught up in the endless plots and escape strategies we often use to defend ourselves against the threatening hues and density of depression's bruises and currents. Sometimes depression creeps along right next to us; at other times we find ourselves swallowed by the inability to get out of bed. Over time, however, we begin to see that trying to escape from our experience is impossible and exhausting. Cure comes through releasing our chronic identification with our moods. This chapter describes three pearls of wisdom that can help us reenvision our approach to and understanding of the symptoms we call "depression."

Depression is one of the most challenging psychological symptoms because, although it seems to be characterized by a lack of vitality and repression, it often involves something much more subtle happening within the mood—namely, our being caught up in stories that maintain the momentum of the mood. Waking up in the early morning and obsessing about our lives, lying in bed worrying, avoiding social inter-action because of projected fear, not paying attention to present expe-rience because of being caught up in inward thoughts—all of these characterize this mood. It's the energy we invest in our stories about our mood and ourselves, as well as our attempts to lean away from painful feelings, that gives rise to the exhaustion and fatigue so preva-lent in depression.

The endogenous physical roots of depression, especially when it can be tracked through family patterns, deserve some attention from this perspective as well. The physiological symptoms of tiredness or numbness often hit first, and then the mind will look for reasons or stories to confirm what the body is experiencing. I can wake up one morning with a feeling of severe fatigue, and then attribute it to all kinds of events (my job, my visit with my mother) when in fact it is just a metabolic shift. The impact of physical symptoms and sensations associated with depression is also affected by how we interpret them. As one of my colleagues recounted:

> I have experienced depression in this physical way, and then experienced my mind trying to explain it away versus allowing myself to just experience it. . . . One time when I did allow the experience to just be an experience (I just sat, staring at the wall for a few hours), the panic that it caused in my father led me to avoid doing it again at all costs (and led to a lot of probably more destructive behaviors that were culturally acceptable, like binge drinking). Clinicians' and family members' fears—and desires for loved ones to behave normally—may sometimes get in the way of a client's recovery. This makes it difficult to get to know what depres-sion actually is, how it happens, and how we can accept that so much of our difficulty comes from what we do with feelings, not from the feelings themselves.

Is it possible to return our attention to something other than our stories about our symptoms or even our favorite escape strategies, especially when the depressed state begins to take over? As clinicians, can we help our clients go deep inside the depression to see just exactly how it is constructed? Unfortunately, most people, clinicians included, often approach depression as something to get rid of; we investigate our stories about depression. But chronic moods like depression are hard to unravel until we move deep into the mind states that give rise to it and then begin to deconstruct our contribution to them, even when we contact the most unpleasant feelings.

PEARLS

What moves me most about psychotherapy, or any healing relationship for that matter, is the empowering and brilliant pearls of wisdom that arise spontaneously within people who are struggling with the deep questions that emerge when we face, head on, the reality of life's predicaments, the reality of how things actually are. Sometimes we have the rare privilege of working with clients who employ their whole being in the service of waking up from constricted and self-imposed forms of suffering. In working with others and in struggling with my own phases of depression, I've found that healing occurs (1) in the context of relationship and (2) by seeing how the mix of feelings and stories within the mood are *self-imposed* entanglements. This chapter describes three pearls of wisdom that have helped me personally and professionally.

Pearl #1. Experience is not unique.

I often ask clients to pay attention to their moods without identifying with them. I have them close their eyes and notice what is being felt as they stay with their breathing. "Now," I'll say, "see if you can notice your feelings *with* a sense of I, and then *without* a sense of I." When dealing with symptoms like depression, it's amazing for people to notice moods with and without a story attached to them. Our stories are constructed to reinforce a sense of "me," and the more we identify with our symptoms of depression, the more they seem like a unique part of our identity. But when we see a mood as a mood, a feeling as a feeling, a thought as a thought, we come to see that experience need not refer back to a sense of *I*, *me*, or *mine*.

Pearl #2. Everything changes.

In order to avoid the truth that all things arise and pass away, we hold onto the stories we create for ourselves. Furthermore, identifying with our symptoms reinforces the stories we tell about ourselves, and this separates us from life. Although this is most evident in depression, it is also a universal and consistent phenomenon. As therapists, we must be skillful and creative in helping our clients to explore their experience and to see how our "addictions" to our stories are attempts to deal with impermanence. When we are relaxed and attentive, the stories we have about ourselves and others can move through awareness more easily, and we can begin to see them as nothing other than stories.

Pearl #3. Nothing belongs to "me" or is "mine."

The culture of psychotherapy, at least from the lay perspective, sets up expectations that a "unique story of me" will lead to the flash of insight that cures all. When we look into pain or numbness, even in states of dissociation, it's important to begin to see that feelings and sensations do not refer back to a sense of self—they are phenomena that arise in conditions that are impersonal. The stories we have for our experiences make them personal. These stories we have also create a kind of mis-identification that separates us from what is actually occurring in the body in the present moment. Suffering is the gap between how things actually are and how we think they should be. For example, if I think of myself as busy, strong, confident, and always available to others, I bring this perspective to feelings of sadness or exhaustion, and this perspective, although hidden, influences the way I approach and configure my feelings. In the act of perception, my feelings are condi-tioned by my core beliefs. Most of the time we create suffering for ourselves through our stories, and those stories serve to divorce us from the raw impact of life. Depression has within it a narrative that needs to be brought to the surface and then let go of. Maybe the story is about low self-worth or hurt or old pain—regardless of the underlying theme, once we feel our way into experience, the stories need to be dropped.

Though these pearls of wisdom sound more like philosophical achievements, they were an important part of my work with Gary, who was severely and chronically depressed. Gary brought us both to a deeper level of psychological understanding, wisdom, and compassion, and he taught me that the most radical and helpful approach to healing depression comes through a transformation of perspective that allows us to accept even what is unbearable.

CASE EXAMPLE: GARY

Gary arrived at our first meeting with soaking wet pants and shoes after forgetting his umbrella on the bus. "I was so immersed in a crossword puzzle," he explained, " that I forgot I had my umbrella with me, I didn't realize it was raining, and I didn't think about the length of the walk to your office. I'm not sure I've looked away from my crossword puzzles in a long time." He looked down at his pants. "Oh yeah, they are soaked."

We spent most of the first session talking together about how inward Gary felt on the bus, "paying attention to nothing, not looking at anyone, not noticing anything." It was like the world happened behind Gary's eyes; he neither participated in nor noticed anything other than his local activity. It was obvious why his wife, a family doctor like Gary, sent him to me. Gary had taken a leave of absence from his medical practice and was working for his brother in a quiet office with a computer and almost no contact with colleagues.

What was most moving about Gary's depression was that his interior life was flat, his exterior observations so minimal, and his energy so low. I couldn't even imagine how he helped his two young children get dressed, let alone himself. His family was falling apart and he had no friends.

Gary's wife was growing increasingly frustrated with his sunken mood, lack of energy, and absent composure. Visibly upset by the intervention from both his wife and brother, Gary asked me if he could attend a mindfulness meditation course I was leading at a local yoga studio. I invited him to a daylong meditation session I was facilitating, followed by an evening lecture.

Gary sat perfectly still through the entire day of meditation, following the instruction to feel the incoming breath and the outgoing breath and to simply and gently return awareness to the breath when there was any distraction in body or mind. If the breath was agitated or if the mind was distracted, I asked the participants to simply notice these agitations and return to the feeling of breathing without judgment or commentary. All day, we sat still meditating on the breath, interspersed with periods of silent walking.

At the end of the day, Gary left alone for dinner and returned for the evening lecture, where he sat in the last row but with the most present awareness I'd seen. I noticed his height for the first time and also his hairstyle and the color of his eyes.

At our session the following week, he talked about how it was enjoyable learning how to sit in meditation, something he'd always wanted to try, especially because he "didn't have to engage with anyone."

Later that night, Gary had a dream in which he was in a desert, dressed in a snowsuit and sweating like crazy. He woke up with his duvet drenched "and the strange feeling that everything made sense even though the understanding wasn't there yet."

Reflecting on both the dream and the day of meditation, Gary realized that the kinds of struggles each participant was going through were not so unique—just as anyone, not just him, who was dressed in a snowsuit in the desert would sweat (*pearl #1*). "It's just the nature of the mind to get swept up, polluted, or even go absent," he said to me. "When I heard others talk about how they related to their own minds, I realized we shared the same troubles and that the troubles are not that unique. Most of us don't know how to work with our mind."

Then, in the kind of flash that can only happen when someone is very present and awake, he shifted his posture into a more erect and vibrant form and said, "I feel dead. I really feel empty. But maybe it's not about all the issues you and I have talked about. Maybe this dead feeling is just impersonal, maybe it's just the mind or physiology or brain acting a certain way that I just haven't seen. I keep thinking that some explanation from my past will get rid of this depression or that you'll hear something about my relationship with my wife that will light up a giant torch. I know I am depressed but maybe *I* am not depressed. Maybe there is just this thing, depression, happening, and I needn't be so identified with it. What do you think?"

Truthfully, I was taken aback. I was moved by how clear his description of his situation had been. The dream and the meditation session showed us both how thoughts and feelings are not necessarily so unique; we all struggle with distractions, emotions we can't understand or tolerate, disruptive sensations, and recurring fantasies. Like someone sweating in a snowsuit, the trouble is not with the mind or body, with sensations and thoughts, but rather with our ability to feel and think and become aware without being entangled in everything that moves through awareness.

Practice

In meditation practice, we allow thoughts and feeling to arise and pass away, and when they don't—when we get entangled in their turbulence—we simply come back to the breath, over and over again. This mind-training is just like learning a new language or a new musical instrument. We don't measure our progress in meditative practice by how peaceful we are but rather by how well we can decenter from the mental habits that keep us fixated or, in this case, shut down and inattentive. Noticing how thoughts and feelings, images and sensations arise and pass away in awareness helps us when we start overanalyzing, getting lost in daydreams, or, in Gary's case, getting entangled in personal commentaries and constant worry.

"I keep thinking the worries are mine," Gary said in a subsequent session. "That the thoughts are mine, every problem is mine, or I am bad. But when I heard so many others struggle also, I realized that we all think these things. But some of us can see them come and go and others just fall headfirst into them."

The more Gary explored the impermanent nature of feelings and thought, the more he found ease in his own mind (*pearl #2*). As he contemplated impermanence, it dawned on him that it was not just his thoughts that were changing but that *everything* was changing, everything expires. This motivated Gary to see his relationship with his family as structured in time, precious here and now.

One day, when Gary was relaxed, I asked him if we could just sit still and listen to the birds in the yard beyond the window. "It's amazing," he said. "For a moment I heard the sound of the bird and the cars going down the street without much commentary. It's amazing. Why is it so hard to relax around everything, to let things be, let things happen? They happen anyway. My ideas about everything just get in the way."

A few weeks after his initial insights, Gary's daughter asked if they could ride their bicycles to her school that morning rather than drive. Rarely giving such questions much thought, Gary usually said no because he didn't want to go out of his way. He described the scenario like this: "She asked if she could ride and so we went to the garage and put on her helmet and took out her bike. I was embarrassed by the fact that her bike and helmet were too small—have I been absent for that long? Have we not ridden together? When was the last time?"

Tears came to Gary's eyes as he told the story. Tears came to mine as well. He spoke quietly and with an attention more precise than usual. "We rode down the hill and as it curved left, I watched her handle the speed bumps so easily. I looked at her riding. I looked at her in her helmet, her legs that were way too long for the pedals, and her blue knapsack. Suddenly, it was like a veil lifted from my face, from my eyes. I *saw* her, I really saw her. She was riding in front of me, riding so well, and I really saw her, my daughter, riding there in front of me. I can't explain what happened, it was like I woke up, I had a kind of visionary moment, like the one mystics talk about but it was about her, about my own child. I was riding behind her and suddenly I really saw, like it was the first time. So beautiful. A thought came to my mind . . . I am so lucky."

Gary and I were both in tears. Through paying attention and working though his distracted and dead-end habits, Gary's eyes, heart and mind opened to his daughter, opened to life. This moment interrupted the momentum of the old stories about himself and his experience that had consumed him.

This episode taught me how depression can be a wicked addiction to our own stories, our own internal chatter. When Gary's chatter stopped—when he stopped his internal dialogue—his daughter burst forth. He wasn't trying to stop his thinking or intentionally connect with his daughter but he did take a risk. He let his old stories fall away for a moment. He interrupted his schedule to go with his daughter, to follow her flow, and in doing so he entered his life again.

Our stories are constructed to reinforce a sense of "me" and the more we are identified with our symptoms of depression as personal, the more they seem so. But **when we see a mood as a mood, a feeling as a feeling, a thought as a thought, we come to see that *experience need not refer back to a sense of I, me or mine*** (*pearl #3*).

As therapists, we must be skillful and creative in order to help our clients explore their experience and see how impermanence is an absolute truth and that many of our addictions are attempts to deal with impermanence. When relaxed and attentive, the stories we have about ourselves and others can move through awareness more easily and we can begin to see the stories as nothing other than stories.

CONCLUDING COMMENTS

We live in a "quick-fix" culture that is manically defensive against depression; we want to be fast, light, quick, and efficient, and depression turns us slow, low, blue, and deep. Of course we want depression to give way to a balanced and engaged life in the heart, yet at the same time, our depression may have something important to offer, so we must turn to it without being entangled in it, in order to learn about what it wants.

After years of studying psychotherapy and undergoing my own therapy, I found myself caught in depressive symptoms much like Gary. I knew much about the patterns of the depression and the "why" and "how" of what I was experiencing, but I did not have the ability to sit still and let the mood move through me. It was during this time I turned to meditation practice. I realized that just knowing *about* myself did not give me the skill set needed to actually let things be, let things go.

The three pearls of wisdom allow us to turn toward depression with a different lens, an altogether accepting and gentle attitude. "One thing you do learn in therapy," wrote James Hillman (1989), "is how, when you have a depression, it belongs to you, but you don't identify with the mood. You live your life in the depression. It doesn't completely stop you. It only stops you if you're manic. Depression is worse when we try to climb out of it, get on top of it."

When we stay with depression without completely identifying with it, we can begin to respect and appreciate its contours and lessons, and its symptoms can in turn reveal some profound lessons that bring balance and creativity. Duke Ellington, Nina Simone, Vincent van Gogh, C. G. Jung, Pablo Picasso and many others went through long "blue" periods in which some of their most meaningful and provocative work emerged. We need not turn to the blues with an attitude of control or escape but rather enter the shades of blue without identifying with them and with the knowledge that whatever is being felt is certainly not permanent unless we characterize it as such.

Mindfulness meditation teaches us how to stay with feelings, track thoughts, and be with strong moods without identifying with them. It teaches us how to be *in* life rather than caught in our *ideas* about how things are or should be. Mindfulness is the intention to be (1) present, (2) without judgment, and (3) without commentary. Once we can sit still with whatever it is we are experiencing, we gain insight into the way the mind constructs our experience. Mindfulness slows down this construction process. Out of this kind of stillness and emotional balance, we gain deep insight into the way our challenging mind states affect others. Gary's pearls of wisdom are not just about his own transformation; they also woke him up to the beauty of his daughter, the importance of his family, the preciousness of this life.

BIBLIOGRAPHY

Hillman, J., and Moore, T. (1989). *A blue fire.* New York: Harper Perennial.

Stone, M. (2008). *The inner tradition of yoga.* Boston: Shambhala Publications.

Stone, M. (2009). *Yoga for a world out of balance.* Boston: Shambhala Publications.

BIOGRAPHY

Michael Stone, MA, is a psychotherapist in private practice in Toronto. He lectures and leads workshops in conference, academic, and clinical settings internationally, and he is a sought-after speaker on the subject of psychology and meditation. He runs Mindfulness Meditation in Clinical Practice, a yearlong Leading Edge Seminars study program in Toronto that brings together meditation practice and clinical theory and technique. His research and teaching focus on the relationship between Eastern and Western approaches to the mind-body relationship and spirituality in clinical practice. Stone also teaches yoga and leads Centre of Gravity, an urban community of yoga and Buddhist practitioners in Toronto interested in the integration of committed practice and social action. For more information, visit www.centreofgravity.org.

Section Two:
Trauma

Chapter 4
Working With Entrenched Reactive Symptoms Following Traumatic Experience

Dusty Miller, EdD

Most of my clinical work over the past 30 years has been with people who are deeply embedded in old pain, women and men whose emotional wounds don't heal easily. They are generally diagnosed with posttraumatic stress disorder (PTSD), borderline personality disorder, substance abuse, and bipolar disorders. They bounce from group to group, program to program, therapist to therapist. They've been subjected to every new treatment model that comes down the pike. These clients are trapped in a variety of self-sabotaging patterns. They have challenged many bright, willing therapists.

PEARLS

Pearl #1. Focus on the issue of self-protection.

Although clients who have been traumatized must have the opportunity to tell the details of how they were victimized, they are actually *harmed* by repeatedly retelling the details of the victim story. However, trauma survivors have quite often missed the opportunity to tell the most important part of the story—that is, the experience of *not having been protected.* Instead of allowing the focus to be on the details of the violation, I zero in on the formative experience of not being protected. Frequently, healing is blocked by the pain of the betrayal—

the traumatic experience going unnoticed, the person feeling unheard or disbelieved.

Traumatized people need us to bear witness to how alone and helpless they felt when no one protected them. This is true for all sorts of traumatic experience—for victims of childhood trauma, adult violations, war trauma, or shattering loss. Therapists should ask the client how the central role of nonprotection in the original wounding experience gets reenacted. The old trauma story needs a new angle; you get there by helping the client to identify how she (or he) is *currently not protecting herself.*

Acknowledge, and then work with, the reenactment of nonprotection. Help clients explore the ways they continue to not protect themselves, as well as their wish for the therapist/group/spouse/friend to be able to completely protect them, to magically create a happy childhood. The longing to be rescued and protected often gets covertly loaded into the therapeutic relationship. Then the reenactment of nonprotection follows—the helpless therapist can't deliver a belated happy childhood. When this inevitable disappointment is not made explicit by the therapist, the client is plunged back into the pain and rage of the original betrayal. Figure out with clients how the longed-for protector can become the clients themselves.

Pearl #2. Look for addictive behavior and addictive thinking.

No matter what the diagnosis, where there's entrenched, long-standing, intractable pain, explore the likelihood that there is addictive behavior and addictive thinking. There are probably a hundred good reasons why survivors of shattering experience use addictions—of all kinds—to escape pain. You and your client need to face the fact that whatever the addiction is, it eventually rules daily life. Your work is to help clients name their specific addictions and identify how the daily life patterns control their life.

The consequences of addiction replicate the dynamics of abuse and nonprotection: The client becomes isolated, out of control, miserable, and ashamed. The good news is that once you name the addiction, you can draw on decades of accumulated best-practice intervention from the world of addiction treatment. This will inevitably expand the client's support network to include others struggling with addiction, and you won't be in the impossible position of being the only one holding the lifeline. This will help you avoid being in the role of rescuer.

Pearl #3. *Help your client connect with a larger community.*

One-on-one relationships are never adequate, whether they are with the therapist, a best friend, a partner, or God. In fact, relying too much on the dyadic therapeutic relationship can cause harm, often replicating the original experience of not being protected. No matter how isolated someone seems to be, perhaps the single most important task for the therapist is to help the client access a community of support.

This often requires getting creative about the definition of community. Volunteering in a soup kitchen or an animal-rescue organization creates community. Going to a 12-step group means hooking up with a community. Blog sites, chat rooms, coffee shops, and doggie play-groups all exemplify community options. You and the client have to figure out the best fit for her or him. Then you need to keep finding ways to reinforce any attempt the client makes to engage in community. Therapy sessions may get repetitive and a little dull, but your job is to talk about current daily life efforts the client is making—or isn't—to become connected to others. Your job is also to become less and less central to the client's survival and well-being.

CASE EXAMPLE: BETH

I will always be grateful to a client who, early on in my trauma work, helped me lay the foundation for the three clinical pearls described above. Beth was sent to see me at the end of her year in a halfway house for incarcerated women. She, like all the other women living at the house, was in recovery from drug and alcohol abuse. I was working in Lynn, Massachusetts, one of the most drug- and violence-choked communities in the state. Beth had gotten clean from alcohol and heroin, and had stayed clean and sober for a year. She was now getting ready to reenter the world.

The counselors at the halfway house were concerned because Beth remained unwilling to share much of anything personal with the other women in the house or with the staff. In fact, she had not made much of a connection at all with the other women in the house. She dutifully attended 12-step meetings but remained very shut down. Her isolation made it seem likely that she would relapse when she left the house.

When I first saw Beth sitting in the waiting room, she looked small, fragile, and very fearful. But from that first moment, I began to learn that this small, wispy young woman had a will of steel and a powerful set of defenses. Our first impasse occurred in the very first moment of our relationship, when I held out my hand to shake hers. She refused. She was shaking with fear, but she was not going to let me force her into an interaction she did not welcome.

I was impressed from the very beginning by the intensity of Beth's fear and rage. She was coming to see me only because she felt forced to do so. She disliked me and all the other would-be "helpers" in her life. Working with her was going to be a challenge, and she let me know that from the get-go.

My practice has always been to slow clients down in the first session or two, trying to block too much sensitive disclosure before they have had the chance to assess me. They have the same need I do—we are both gradually assessing each other. Before someone spills too much and then feels too vulnerable, I try to develop some sense of mutual respect. With Beth, the first session turned into a series of painful and shocking revelations that she would not let me block. She wanted to give me the whole story immediately, and she would put up with no interruptions from me no matter how skillful I tried to be.

Score 1 for Beth and 0 for me!

Beth's life story was a rough one. She recited the violence and sexual horrors she endured at her father's hands, the violence inflicted on her mother and younger siblings. None of the story was that new or different for me. I had been working for a while with trauma survivors. But Beth's story was just a little more extreme. The enormous rage she felt toward her father was also notable. In fact, it was frightening. I came to believe that she was capable of making a murder attempt, although she did not disclose a concrete enough plan for me to feel that I had to notify the police.

My immediate challenge at the end of the first session was to persuade Beth that therapy was not completed. She had told her story, she said angrily, and thus had fulfilled the requirements of the halfway house staff. What else was she supposed to do?

My gentle attempt to talk her into sharing more than just her story was met with extreme irritability. She only agreed to return for a second meeting because she thought she had to. She knew that her discharge depended on a certain amount of compliance, and so she sullenly made another appointment.

In our second session, I learned that although Beth had remained clean and sober, she had devised many new ways to harm herself, including seeking out situations of extreme danger. She even managed to find employment that guaranteed extreme danger—being a bicycle messenger in the city of Boston, where everyone drives homicidally!

But there was something at the core of her story that caught my attention. There was an important message that she had repeatedly received from her father that seemed to capture her (*pearl #2: Look for addictive behavior and addictive thinking*). She had been trained by him, in a sense, as a "warrior"—a warrior who had to learn to withstand extreme torture. Now she was tough as nails, and she was inflicting suffering on herself. Just as she had been abused and never protected, now she was enacting the same scenario but playing *all* the roles, including the nonprotecting bystander.

I decided I wanted to share this observation with her. After a few sessions, all feeling very slow and nonproductive, I decided to take a big risk. "You seem to be acting on your father's orders, still," I commented. "You're doing to yourself what he did to you, your siblings, your mother. So you're loyally carrying him around with you, the internalized abuser."

Beth was enraged by my observation. She took in what I said, but the tide did not change until we began to talk more about the gross lack of protection in her history. She was very quiet at school, and no one in the family dared to help her. Neighbors who noticed anything about the family must have looked the other way.

"You have become your own nonprotecting bystander," I said to her one day. "You hurt yourself, and no one—including you—steps in

to protect you. You are still a lonely, hurting warrior following your father's orders." (*pearl #1*)

Suddenly, there were tears, long overdue. Now we began to really work *together*.

Naming the addictive nature of her patterns self-harm was relatively easy. Beth already understood the dynamics of her former addiction to heroin. Now we could track the addictive pattern of her current self-harmful activities.

"When you feel helpless and angry, you use these newer methods of escape—like hurting yourself physically—just the way you once used your addiction to alcohol and drugs," I pointed out. "And just the same way you experienced a numbing of pain when you were in your substance-abuse cycle, now when you engage in one of your new methods of self-harm, you feel relief, right?" Beth agreed. She also admitted that it was part of a familiar addictive cycle to keep herself from really engaging with others. She stayed isolated so she could be devoted to and uninterrupted in her addictive behavior. Like every addict, her addiction replaced relationships with people. As we began to name the pattern, Beth was able to apply her previous success in staying abstinent to her newer methods of self-harming.

Creating community was difficult. After a lifetime of feeling betrayed and mistrustful, Beth had been unwilling to open up and make connections in 12-step meetings. She had refused to allow the other women at the halfway house to get close. I felt helpless in my various efforts to persuade her to take some risks in trusting others.

Then, through pure serendipity, Beth had an accident. Zooming through the streets of Boston for her bicycle-messenger job, she was hit by a car and broke her leg. **The good news about this was that the other women in the house were eager to help her with simple physical things she couldn't manage. And she had to let them. Gradually, she began to let these women get a little closer, just as she was letting me in bit by bit** (*pearl #3: Help your client connect with a larger community*). I was able to focus our conversations on how it felt to let others get close to her. She was beginning to see that not everyone was going to fail her or ignore her need for protection.

After about 12 sessions, Beth was truly beginning to make friends. She was now on the road to real change.

Often such a serendipitous experience of community is not handed so easily to the therapist. If this accident had not precipitated Beth's becoming more open to those around her, I would have kept looking for other possibilities. I would have looked at what she already valued about herself and tried to build on that in making suggestions for community-building. Given her warrior style, I might have, for example, coached her to get involved in some form of self-defense training requiring vulnerability and cooperation.

Beth and I parted ways when I moved and had to leave my practice. I kept in touch for about a year with her new therapist, who reported that she was continuing to make friends and had remained abstinent from her previous addictions. She was working at a job that did not require daily risking of her life. Her obsessive preoccupation with revenge against her father had also abated. She was able to use therapy to grieve the losses of childhood and to embrace her adult life.

CONCLUDING COMMENTS

I wouldn't have been able to stay with this very challenging work for all these years if I hadn't had eventually worked through some of the same traumatic experiences I have in common with my clients. I had the chance to experience healing through the unconditional positive acceptance and love of several therapists. Judith Jordan, cocreator of the Stone Center's relational therapy model, offered insight and strength through her writing and her deep kindness while she was my therapist.

I also had the inspiring experience of participating in several social-justice movements, including the civil-rights and women's-liberation movements. These activist communities helped me see that only in community was it possible to successfully fight injustice and develop resilience.

My family-therapy mentor, Evan Imber-Black, guided me skillfully through my professional training and helped me know which tools to choose and which to discard. At the core of what Evan taught me was an abiding faith in the self-healing strength of the client. I found soul mates in my family-therapy diaspora; the work of Michael White, Rachel Hare-Mustin, Gary Sanders, Laurie MacKinnon, and Bill Lax created a powerful web that has lasted through the years.

And after many false starts, I finally was able to fully comprehend and celebrate what the 12-step movement has given to millions of addicts. I have found many ways to join that experience with what I already knew as a mental-health professional and client.

BIBLIOGRAPHY

Miller, D. (2001). *Addictions and trauma recovery: Healing the body, mind and spirit.* New York: Norton.

Miller, D. (2003). *Your surviving spirit: A workbook of spiritual resources for coping with trauma.* Oakland, CA: New Harbinger.

Miller, D. (2003, July/August). The end of innocence. *Psychotherapy Networker*, 24–33.

Miller, D. (2005). *Women who hurt themselves (10th anniversary edition).* New York: Basic.

Miller, D. (2008). *Stop running from love: 3 steps to overcoming emotional distancing and fear of intimacy.* Oakland, CA: New Harbinger.

BIOGRAPHY

Dusty Miller, EdD, is the author of the pioneering book for consumers on self-harm and trauma, *Women Who Hurt Themselves.* She is the coauthor of the ATRIUM-model treatment manual *Addictions and Trauma Recovery: Healing the Body, Mind and Spirit* (W. W. Norton, 2001). She has also published two self-help manuals: *Your Surviving Spirit: A Workbook of Spiritual Resources for Coping with Trauma*, and *Stop Running From Love: 3 Steps to Overcoming Emotional Distancing and Fear of Intimacy.* She has published numerous journal articles on addictions and trauma, including feature articles in *Psychiatric Quarterly* and the *Psychotherapy Networker.*

Chapter 5
Healing Attachment Trauma With Attachment (. . . and then some!)

Diana Fosha, PhD

With attachment trauma, the good news is the bad news—as Bob Dylan sang, "What drives me to you is what drives me insane" (Dylan, 1976). Attachment—wired-in and salient "from the cradle to the grave" (Bowlby, 1977, p. 203)—is a powerful force: for good when secure, problematic when not. Whereas secure attachment is foundational for resilience and optimal development, disrupted attachment wires in a vulnerability to trauma. In therapy, however, when explicitly worked with and experientially entrained, attachment can be a powerful force for healing and repair once again.

PEARLS
Reflecting an understanding that moment-to-moment dyadic affect regulation and the adaptive processing of emotion are not just important to attachment, but, in fact, are the very constituents of it (Schore, 2001), my three clinical offerings are all under the aegis of an attachment-informed therapy. They address and seek to redress the twin issues of attachment trauma: affect dysregulation and the drenching of the self in shame. What I am writing about here is best understood in the context of an approach I have developed called "accelerated experiential-dynamic psychotherapy" (AEDP). You can learn more about AEDP in published work (e.g., Fosha, 2000, 2003, 2009 in press) or by going to the AEDP website (www.aedpinstitute.com).

Pearl #1. Surprise the unconscious: Be a detective for transformance strivings.

Given that we are wired for growth, for healing, and for self-righting (Doidge, 2007), we might as well put that wiring to good use in treatment. Until recently, the mental-health field, hyperfocused on pathology, lacked concepts to guide clinical use of these powerful motivational strivings. "Transformance" is a construct that seeks to rectify that lack—it is the motivational counterpart of resistance, driven by hope and the search for the vitalizing positive affects that accompany all affective change processes (Fosha, 2008).

Thus my first pearl. Be on the lookout for transformance, and make use of it when you detect it. Your job as a transformance detective will be immeasurably assisted by the fact that transformance at work is visible: It is invariably accompanied by positive affective markers. By "positive" I do not necessarily mean happy, but rather that whatever we are feeling, even if painful or difficult, feels right and feels true, and is full of vitality (Fosha, 2008, 2009, in press). As an AEDP therapist, I am an assiduous detective for evidence of transformance in glimmers—or actual rays—of resilience, strength, courage, hope, integrity, curiosity, and unsuspected capacities. Healing is a force that operates moment to moment; it is not just the outcome of a successful therapeutic process. From the get-go, I invite my clients into a healing relationship: Compassion toward suffering, delight in the person of the client, and empathy for his or her experience are all part of that invitation. The welcoming and valuing of emotions is another important part.

Mary Main spoke about the efficacy of the Adult Attachment Inventory (AAI), one of the most robust research tools ever developed, as being based in "surprising the unconscious" (Main & Goldwyn, 1998). One way to get a lot of therapeutic traction is to surprise the client's unconscious, conditioned as it is by past experience. Their resources overwhelmed, clients come into therapy prepared to have the worst in themselves exposed. To be met not only with compassion and empathy but also delight and appreciation of their strengths and qualities is the last thing that a client—down and out, feeling scared, overwhelmed, and defeated—expects. To do so is disarming and rapidly undoes defenses, yielding access to more viscerally felt, right-brain-mediated emotional experiences, which, in my work, constitute the stuff of therapy.

Pearl #2. Undo the client's aloneness in the face of intense emotional experience.

Aloneness—unwilled and unwanted aloneness—in the face of unbearable emotions is central to AEDP's understanding of how psychopathology develops and, a fortiori, to how attachment trauma comes to burrow its way in the psyche.

When the parent can support and help the child deal with intense emotions, secure attachment is the result. Secure attachment reflects the capacity to "feel and deal" (Fosha, 2000, p. 42). If the parent is accepting and there to help, the child feels secure that his or her emotions will be met and not experienced as being "too much" or "weak," "disgusting" or "shameful," "evil" or "destructive." The latter is precisely the experience of kids whose attachment figures are undone by their emotions: Because the parents themselves cannot feel and deal, they cannot help their kids do the same.

Kids with insecure or disorganized attachment learn that their emotions trigger their attachment figures' own attachment trauma. The child's emotions not only render the attachment figure incapable of helping, but may also sometimes lead to outright attack, rejection, or neglect. If the attachment bond is to be salvaged, the child has to institute what Bowlby (1980) called "defensive exclusion": He or she must exclude from his or her repertoire any emotions that dysregulate the attachment figure. Doing so preserves the attachment bond but at a cost. The child is left alone with emotions that were overwhelming to begin with, and that become even more so, compounded as they are by disruptive attachment experiences. Compensatory protective mechanisms emerge in the context of such affect regulatory lapses. Insecurely attached kids institute defenses that lead them to either "feel but not deal" (resistant attachment; Fosha, 2000, p. 43) or "deal but not feel" (avoidant attachment; Fosha, 2000, p. 43). In disorganized kids, these strategies eventually fail and "not feeling, and not dealing" (Fosha, 2000, p. 44) turns into disorganization or dissociation.

Clinically, in order to render defense mechanisms no longer necessary and to gain access to the emotions that have gone offline, it is crucial to undo the client's unwilled and unwanted aloneness. With traumatizing experiences, "being with" is necessary but not sufficient. When it comes to the regulation and processing of heretofore feared-to-be-unbearable emotions, active engagement—that is, sleeves-rolled-up feeling and dealing right along with the client—is what is required. This active engagement on the part of the therapist has two components: One is the armamentarium of experiential and emotion-processing techniques; the other has to do with the judicious, mindful use of the therapist's own affect. Dyadic affect regulation means exactly what it says: It takes two to tango. As the attachment-figure partner of the therapeutic dyad, the therapist cannot do adaptive dyadic affect regulation with a "still face" (cf. Tronick, Als, Adamson, Wise, & Brazelton, 1978). The therapist's affective engagement and affective responses to and along with the client are integral to dyadic affect regulation, which in turn is central to healing attachment trauma.

Pearl #3. Promote the client's felt sense of "existing in the heart and mind of the other."

It is not enough for you to feel empathic; for it to count, the client must receive and experience that empathy. Peter Fonagy has written eloquently of how feeling understood is a biological imperative (Fonagy et al., 1995). The child's sense of "existing in the heart and mind of the other" (Fosha, 2000, p. 57)—and doing so as oneself (i.e., not as a projection), I might add—is foundational to an individual's sense of security of attachment and thus resilience in the face of adversity. The child internalizes this sense of existence when all goes well in secure attachment through dyadic affect regulation and a million shared experiences. It is this sense of ourselves existing in another's heart and mind that is at the root of what allows that other to respond sensitively, empathically, and contingently just right to our needs, experiences, and communication.

In individuals with attachment trauma (Lipton & Fosha, in press), that felt sense can't be had: Their felt sense is more that they or their feelings don't exist for the other (avoidant attachment), or that they exist only as a projection (disorganized attachment), or as a narcissistic extension (ambivalent attachment) of the caregiver. Recipients of such disturbing responses need to erect defensive barriers to protect their core from corrosive shame and from being overwhelmed. It is precisely these defensive barriers, their usefulness long gone, that need to be addressed if the security-engendering qualities of the therapist— assuming that they are in operation—are to be taken in by the client and put to transformative use.

Thus, my third clinical offering has to do with exploring the client's receptive affective experiences of the therapist's presence, care, compassion, and love—in other words, what it feels like to feel under- stood, cared for, or delighted in (Lamagna, in press). Crossing that receptive barrier requires that you challenge taboos against self-disclo- sure (Prenn, 2009; in press). It requires that you (a) explicitly express how the client exists in your heart and mind, and (b) actively explore the client's experience of you—all the more so when the experience is positive, as secure attachment-engendering experiences are (Schore, 2001). A simple way of doing this is through raising the question "what is your experience of me?" and then experientially exploring that experience with the same interest, curiosity, and rigor as you would any other emotionally laden experience.

CASE EXAMPLE: SALLY

Sally, a single professional 35-year-old, sought treatment when her chronic depression exploded into acute feelings of pain, despair, and hopelessness, accompanied by suicidal ideation. Though she had always had friends, she had never had an intimate relationship. As she put it, "I've never even been kissed."

Sally manifested her avoidant-attachment dynamics from the start. Intimate contact was fraught with danger and thus avoided. Her feel- ings and her yearnings for emotional connection had been met with dismissal and disgust by her parents. Wary of the pain and shame that, in her past experience, invariably accompanied emotional closeness, Sally banished her emotions and yearnings for connection. She devel- oped a brittle self-reliance that, in turn, led to the isolation and crushing loneliness that brought her to treatment. The following vignettes, transcribed from a videotape of the session, are from my ninth session with Sally.

Vignette #1. Dyadic Affect Regulation of Painful Feelings (Not Being Alone)

In this segment, Sally approaches very painful dark feelings, which are both expressed and defended against. My tone, affectively congruent with the experiences Sally described, bypassed her defenses. A deeper affect was entrained, allowing Sally greater access to right-brain-mediated affective experience.

"Life is just empty for me," Sally said in a disconnected, matter-of-fact tone of voice. "Is there more than this? And if there is no God . . . that's my light at the end of the tunnel. . . . If you take this light away, it's pretty dark."

"It's dark," I said, in a soft, deep, somber tone.

"Yeah." Sally's tempo was slow, and her despairing affect deepened. But then her defenses kicked in: Her speech sped up and took on a pressured, cynical tone. "So what's the point? You go through life proving, you go through life working. I mean this is . . . . "

I slowed down the pace again. "Okay . . . if for a moment . . . if you let yourself stay with this feeling, the sense of emptiness, this inner sense of . . . " I took a deep sigh and maintained a grave tone of voice, "having to work *so* hard to keep something away . . . . "

"Yeah. . . . " Sally slowed down again and sobered. "It's tiring." (This reflected a deepening of the experience.) "I don't know . . . sometimes I wonder, *Is this it? Is this what life is about?* . . . It feels empty," she said, in a pained tone.

I matched her slow, pained tone of voice. "In this dark moment, what is that emptiness like?"

"It's black," Sally said. She paused for a long moment, with a deep affect of despair.

"Black. . . . "

"It's like . . . I don't have to be here . . . if I thought of it that way." (This was a reference to her suicidal ideation.)

Vignette #2. Transformance in Action

Having bypassed Sally's defenses against these painful emotional experiences, I made explicit that something significant had happened: Not only had Sally experienced her painful feelings, but she also had shared them with another, who received them. I asked her what it was like for her to share these feelings with me.

Immediately upon asking, there was a transformation: Sally's affect brightened considerably as she spontaneously initiated an experiential exploration of togetherness. Little in her procedural past indicated prior experiences to support such intimate and confident relating. Nonetheless, in response to my invitation to explore, Sally issued an invitation of her own. **She beckoned me to join her in her transformational journey of sharing her darkest places with another, and she affirmed that it was a positive, acceptance- and curiosity-filled experience** (*pearl #1: Surprise the unconscious: Be a detective for transformance strivings*). The positive affect that lit up the way was a marker of the transformance strivings in action (Fosha, 2008, in press a, in press b). So was the initiative and creativity evident in this exploration.

"This profound dread-filled place," I said with a deep sigh, "this blackness . . . this isolation . . . what is it like to talk about it with me? What's it like for you?" (This was an invitation for Sally to elaborate her experience of what it was like to share her until-now-private pain.)

"Well, it's sort of like . . . it's like we are walking or hiking," she replied, beginning to brighten, "and we are walking through this cave that's get darker and darker, and gets really, really dark." (This was an acceptance of my invitation.)

"Mm-hmm . . ."

"And . . . there is this little hole in the wall maybe." She made a circle shape with her hands. "And I kind of like go like this to you," she said, making a beckoning motion with her hand.

"Uh-huh."

As she continued, Sally became more animated. "And I open this door and it already feels like we are crowded in like this, and there is this tunnel with this wide opening that's getting narrower and narrower, and there is a door to that hole and I am opening this door and I am telling you, 'Dr. Fosha, look inside, open the door.'"

"You're inviting me to share where you live . . . inside."

"Yeah, that's how I feel. . . . I guess it's nice to show someone that this is how I feel. . . . I guess since you sort of made me think more about who I am, I feel you are a part of it too because you sort of sparked it in me. . . . So I feel like you are part of it, part of the process of me showing you me, putting the mirror in front of my face, and me even looking at myself and examining."

*Vignette # 3. The Felt Sense of Existing in the Heart
and Mind of Another*

Given how attachment trauma compromises the transfer of information between the hemispheres (Schore, 2009), it is not enough just to have a new experience; the client needs to know that he or she has had it. That is the aim of the therapeutic work that follows. Note Sally's focus on my not only being willing to be with her and her feelings, but also actually actively *wanting* to do so. The child's feeling that the parent wants to be with him or her is a key antidote to experiences of shame (Hughes, 2009; Kaufman, 1996; Trevarthen, 2001).

"Where am I?" I asked, in a slow, deep tone. "How am I in this journey?"

"In this whole scenario?" Sally asked.

"Uh-huh."

"You're sort of right behind me," Sally replied. (This comment indicated that she was in charge of the process.)

"So what does that feel like?" I asked. "At this time when we're in this cave, going to this place that's darker and darker and darker . . . you turn and I am there behind you, and you are telling me about it, and I . . . I see it with you."

"Yes, it's the first time, you're the first. . . . And it feels like you don't mind seeing it, I feel you are not offended, you are not taken aback by it. . . . You want to see it, and I am showing it to you, so there is an understanding I get from you that this is where I am coming from. . . . I guess there is a nurturing understanding about my situation. . . . you are trying to get a better understanding of who I am, so I am allowing you to look at it." (This was an articulation of her new experience of being with an other who wants to be with her.)

"Yeah."

"And you're a very safe person to show it to because . . . because you try to understand and you don't make light of it. It's okay for me to show you. . . . It makes me feel that I can show it to somebody, so it makes me feel like there is someone with me. . . . Maybe you don't quite understand what's happening when I open the door, but . . . I am sharing with someone that 'this is what I have to live with, this is how I really feel.' . . . And I never show people that side of me so . . . I don't know, it just feels . . . " (at this point she had tears in her voice) " . . . comforting. It feels like a little bit of a relief too." Fighting back tears, she continued, "Like maybe there is somebody else in this world who might have an understanding of who I am." She cried as she finished the sentence.

"You are telling me . . . that what is developing is the sense that, in a way, this is your journey, but in a way it's our journey and I am there with you in some way," I said (*pearl #2: Undo the client's aloneness in the face of intense emotional experience*).

"Yeah, definitely," Sally replied, nodding through her tears. "I couldn't put it into words but . . . it's like you just said, that we are going through this thing together."

"I wonder what you see . . . what you see in my face, what you see in my eyes in response to what you are telling me." (This was crossing the receptive barrier of the client's perception and experience of the other.)

Sally looked very carefully at my face, much like a baby surveying the mother's face. "Oh, it's like we are in this trip together so . . . I feel like there is a connection, you know . . . a connection, and there is an understanding . . . a compassion. I feel a certain amount of . . . the feeling of trust. . . . Because honestly, your face, you know, like every time I talk to you, you look like you're really feeling it." At this, Sally laughed, scrunching up her face in imitation of my expression. "Like you really get a good feeling for where I am coming from, it's like you almost got a pained look on your face." (Here the negative affect became transformed into positive affect.) "It's funny though, but it makes me feel like someone out there understands, so I don't have to dwell on it." Sally smiled, and her tone was upbeat.

"Mm," I matched her mood, with a smile in my voice.

"It's a relief, thinking that there is another someone in this world who understands where I am coming from. . . . It feels good." Now her voice was energetic, and her mood became increasingly bright. "I don't feel all alone in that world, someone's looked at it, so that I am not by myself. When I discovered that this is how it made me feel, I told my friend, it's weird, but I was all happy after last session. . . . **Because it's like, 'Oh, someone knows, I don't have to hide it all the time, someone else knows out there.'"** Sally let out a big sigh of relief and flashed me a bright smile. **"And I can move on. . . . It's nice that I can be real with you—I don't have to be anything I don't want to be. I can be me. I can be myself."** (This was Sally's experience of *pearl #3: Promote the client's felt sense of "existing in the heart and mind of the other."*)

"I know what you mean," I replied.

"I can be myself and it makes me feel. . . . It feels a little like when you show people this side of you, this private part of yourself, it makes you feel a little bit lighter." She took a deep breath. "You know, I can breathe a little bit better too."

This session with Sally proved to be pivotal. Her new experiences with me, marked by the positive affects associated with transformance strivings, led to a more consistent willingness to be open, which enabled us to stay connected and endure the emotional storms associated with working on the painful aspects of her past. It also inspired Sally to work hard to overcome her fears of rejection and have the courage to risk being in a relationship.

Reflecting the consequences of an avoidant attachment style, Sally was isolated, lonely, depressed, and intimacy-phobic when she started therapy. She developed a secure and resilient therapeutic relationship early in the treatment, which deepened over time. At termination, she was involved in a loving, committed relationship.

One of the last pieces of therapeutic work involved helping Sally share with her partner the nature of her struggles and enlist her partner's help in countering her avoidant tendencies. Her partner not only was willing to lend a hand, but also felt moved and honored by the trust. At follow-up, a year after the termination of treatment, Sally continued to be free of chronic depression; occasional bouts of depressive feelings were short-lived. She continued to be deeply involved in her relationship, where emotional communication and closeness were valued by both partners. The sharing of emotional experiences to deepen intimacy and solve problems, initially a new experience with me, became an ongoing aspect of Sally's everyday interpersonal life.

CONCLUDING COMMENTS

Transformance strivings are everywhere, and a theory informed by transformance allows a knowledge of and sensitivity to markers of health and healing, thus making the most of them. In my work with Sally, her explorations and her positive feelings were taken to be substantive and important markers of healing and self-righting, not to be avoidance of the darker side.

The pivotal moment that captures the healing mechanism is when clients, despite a lifelong avoidant attachment style, initiate close emotional contact and actually beckon their companion to accompany them on a journey where they will share the darkness that they live with. In that moment, transformance in full operation: Confident that they exist—as themselves—in the heart and mind of the therapist, clients find that their aloneness in the face of unbearable emotions is undone. The therapeutic relationship acquires the features of security that allow us to do the hard work of processing previously unbearable emotions until they too are transformed and yield their gifts of adaptive action and resilience for clients to make use of moment to moment, day to day in their lives.

BIBLIOGRAPHY

Bowlby, J. (1977). The making and breaking of affectional bonds: Aetiology and psychopathology in the light of attachment theory. *British Journal of Psychiatry, 130,* 201–210.

Bowlby, J. (1980). Attachment and loss: Vol. 3. *Loss, sadness, and depression.* New York: Basic.

Doidge, N. (2007). *The brain that changes itself: Stories of personal triumph from the frontiers of brain science*. New York: Penguin.

Fonagy, P., Leigh, T., Kennedy, R., Matoon, G., Steele, H., Target, M., Steele, M., & Higgitt, A. (1995). Attachment, borderline states and the representation of emotions and cognitions in self and other. In D. Cicchetti & S. L. Toth (Eds.), *Emotion, Cognition, and Representation: Rochester Symposium on Developmental Psychopathology VI (Rochester Symposium on Developmental Psychology)* (pp. 371–414). Rochester, NY: University of Rochester Press.

Fosha, D. (2000). *The transforming power of affect: A model for accelerated change*. New York: Basic.

Fosha, D. (2003). Dyadic regulation and experiential work with emotion and relatedness in trauma and disordered attachment. In M. F. Solomon & D. J. Siegel (Eds.), *Healing trauma: Attachment, trauma, the brain and the mind* (pp. 221–281). New York: Norton.

Fosha, D. (2008). Transformance, recognition of self by self, and effective action. In K. J. Schneider (Ed.), *Existential-integrative psychotherapy: Guideposts to the core of practice* (pp. 290–320). New York: Routledge.

Fosha, D. (2009). Emotion and recognition at work: Energy, vitality, pleasure, truth, desire & the emergent phenomenology of transformational experience. In D. Fosha, D. J. Siegel, & M. F. Solomon (Eds.), *The healing power of emotion: Affective neuroscience, development, clinical practice*. New York: Norton.

Fosha, D. (in press). Positive affects and the transformation of suffering into flourishing. In W. C. Bushell, E. L. Olivo, & N. D. Theise (Eds.), *Longevity, regeneration, and optimal health: Integrating Eastern and Western perspectives*. New York: Annals of the New York Academy of Sciences.

Hughes, D. A. (2009). The communication of emotions and the growth of autonomy and intimacy within family therapy. In D. Fosha, D. J. Siegel, & M. F. Solomon (Eds.), *The healing power of emotion: Affective neuroscience, development, clinical practice*. New York: Norton.

Kaufman, G. (1996). *The psychology of shame: Theory and treatment of shame-based syndromes* (2nd ed.). New York: Springer.

Lamagna, J. (in press). Of the self, by the self and for the self: An intra-relational perspective on intra-psychic attunement and psychological change. *Journal of Psychotherapy Integration*, Special Issue on Attachment in psychotherapy.

Lipton, B. & Fosha, D. (in press) Attachment as a transformative process in AEDP treatment of relational trauma: Operationalizing the intersection of attachment theory and affective neuroscience. *Journal of Psychotherapy Integration*, Special Issue on Attachment in psychotherapy.

Main, M., & Goldwyn, R. (1998). *Adult Attachment Scoring and Classification System*. Unpublished manuscript, University of California, Berkeley.

Prenn, N. (2009). I second that emotion! On self-disclosure and its metaprocessing. In A. Bloomgarden & R. B. Menutti, (Eds.), *The therapist revealed: Therapists speak about self-disclosure in psychotherapy* (pp. 85-99). New York: Routledge.

Prenn, N. (in press).Mind the gap: AEDP interventions translating attachment theory into clinical practice. *Journal of Psychotherapy Integration*, Special Issue on Attachment in psychotherapy.Schore, A. N. (2001). Effects of a secure attachment relationship on right brain development, affect regulation and infant mental health. *Infant Mental Health Journal, 22,* 7–66.

Schore, A. N. (2009). Right brain affect regulation: An essential mechanism of development, trauma, dissociation, and psychotherapy. In D. Fosha, D. J. Siegel, & M. F. Solomon (Eds.), *The healing power of emotion: Affective neuroscience, development, clinical practice*. New York: Norton.

Trevarthen, C. (2001). Intrinsic motives for companionship in understanding: Their origin, development, and significance for infant mental health. *Infant Mental Health Journal, 22,* 95–131.

Tronick, E. Z., Als, H., Adamson, L., Wise, S., & Brazelton, T. B. (1978). The infant's response to entrapment between contradictory messages in face-to-face interaction. *Journal of the American Academy of Child and Adolescent Psychiatry, 17,* 1–13.

BIOGRAPHY

Diana Fosha, PhD, the developer of accelerated experiential-dynamic psychotherapy (AEDP), is the director of the AEDP Institute in New York City, where she practices and teaches. She is the author of *The Transforming Power of Affect*, and editor, with Dan Siegel and Marion Solomon, of *The Healing Power of Emotion: Affective Neuroscience, Development and Clinical Practice* (W. W. Norton, 2009). A DVD of her live clinical work is in the APA's *Systems of Psychotherapy* series. For more information, visit www.aedpinstitute.com.

Chapter 6
Pearls from the Early Days of PTSD Studies

Babette Rothschild, MSW

At the time I first started working with traumatized individuals, the field of traumatic stress was still in its infancy. It was 1989 and I was living, studying, and working in Denmark. My decision to move to Scandinavia was motivated by the potential of an intriguing program in somatic psychology developed at the Bodynamic Institute in Copenhagen. A dynamically trained clinical social worker and body psychotherapist since 1976, I wanted to expand my knowledge and skills. I was drawn to Bodynamic's innovative theory and methodology, which linked motor development and neurophysiology to mental health. Their approach to stabilizing trauma survivors particularly piqued my interest.

PEARLS
Of the three pearls discussed in this chapter, the first and second derive directly from my years of training at the Bodynamic Institute. The evolution of the third pearl is somewhat different, however. It is not something I was taught and it is not a technique, but a principle. The concept dawned on me gradually over my early years of direct (as a therapist) and indirect (as a supervisor, trainer, and consultant) work with trauma clients.

Pearl #1. Teach clients somatic mindfulness.

Though they have been a focus in the body psychotherapies and Gestalt therapy for close to a century, mindfulness and somatic awareness have become more popular in mainstream psychotherapy since the turn of the twenty-first century. Awareness of body sensations is just one of the four facets of the practice of mindfulness, which has been integral to Buddhist meditation for thousands of years. Somatic mindfulness is the body-awareness component. It can be useful for any individual, whether in therapy or not. However, it is particularly valuable for many who continue to suffer from trauma, helping them access greater self-knowledge and self-control—so long as they can learn and practice it without distress or a worsening of symptoms. Somatic mindfulness has the potential to enhance containment and stabilization, as well as to anchor awareness in the here and now. The latter is particularly important for those who suffer from posttraumatic stress, as one of the main features of the disorder is a blurring between past and present. For that difficulty, body awareness can be particularly helpful because experiencing body sensations is a here and now activity. Remembering a sensation from the past is not the same as actually experiencing that sensation in the present.

Pearl #2. Develop client boundaries.

Many experiences of trauma involve a loss of the sense of boundary—of the integrity of the edges of the body. Incidents that involve intrusion, such as assault, rape, physical abuse, and some surgery experiences, can compromise a person's security within his or her own skin. A portion of people with boundary problems are not able to feel all or parts of their body at times or have trouble knowing where they stop and where the environment or another person begins. Others are overly aware of their personal space and feel easily intruded upon. Depersonalization is an extreme form of boundary problem. Reclaiming the sense of integrity of one's body as well as being better able to control the distance between self and other will help many victims of trauma to stabilize and manage their daily life.

Pearl #3. Contain your curiosity.

The historic and current thrust of trauma therapy almost always includes the processing of trauma memories no matter the method or model applied. For many therapists, the memory work is trauma therapy. Many would find being a trauma therapist less stimulating and interesting without memory work. However, those of us who work with traumatized individuals must be prepared to treat some—possibly many—of them without ever knowing the details of the traumatic incidents. With some clients, working with trauma memories is contraindicated and could actually do them more harm than good. This is not something that is discussed very much in trauma literature or at typical training programs or lectures on trauma treatment. But most trauma therapists have seen a portion of their clients go downhill as they remember. For these clients, remembering traumatic events causes destabilization or even decompensation. Under such circumstances, a focus on here-and-now stabilization and safety is the better strategy. In the case example that follows, the decision of whether to do memory work was easy—the client preferred to avoid his past traumas. Indeed, that is the primary reason for a therapist to contain curiosity: because the client does not want to address the past. No one should ever be forced to revisit his or her past, and pressure to do so can lead to further trauma or the creation of false memories. Other individuals may not be stable enough to risk the distress of a memory focus. No matter the reason for steering clear of trauma memories, containing curiosity is a necessary resource for any trauma therapist.

CASE EXAMPLE: CARSTEN

Twenty-two at the time I first met him, Carsten was a university student trying to figure out a career he could pursue. He was my first Danish client, and one of the few I had clearly identified with the still rather new diagnosis of posttraumatic stress disorder (PTSD). His advisor made the referral because of Carsten's sometimes crippling agoraphobia. He was rarely able to leave the house he shared with his mother and his dog without company, and he was afraid to live on his own. In addition, he had difficulty riding the bus. His immediate family included an older sister who lived close by. His father had died of a heart attack a few years earlier. Carsten had a couple of fairly close friends with whom he would play sports or go to the local pub. He had dated a few girls but had never had a relationship of any significant length. His interest in the young woman he was currently dating was only moderate. Though able to date and form relationships, Carsten only shared his innermost thoughts and feelings with his mother.

For the most part, Carsten's health had been good throughout his life. His tonsils were removed in 1973 when he was 6 years old. At that time in Denmark, there was little awareness of and sensitivity to the emotional needs of young patients. Though he did not remember his hospital stay, Carsten knew the story from his mother: He was terrified when they wheeled him into the operating room and screaming when he woke up from the anesthesia. Following the surgery, he became very anxious when separated from his mother. Carsten believed that experience laid the foundation for the agoraphobia that gripped him following the sudden death of his father.

The Therapy Process

Carsten longed for a life of independence, free from the constraints of agoraphobia, panic, and anxiety. Though he knew the tonsillectomy and his father's unexpected death had had severe emotional consequences for him, he was loath to open what he called the "Pandora's box of my past." We agreed that increasing his self-control, especially over his somatic symptoms, would be an important means to his primary goal. Body awareness would facilitate increased self-knowledge and greater symptom control. We would also work with boundaries so he could have a greater sense of self-control within relationships, both with his mother and his peers.

My biggest challenge was the way I had been trained to work with trauma. Until that time, reviewing traumatic memories was the only way I knew to help someone with trauma. Carsten, however, not only was not stable enough to risk that, but also was vehemently opposed to the idea. Where did that leave me? Like most of my colleagues, I was drawn to psychotherapy by a natural curiosity about the lives of others. **It was a challenge for me to resist the temptation to explore these two serious and intriguing traumatic events and instead respect Carsten's wishes. Could I adequately contain my curiosity (*pearl #3*)?**

During our first therapy session, Carsten talked about his panic attacks and I helped him to identify a pattern. Typically, the attacks would begin during his school day and then increase. Eventually he would call his mother, who would calm him. It was very rare for him to talk to anyone else about his anxiety.

To explore Carsten's body awareness, I had him focus on his body and report sensations as he noticed them (*pearl #1: Teach clients somatic mindfulness*). With little effort he found he could feel his heartbeat and breathing. While paying attention to those, per my encouragement, Carsten remembered that usually during panic attacks his heart rate would climb and his breathing would become restricted. He also remembered a warm flush throughout his body. In just the first part of the session, Carsten's mindfulness was increasing and being associated to his difficulties.

To further teach body awareness and increase his stabilization, I focused on Carsten's current posture. I could see he was quite slouched in his chair. When I brought this to his attention he admitted it was a typical way for him to sit. This awareness gave us something to work with that might help him change his anxiety pattern. I suggested that he slowly straighten up, *really* slowly so that he could feel the muscles along his spine contract. Slowing the pace might make it possible for him to notice what—if anything—changed in his breathing as he sat up. It was somewhat tiring for him to straighten his spine in this way. However, he noticed that his breathing actually became easier and fuller.

I then had him do the opposite—slowly ease himself back into a slouch. It takes muscle strength to do this slowly, so it was also tiring. He was tempted to just collapse, but he stuck with it. Going back and forth between slouch and straight a few times helped to deepen his postural awareness and got him thinking. He wondered if during panic attacks he was also slouching. And, if so, would straightening up free his breathing? We decided that practicing shifting postures in general, and in particular when he was having an attack, might be a good homework assignment.

For the fifth session we decided it was time to begin work with boundaries. Carsten had become quite aware of his body and was able to use his increased skill with somatic mindfulness in coping with his anxiety and panic attacks. Now he wanted a better command of his personal space, so working with boundaries was a natural next step. We started with a boundary basic familiar to most therapists. The exercise involves experimenting with the distance between the therapist and client. As I had originally learned it in the U.S., the task entailed noting any thoughts or feelings that indicated comfort and discomfort with the changing space between the participants. The Danish trainers, though, enhanced it by including the dimension of somatic mindfulness. With that addition, I found the simple exercise became even more useful. Applying what I had recently learned, I asked Carsten to pay particular attention to his body sensations, taking note of both pleasant and unpleasant shifts.

To begin the exercise, we stood at opposite ends of the room. As I walked toward him, Carsten was to raise a hand and say "stop" when he felt something change in his body. The first time we tried it, he reported feeling "threatened." I asked him if he could identify the body sensations that coincided with *threatened*. What were the sensations that allowed him to identify that feeling? Pivoting his body slightly to the left, he said, "I feel a little nausea and I want to turn away from you—that's how I know I feel threatened." This was a great first effort. I suggested that we try again and when he felt that twist, that he do it slowly and see what else was going on in his body. After a few tries, he was able to identify tension in his neck, shoulder, back, and stomach, all of which constituted what he called "threatened." **As we attempted different distances, sometimes with him walking toward me, he began to identify—from his body sensations as well as his thoughts and feelings (the broader scope of mindfulness)—what was comfortable and uncomfortable for him. He was becoming aware of his boundaries** (*pearl #2*).

At our next session, Carsten remarked that he had noticed specific somatic differences when his mother was in varying proximity to him.

He was pleased with himself but also distressed as he began to suspect he would need to keep more distance from his mother than she might easily accept.

A few sessions later, we worked with a different aspect of boundaries. I gave Carsten a skein of yarn and asked him to use it to describe his sense of his personal space. Relying on mindfulness, he used the yarn to outline the amount of room he needed to feel comfortable, which included more than three quarters of my office. I was to remain outside of his "space." Inside this yarn boundary he felt at ease: heart calm, breathing easy, temperature normal, muscles relaxed. My office was fairly big, so being outside his circle meant that I was quite a distance from him. After a while he began to feel a little lonely and invited me closer. When I walked forward past the yarn, he inhaled sharply. I stopped and asked, "What happened?"

Carsten flushed and replied, "I felt your step in my stomach. My heart is racing and my face is very hot." This comment precipitated a discussion about personal space and physical distance. Next, Carsten asked me to step back outside of the yarn, but then he felt lonely again. He was torn: How could he have people close and have his boundary at the same time? He looked at the yarn. I waited. He asked if he could draw the yarn in. Of course he could, it was *his* space. So he pulled the yarn—his boundary—in and then asked me to step closer, but stay outside of the border. No reaction this time; he stayed calm and cool.

Before we finished, with his permission, I stepped over the yarn boundary again, precipitating another reaction. We discussed the fact that others invade our boundary all the time, and the more actual space we feel we need, the easier it is to feel intruded upon. He wondered if that might have something to do with his reluctance to ride the bus. I agreed: If his personal space was too big, lots of people were going to be inside it. So, holding his boundary closer to his body would probably give him a greater sense of private personal space. Carsten caught on immediately. Rather than asking me to step back out of his space, he again pulled his yarn—and his boundary—closer to himself. This gave him an immediate and tangible physical sense of relief, which he emphasized with a big sigh: "Whew! That feels better."

He liked the idea that he could better protect his space by pulling in his boundary rather than by pushing people outside of it. This successful experiment in the therapy session became the inspiration for Carsten's next homework assignment—applying the same technique (sans yarn) to find out if it would help him feel more comfortable at school and when he rode the bus.

After we had worked together for about 6 months, Carsten entered my office with straighter posture and a new spring to his step. He smiled as he told me that he had experienced his worst panic attack ever a few days ago at school. He proceeded to describe the course of the attack in precise, mindful detail. "It began with tension in the back of my head and shoulder blades, out into the backs of my arms and up to my jaw. My stomach and chest were tight. My arms and feet were prickling, but my head was unusually clear. I forced my breathing to slow, even while my heart raced. Next I got hot all over and broke out in a sweat—but a warm, not cold, sweat. After that, the tension started to ease and my heart slowed down." He was extremely proud of himself: "It was awful, *and* it was fantastic. I handled it!"

Of course, Carsten hoped that he would not have such an unpleasant experience again. But he no longer feared it in the same way, as he was confident he could handle it: He would be mindful of his bodily reactions and exercise patience while he allowed them to run their course. From that point on our work together changed. Over the next few weeks, Carsten's confidence grew. No longer afraid of his anxiety, he felt increasingly ready to go out into the world with his newfound tools. We said goodbye with the understanding that he could return if he ever wanted or needed further help. A few months before I moved back home to Los Angeles, Carsten contacted me. The skills he had gained earlier had held. He was pursuing an interesting career and was living with a caring woman.

CONCLUDING COMMENTS

None of these techniques addressed the traumatic roots of Carsten's anxiety, panic, and agoraphobia, so why did he get better? Part of the answer is found by understanding the importance of control for trauma survivors.

For someone to experience trauma, he or she must be out of control. People don't get traumatized when they can fend off the attacker, prevent a loved one's death or injury, or step back from a precipice. So anyone suffering from trauma is also dealing with issues of control. Moreover, the symptoms of trauma and PTSD increase the experience of being out of control, as they are usually difficult to manage. This was certainly true for Carsten. Teaching him how to use mindfulness and increase his command of his boundaries greatly increased his control over his body as well as over his environment, especially with regard to his personal relationships. This was a major factor in his improvement. As his quality of life improved, so did his confidence, and vice versa. The pattern of his life changed from the vicious cycle of traumatic stress into a sequence of success building on success.

I can see no better goal for trauma therapy than helping our clients to improve the quality of their lives. Of course, by agreeing to avoid his memories I may have colluded in depriving Carsten of even greater improvement. On the other hand, because of his instability combined with his own fear to face his past, pushing such an agenda could have backfired and led to a severe decrease in life quality. Therefore, I chose to follow what I believed was the more sure—and more respectful—route. By containing my curiosity I helped Carsten to reduce his overall stress and gain control over his body and symptoms, enabling him to pursue a normal life.

AUTHOR'S PUBLICATIONS

Rothschild, B. (2000). *The body remembers: The psychophysiology of trauma and trauma treatment*. New York: Norton.

Rothschild, B. (2003). *The body remembers casebook: Unifying methods and models in the treatment of trauma and PTSD*. New York: Norton.

Rothschild, B. (2006). *Help for the helper: The psychophysiology of compassion fatigue and vicarious trauma*. New York: Norton.

Rothschild, B. (2009). *8 keys to safe trauma recovery: Take-charge strategies for empowering your healing*. New York: Norton.

Rothschild, B. (in press). *Trauma essentials: A go-to guide for clinicians and clients*. New York: Norton.

BIOGRAPHY

Babette Rothschild, MSW, has been a psychotherapist and body psychotherapist since 1976. She is the author of four professional books and one self-help book, as well as editor of the W. W. Norton *8 Keys* self-help book series. After living for 9 years in Copenhagen, Denmark, she returned to her native Los Angeles, California, in 1997, where she continues to write while maintaining a busy international schedule of lectures, trainings, supervision, and consultation.

Section Three:
Anxiety

Chapter 7

The Art of Persuasion in Anxiety Treatment

Reid Wilson, PhD

It is well established that cognitive-behavioral therapy (CBT) is the treatment of choice for the anxiety disorders. Yet to engage the client in treatment, even skilled CBT clinicians face the daunting task of changing anxious people's rigid belief system regarding how to cope with distress. This is no tabula rasa. Typical clients have long established a mix of avoidance and resistance that is the most successful potion they can conjure up to keep uncertainty and distress from boiling over. They seek help not because their current strategy fails to reduce distress, but because the decision to resist and avoid is generating a new set of problems. The fearful flier can't accept the new job that involves distant travel. The socially anxious professor can't present in grand rounds. The woman with panic disorder doesn't want to remain on medications while pregnant or nursing.

Anxious clients enter treatment with two conflicting stances. The first is that they want to change, have attempted to change on their own and failed, and seek the therapist's guidance. The second is that they do *not* want to feel uncertain or anxious. That is the conundrum I have been studying for 30 years. And here, as succinctly as possible, I share with you three pearls of wisdom from that study.

PEARLS

My career-long attention has been toward self-help. These three pearls, therefore, are directives to the client. They counter the biggest obstacle to therapeutic change: the client's dysfunctional belief system.

Pearl #1. Focus solely on a new frame of reference, not on techniques.

My immediate goal in the therapeutic conversation is to shift clients away from content—"it's about my heart/ my debt/ the safety of the plane/ germs"—and onto the very best strategies to recover from their anxiety disorder. These strategies will always focus on the point of view that currently motivates their actions. Most decisions by anxious clients are motivated by two intentions: (1) to only take actions that have a highly predictable, positive outcome, and (2) to stay comfortable. If you lead with technique or skill practice without accounting for these implicit goals, you will encounter resistance.

Repetition of a new behavior is essential for long-lasting change. But a belief system will always trump exposure practice. You hear this from your clients when they enter treatment. Those with panic disorder will say, "I go to the grocery store. At least three times a week! And I stay there, anxious as hell, sometimes for 45 minutes to an hour. But I'm still no better!" Why? Because as they stand in the threatening situation, their self-talk includes, "God, I hope I don't have a panic attack. I wish I could get out of here. I *hate* this feeling." They resist because they are driven by a point of view expressed by this instruction: "Get safe and get comfortable."

Clients need to frame a new therapeutic view of their problem and its solutions. When they can change their perception about how one beats anxiety, they will invent their *own* homework assignments, as you will see in this chapter's case example.

My primary job is to change my client's mind. Persuasion is an art and a science. It begins with empathizing with clients' beliefs and normalizing those beliefs as universal. *Everyone* seeks comfort. And *everyone* wants to feel confident about certain outcomes. Most people who experience traumatic events—a near drowning, a panic that resembles a heart attack, blanking out in the middle of a conference presentation—initially react by seeking comfort, safety, and reassurance. Persuading clients to change must also include a *convincing* explanation that their solution to the problem—avoiding and resisting, and seeking comfort and certainty—perpetuates their problem. Anything that is resisted will persist; therefore, the best perspective is a paradoxical one: When facing a problem, one must go *toward* uncertainty and distress.

Pearl #2. Create an offensive strategy—seek to be clumsy, awkward, uncomfortable, and uncertain.

Powerful therapeutic frames of reference related to anxiety must be in absolute opposition to clients' current beliefs. The anxious belief is such a stable, protective, well-constructed fortress that it will easily subvert softer alternatives.

Here is how typical clients respond to a task you assign: "This therapist sounds like she knows what she's doing. I guess I'll try it. But I'm worried about how it's going to go. I don't want to get *too* anxious. And I hope this is going to work—that it helps me start feeling better soon. And I hope I don't go through what I did last time, when I still didn't perform very well." This stance directly undermines the therapeutic efforts. Remember, belief trumps behavior. With anxiety, the belief is always "I should defend myself." Thus, clients stay safe by backing away from challenges, by playing it safe. To take back territory lost to anxiety, they must push forward aggressively into arenas where they previously surrendered. When I offer a behavioral assignment, I subsume it *underneath* the primary goal of generating such an offensive strategy. Since anxiety *requires* that the person seek out comfort and certainty, clients should voluntarily and purposely seek out the sense of feeling clumsy, awkward, doubtful, and distressed. "Courage first; comfort last," should be their motto.

Understanding this concept intellectually is easier than implementing it. The best way is to act instead of think. I help clients adopt rules that they follow *unquestioningly* during their threatening events. It is a poor therapeutic strategy to wait until the moment of threat to choose a response, because the mind tends to regress back to a defensive mode at these times. Instead, they are to generate firm rules during the treatment session and activate them at the threatening moment. These rules, of course, are paradoxical. My goal is to convince clients of the following:

- Shooting for *clumsiness* is a winning strategy.
- *Wanting* to feel awkward and uncomfortable will counter their dysfunctional strategy of trying to get better while they simultaneously stay comfortable.
- *Seeking out uncertainty* gives them a competing alternative to their impulse to become quickly certain of a safe outcome.

Pearl #3. Help clients believe they can cope with failure.

The most difficult-to-handle fears of anxious clients are those of catastrophic consequences. The panic-prone client will say, "I think I now can cope with a #6-level panic. But what if I have a #10?! I can't handle that!" The fearful flier: "I think I can handle a flight now, but what if we have to sit on the tarmac for 4 hours? I can't handle that!" The socially anxious: "I'm prepared to give my report now. But what if they start peppering me with questions? I can't handle that!"

These stances invite clients to worry, over-prepare, avoid, and resist. All of these crutches perpetuate their anxiety regarding a threat. One strategic mistake therapists make is to rely on cognitive methods to challenge the likelihood of such catastrophic events. Although these approaches can be useful, they have a major limitation: You can never reassure anxious clients enough. First, anxious people tend to seek *absolute* certainty, not relative certainty. I remember feeling like I did a bang-up job convincing one client of the safety of commercial flights. I concluded with, "Do you have any idea of the probability of dying on a plane? Think about this: If you flew every single day of your life, it would take 26,000 *years* before your number would be up." "Yeah?" he said. "But what about the guy sitting next to me? What if his number is up!?" We can never give them the absolute certainty they demand.

Even if I convincingly persuade clients of the unlikelihood of a catastrophic outcome, that reassurance is unstable. In a threatening moment, the anxious mind races to worst-case scenarios, overriding any softer message of "it probably won't happen."

So, instead of emphasizing the low probability of catastrophes, it is better to switch the attention to coping strategies. Most studies of resilience—the ability to spring back from adversity—indicate that the critical variable is self-efficacy. Here's the overarching position I shoot for: "Whatever happens, I'll handle it." To accomplish this, I don't necessarily challenge whether the bad event will occur; I challenge the client's *perspective* about that outcome. Albert Ellis, one of the great pioneering innovators of cognitive treatment, taught people to degrade events from perceived catastrophes to manageable events. Clients have the ability to shift their perception of an upcoming event from "humiliating" down to "embarrassing," from "the end of life as I know it" to "pretty tough for a while." To reach that perspective, I help my clients detail all their feared outcomes and extend a timeline out into the future, outlining their possible coping strategies. Clients initially fight that protocol because to be so concrete increases their anxiety. But the research is clear: The more specific you are about the variables associated with a future feared event, the easier it is to generate coping strategies. That leads to self-assurance: "I can handle it."

CASE EXAMPLE: MATT

Matt, in his mid-30s, came from out of state to attend my 2-day treatment group for obsessive-compulsive disorder (OCD). I knew nothing of his history, and I never asked about it. All I had was a written referral from a health professional, confirmation of the diagnosis, and a list of his obsessions and compulsions. Two distinct central obsessions dominated his waking life: that he would become contaminated, and that he would not understand some critical information. His compulsions included repeating behaviors in sets of 4, 8, 16, or 20; touching items in a specific sequence; counting; and rereading in a certain numbered order. He further protected his safety by avoiding as many threatening events as possible. The week before treatment his Yale-Brown Obsessive Compulsive Scale (Y-BOCS) score was 23, indicating the highest end of moderate severity.

The group treatment consisted of 12 hours of cognitive therapy focused on persuading eight clients to change their relationship with OCD. This protocol was reinforced by behavioral assignments during both of the 90-minute lunch breaks as well as the overnight break between sessions. Within the first 3 hours, I had constructed a new frame of reference that depicted OCD as a mental game in which the clients had adopted a 100% defensive strategy. Because one cannot win a game without an offensive strategy, we created an aggressive plan to take territory back from OCD. The Saturday lunch break offered the first opportunity to score points; we used an actual score-card for each event. The primary ways to score were:

- When I say, "I *want* this [anxiety or doubt]," I am clear *why* I mean it.
- When I say, "I want this [anxiety or doubt] to *stick around*," I am clear *why* I mean it.
- When I say, "I want this [anxiety or doubt] to *feel intense*," I am clear *why* I mean it.

I suspected that Matt was going to be a good student of the work, because he peppered me with questions and doubts during that morning session. I wanted skepticism *actively expressed* in the session, so I could acknowledge and handle it. Hidden doubt undermines treatment by supporting passivity.

My hunch was right. Before lunch, each person identified three tasks he or she would practice during the break. As we debriefed, Matt didn't attempt three practices; he completed eleven. He was focusing on a frame of reference, not technique. **He knew the assignment was to *seek out uncertainty* and *seek out doubt*, and to score as many points as he could in that pursuit** (*pearl #1: Focus solely on a new frame of reference, not techniques*). So he continued to generate opportunities to feel contaminated by money, door handles, trashcans, and the floor. He created doubt and distress by glancing at provocative headlines without paying close attention and by breaking his compulsive pattern of counting sequences. He told the group, "Every time the obsessions tried to grab my attention, I'd say, 'This is just noise,' and I'd move on."

On Sunday morning his report of his overnight practices reflected his attention to a strategy of offense instead of simply applying technique. Practice started immediately, as soon as he left the parking lot. "Driving home I looked at things—signs, cars, etc. that had been causing me to count—and I tried to bring on anxiety and counting. But it didn't really happen." Once again, he practiced throughout the evening. But one event proved daunting, and he avoided it until the last moment before driving to the group. This consisted of touching a "contaminated" bottle of alcohol, causing him to contaminate everything else that he touched. This took great courage. On the drive to the group he became overwhelmed by the awful awareness of what he had done. "I started crying, and then I started to hyperventilate. Then my arm went numb, and I couldn't hold the steering wheel. I switched arms, and my other arm started getting numb. Then my leg that was pressing the gas pedal started getting numb and felt like it was locked in place."

"I was still crying, hyperventilating, and then I started talking out loud as if I was telling this story to the others at the session. It was strange. I wondered if I should stop the car but I didn't. This went on for about 20 minutes. Much of the time I was telling myself that I wanted to be anxious—and I was! I wanted it to be intense—and it was! I wanted it to last—and it was! **Because I wanted to get the things on the list that I had given up. I wanted to be in control and not be controlled by my OCD** (*pearl #3*)." Matt's stance here reflected the third pearl: Believe you can cope with failure. The group listed all the things they had given up in their lives because of OCD: time, relaxation, business and education pursuits, family and personal relationships. When these types of lists are strong with valued activities, as Matt's was, it becomes an achievable future that empowers clients to take risks. You will hear them say, "I want [this positive experience] back in my life. I'm fighting for that. Whatever bad happens here, I'll figure out how to handle it." Now, instead of fighting against the anxiety disorder, they are fighting to gain the life they deserve.

About 20 minutes after his anxiety began, Matt calmed down. And then? **He stopped at a diner so he could do a few more exposure practices before he arrived** (*pearl #2: Create an offensive strategy*)! He glanced at headlines on the television, pumped the soap dispenser the wrong number of times, grabbed the door handle without the usual paper towel. "Then I decided that I needed more anxiety." So he ordered a coffee simply so that he could touch cash. What an incredible commitment to winning this game! The entire group was in awe.

During Sunday's lunch break Matt was a whirlwind of practice, managing 23 specific provocative tasks. Remember, the assignment was to practice three tasks, so this assertiveness reflected Matt's sense of self-efficacy—his belief that his actions could help him heal. His words revealed that he was directing his actions through principles: His orientation toward OCD was to get anxious on purpose. Listen to his words: "I didn't feel very anxious, *so I decided* to [engage in another provocative practice]." If a practice *was* provocative enough, then "I started to get anxious—and reminded myself that that was the feeling I wanted." By the end of the break, "I still had a few minutes before the afternoon session so I made another unscheduled stop" for more practices. You go, Matt!

After the weekend treatment group, he continued his offensive strategy, practicing multiple times a day, all subsumed under his overarching strategy to push into OCD's territory. If he noticed any hesitation, he would coach himself, "I've got to do it. I need the anxiety! I need it to last, and I need it to be intense."

Seven days after treatment, Matt's Y-BOCS score had shifted dramatically down to an 11—within the mild range—from his 23 when the weekend began. At a month post-treatment his score was 10. By month two, his score dropped to a mild level of 8, where it stabilized through the one-year follow-up.

CONCLUDING COMMENTS

Those with anxiety disorders struggle during times of uncertainty. Worries dominate consciousness, and people respond to worries defensively by avoiding, fighting, running away, or bracing, as depicted in figure 7.1. Treatment introduces clients to unfamiliar, paradoxical strategies. However, these protocols are strengthened by two powerful forces: clients' positive intentions and inner resources. Positive intentions include a commitment to take back their life, including produc-

tivity, intimacy, relaxation and pleasure, and exploration of new territory. Inner resources include the ability to seek perspective on a
problem so that they can coach themselves regarding the best actions.
Everything new involves doubt. Therefore, clients must also be willing
to be scared and act anyway; that's courage. To seek any of these activities clients must find within themselves the willingness to tolerate
doubts about the outcome and to lose as well as win. One of the func-
tions of treatment is to help clients access their positive intentions, to
offer them a new, therapeutic perspective, and to coach them to be
courageous until they are capable of coaching themselves.

FIGURE 7.1

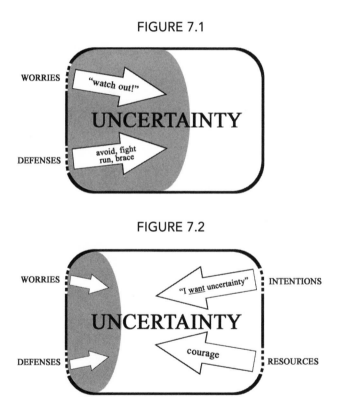

FIGURE 7.2

As illustrated in figure 7.2, during moments of uncertainty related to
their anxiety disorder, clients take back territory from the disorder by
pushing forward with a willingness to be uncertain and the courage to
tolerate an unknown outcome. In that protocol you find all three of

the pearls I intend to pass on to my clients: Lead with a paradoxical frame of reference, push into your awkwardness and doubt, and be willing to lose in order to win.

BIBLIOGRAPHY

Foa, E. B., & Wilson, R. R. (2001). *Stop Obsessing! How to Overcome Your Obsessions and Compulsions* (2nd ed.). New York: Bantam.

Wilson, R. R. (2003). *Facing Panic: Self-Help for People with Panic Attacks*. Silver Spring, MD: Anxiety Disorders Association of America.

Wilson, R. R. (2009). *Don't Panic: Taking Control of Anxiety Attacks* (3rd ed.). New York: Collins Living.

BIOGRAPHY

Reid Wilson, PhD, has specialized in the treatment of anxiety disorders since 1980. He is the author of the classic self-help book *Don't Panic: Taking Control of Anxiety Attacks* and coauthor with Edna Foa, PhD, of *Stop Obsessing! How to Overcome Your Obsessions and Compulsions.* He designed and served as lead psychologist for American Airlines' first national program for fearful fliers. Wilson served on the board of directors of the Anxiety Disorders Association of America for 12 years. His free self-help website, www.anxieties.com, serves 385,000 visitors (16 million hits) per year.

Chapter 8
Tools for Treating Anxiety: Optimizing the Chances for Success

Margaret Wehrenberg, PhD

In my early years as a therapist I learned the hard way that developing complex or interesting psychodynamic themes with clients about their lives left me with excellent theories and not much else to offer them right away. I too often felt helpless facing the distress of frantically worried clients, unable to give the immediate relief they needed.

I eventually came to believe that change can occur first, allowing clients relief from symptoms while they work at the underlying causes of their problems. My empathy for clients suffering anxiety led me to look for methods to teach them immediately, and I developed a compendium of tools for symptom relief. I noted that clients who needed therapy for deeper issues, such as the impact of childhood abuse, were more willing to continue when they felt their anxiety had abated. I discovered that symptom relief was the necessary beginning of a good course of therapy.

As I learned more about anxiety, I began to recognize a specific kind of client more often: the client who looks serene to acquaintances and colleagues but feels frantic underneath that façade. Many of these clients believe they are frauds and will be found out. With these clients, I want them to see themselves as I do—to recognize how very competent they are to accomplish so many positive things in their lives while under such duress! But I have also often met new clients who have had years of therapy with other clinicians, have acquired deep insight into their situation, and yet have no practical interventions that undo anxiety symptoms.

PEARLS

I am convinced that if therapists apply the simple (but not necessarily easy to master) skills of anxiety management, their work will be the better for it and many people suffering pervasive anxiety will be better served. It has become my mission to share this view with other therapists by writing articles and books and teaching on this topic. I offer in this chapter some of the "pearls of wisdom" that I have developed.

Pearl #1. Make sure you completely understand the "Why now?" when a person enters therapy.

I try to refrain from making assumptions about clients so I can think more clearly about them as individuals. This first major pearl for anxiety treatment reflects the importance of that. There are actually two aspects to the question "Why are you entering therapy now?" The first is "What is happening now?" Inquiring about current lifestyle behaviors—sleep, nutrition, exercise, stressors—can reveal causes of anxiety that can easily be changed. The second aspect of the question looks for triggers in the client's current life situation that are based in his or her history and are escalating anxiety at this specific time, but which may not be evident to the client. Paying attention to these clarifies assumptions I might make about the cause of anxiety.

Most people are not paragons of physical self-care, and certain lifestyle habits—unhealthy diet, poor sleep hygiene, insufficient exercise, alcohol or drug use—can contribute to anxiety. The joke is that if you have anxiety "you can't have CATS"—meaning *c*affeine, *a*lcohol, *t*obacco, and *s*weeteners. I am often surprised at how frequently otherwise intelligent people eat large quantities of potato chips and cola, ignoring good nutrition, and how seldom people exercise. Because many lifestyle factors make anxiety much worse, I now interview everyone very specifically about caffeine consumption, alcohol and drug use patterns, smoking, and use of sugar and artificial sweeteners.

All of these can make people more agitated. (Younger clients especially do not recognize the connections between these and feeling more anxious.)

Caffeine is not just a stimulant that makes worry and stress more intense; it can also trigger panic attacks, even in small amounts. Smoking as an activity is often connected to calming, but deep breathing will do just as well. Many smokers do not notice (until they quit) how each cigarette increases anxiety, as they hear the voice in their heads telling them smoking might kill them. I ask clients to keep simple records that rate anxiety levels before and after each cigarette and also for the day before heavy consumption of alcohol and the day following. Clients are usually surprised at the level of anxiety they feel post-cigarette or on hangover day. This record-keeping connects cause and effect and helps clients decide whether the smoke or drink is worth the anxiety—they often think not!

Sleep patterns and exercise don't cause anxiety but play major roles in recovery. I work with people on sleep hygiene and on developing the will and the habit to exercise aerobically 5 days a week. This may seem simple but it does not happen easily. Therapists can help clients pay attention to obstacles to self-care and help raise their motivation to do what is necessary.

The possibilities for how life history can be activated by current situations, causing anxiety for "unknown reasons," are hugely varied. However, it has never ceased to amaze me that anxiety crosses the line from manageable to unmanageable when triggered by some common things:

- Stress can put people "over the edge" of coping ability if they have an insufficient ability to self-soothe due to a childhood in a cold or chaotic family.
- Clients with children may suffer anxiety when their child hits the age at which the client him- or herself had a trauma. This is so common that it is a useful line of inquiry with clients who have children at home.
- The same is true when the client's child suffers a problem similar to one the client experienced in childhood.

- Clients may become anxious when they have a life experience, like getting fired from a job, that parallels a childhood situation in its emotional qualities.

Whatever a person's life history, consider whether life circumstances today are activating something from history. I do not make assumptions about how to handle the issue until I see how they respond to anxiety-management techniques. Because I know clients need to learn to handle anxiety before they can do more psychotherapy, I have time to assess when and how to work with life-history issues.

Pearl #2. Learn to ignore physical symptoms.

The physiology of panic, social anxiety, and generalized anxiety contributes to the serious distress of anxiety disorders. The pounding heart and shortness of breath of a panic attack convince people they are dying; people with social anxiety blush and sweat and avoid any situation where they might be scrutinized. Generalized anxiety worriers can feel washed over by dread, the sensation that something awful is about to happen. These physical sensations of anxiety are so aversive that people go to great lengths to avoid whatever sets them off. A major presenting problem in all anxiety sufferers is avoiding situations when they would be better off participating in them. Things people often avoid, like driving or flying, speaking up in class, or applying for jobs, are all important things for people to do. To get back into the world means getting out of their bodies—or at least getting their attention off of their bodies.

Pearl #3. Anxiety is a condition looking for content.

As I studied neurobiology, I finally understood the reasons behind what I have told clients for many years: "Your anxiety is a condition looking for content. It is like a separate voice in your mind, inviting you to worry. It does not matter if you have anything to actually worry about. Your anxiety will find something without fail." A brain disposed to ruminating on anxiety, when there is nothing on the horizon that is worrisome, will hypervigilantly scan for what is happening in life until it finds a problem to attach to. Once clients understand the premise that they can control worry rather than get reassurance for their worries, they are truly on the road to eliminating anxiety.

People tend to seek reassurance for specific anxieties, and that is a therapeutic trap. Clients want to know what they are worrying about could never happen. They have sought out parents or friends or spouses to tell them that over and over. But still they worry. Don't try to make therapy reassuring. Rather, teach clients that their anxious brains get stuck on thoughts. The neurobiology of worry makes it clear: Rumination happens for biological reasons, not because some worry starts it. The ruminating brain looks for a specific worry to get stuck on. Anxiety treatment teaches people how to stop ruminating, not how to eliminate a specific worry. Thought-stopping, thought replacement, and worry-management techniques are vital. The more persistently people can interrupt and divert worry, the less their brains will generate it.

CASE EXAMPLE: JERRY

Jerry, an engineer in his late 20s with some years of work experience, was married with an infant son. He came to see me because he was tired of "feeling like a duck"—looking as if he was serenely sweeping through the water of life while underneath paddling like crazy with his feet. (This is a metaphor I hear quite frequently.) Nauseated with fear, his face sweating, he would sometimes get off the phone with a customer and wonder how the person could have missed the quiver in his voice. At times he had to close his office door so no one could witness how shaky he was. He ruminated constantly and the feelings of anxiety robbed his life of pleasure. He was even starting to avoid social gatherings because he did not feel he could set aside worrying long enough to have any fun.

Jerry's demeanor was pleasant but his inner life was far from it. He felt tormented daily by worries that he would not pay the right attention to his infant son, or feed him the right foods, or provide the right stimulation for a perfect childhood. He said he had panic attacks at widely varied times, such as reading email from colleagues or working on a household repair. He had stopped being able to sleep well and finally decided he wanted some help. His wife had researched anxiety online and they decided together he should not use medication, preferring to try therapy.

When I interviewed Jerry, it was clear from his constant, nagging worry that he was suffering generalized anxiety and that his self-identified "panic attacks" were actually bursts of acute anxiety, not full-fledged panic with its heart-pounding tachycardia and shortness of breath. Rather, Jerry felt intensely agitated and jumpy, pacing and preoccupied with a nauseating sense of doom and dread that he could not explain. His anxiety attacks left him feeling physically and mentally weak. I knew he needed physiological relief, but he would also need to eventually focus on his cognitive symptoms of worry and dread.

Jerry's history included being emotionally deserted by both parents when they divorced. He was about 11, and he reported that his mother "just left." Jerry bounced erratically between his mother's and father's houses but really was alone much of the time. He made most of his own decisions about where to go, whom to hang out with, even what to eat and whether to do his schoolwork. He "got his act together" when he got his first job after college, married a woman he admired, and focused on his career. Their first child was born a few months before he came to treatment.

Today Jerry bore the burden of being competent without knowing that he was. Without parental instruction for childhood and adolescent tasks and missing all approval for a job well done, Jerry learned things on his own when he was young. Now he did a lot of jobs well but then doubted the quality of his work. No matter what the task, he would reread instructions, examine charts, review and even redo work, trying to reassure himself that he was doing it "right." (This tendency is familiar to many adults raised in chaotic or disengaged families, such as those with parental addiction. Most feel they are incompetent and that this secret will be revealed someday. They live in dread of that moment.)

The first part of treatment with Jerry involved looking at the "Why now?" (*pearl #1*). He usually tried to get by on 6 hours of sleep, but when he started having restless sleep from the anxiety, he became too tired, so his caffeine use soared. A vicious cycle of tired-caffeine-agitation-poor sleep-tired began. He agreed to cut his caffeine use, including colas, over the course of a week down to a morning mug of coffee, switching to decaf thereafter. Jerry had also stopped working out when his son was born. He believed he had to give his son every minute of his attention when he was home. I wanted to help him clarify his values of parenting to see if his belief was true. He actually believed that his son would be okay if one parent was with him. Jerry and his wife were able to get a workout schedule in place without compromising "parent time" with their son. With less caffeine, more exercise, and some of his worry about parenting gone, Jerry's sleep began to improve. That took some of the edge off his anxiety.

Despite more rest, however, Jerry was so preoccupied with how bad he felt physically that he kept returning to his weakness as a source of concern. When he was washed over by acute anxiety, it left him feeling depleted. He was feeling anxious about feeling anxious, in much the same way that people with panic worry about having another panic attack. I believed Jerry needed a rest from the acuteness of his anxiety. Medical checkups revealed no physical problems, and he agreed to give therapy some time to help with feeling weak. I explained how his brain and his body were not separate, and his brain was generating worry that his body felt. Constant stress and worry can result in feelings of weakness, but he found it hard to disbelieve his body. If he could ignore his physiology for a while and focus on controlling worry, he would notice that he felt better physically.

Unlike with panic disorder, where clients use breathing and relaxation to interrupt panic attacks right from the start of therapy, Jerry needed first to learn to control his cognitions in order to control the physiology. He brought specific worries into therapy, seeking reassurance. One week he fretted about whether to let his son cry while he prepared a bottle and the next he worried about whether he should stay up late to respond to emails colleagues sent during the evening. I saw this as his anxiety being a condition looking for content. Interrupting his worry would require him to learn to control the process of worrying, not just learning to defeat one worry at a time. **As we looked at his worries from one week to the next, Jerry began to see that as soon as he felt relief from one situation, he would start worrying**

about something else. His anxiety was always present, just looking for something to attach itself to (*pearl #3*).

We began to work like weaving a tapestry: interrupting the physiology of acute anxiety while weaving in ideas to control worry. First Jerry learned skills like thought-stopping to interrupt his worries. Planned thought replacement—finding thoughts and activities that were neutral or pleasant—was a challenge for him, but he was quite persistent in applying that method. He liked the method of containing worry to a particular time of day, and picked the first 15 minutes at work alone in his office because then, when he was done with his planned worry time, he would quickly have the distraction of the workday to help keep worry contained.

As he was able to do that, Jerry got better at spotting when his worried thoughts began. To his surprise, he could spot the physical sensation of dread that occurred prior to having a specific worry. He learned that when he felt the physical sensations, he could say, **"This is just my anxious brain," and then do diaphragmatic breathing, which he learned easily, and then quickly divert his thoughts to something calming** (*pearl #2: Learn to ignore physical symptoms*). He could interrupt the worry that he was about to have, even in response to things that previously would have triggered an acute bout of anxiety. Not only did he suffer less from the feelings of dread that nauseated him, but his ability to interrupt worry also gave him a sense of control. Finally Jerry felt he had ideas for getting rid of *worry* instead of getting rid of a *particular* worry.

Jerry was doing so well interrupting and containing anxiety that he abruptly decided not to return to therapy, even though I suggested he still had to consider the "Why now?" part of his anxiety. I believed that his life history of abandonment and the birth of his son were related to his increased anxiety, but I ended our work with an invitation to return any time he desired.

Three months later, Jerry returned to therapy, feeling as if all his progress was wasted and wondering if he really should try medication. His anxiety had come roaring back and he could not see any reason for it. Again, we explored the "Why now?" Lifestyle factors, like cheating himself of sleep, had again played a role, but the "one big change had nothing to do with me," he said. His son had started going to day care. He felt so anxious that first day that he left work early, blaming his nausea on stomach flu, and skipped the next day of work. But, as many people discover, being home all day had made his anxiety worse, not better. He found things to worry about every day and said it was as if he had never learned to control worry. This is fairly common when people learn almost enough but do not fully address the trigger for why they sought therapy at a specific time. "Why now?" is often identified by looking at lifestyle, but life history tells why lifestyle changes become triggers for different kinds of anxiety.

We went to work on identifying Jerry's persistent anxious thoughts. An acute bout of anxiety in a hardware store gave us an important clue to the trigger. He was looking for a replacement for a hinge that was no longer made. He was able to see in retrospect that he started to sweat and feel sick when he had the thought, "I don't know how to choose the right one." All of his life he had made choices with no idea of whether the choice was right. If something worked out well, he told himself it was luck, not his competence. Despite having become competent in so many ways, Jerry always waited for the time when he would choose wrongly and his life would come apart. His anxiety was a condition looking for content, and Jerry's content had a theme based on his life history.

When he was ready to see that he had always felt incompetent and was searching for evidence of competence, he could see why the birth of his son put him over the edge. He had always been a worrier, but responsibility for a child was too much: The stakes of being a competent father were much higher than the stakes of getting a good grade at college or building a bookshelf in his house. Now that he had a son, there was an area of responsibility that came without an instruction manual. How does a father raise a son? Jerry did not know, having no template in his mind for good parenting. Whenever he read something about development he felt better for a while, but then, as children are wont to do, his son changed and Jerry's anxiety crashed back.

Now in therapy we could put into place an important concept for people whose anxiety is a condition looking for content: There are procedures by which you can measure competence and ways to tell when you have done all that is in your control. Competency troubles many with anxiety, whether it is the competence to handle panic, the competence to conduct social exchanges, or, as in Jerry's case, the competence to know if he was doing a "good enough" job. Feelings of incompetence are fertile ground for the "condition looking for content," because people who are uncertain will easily find new worries. They need a process to assess whether their worry is necessary, and they need to follow a procedure by which they can assess their competence. Such procedures can be found or created for any variety of worry, from work life to parenting. We set out to help Jerry find those procedures for his concerns about parenting and being good enough.

First of all, we addressed the content or theme of his worry. Anyone who can find a theme for their worries, as Jerry did, will want to resolve those specific life-history issues with psychotherapy, and there are many methods to work with historical concerns. One of the methods that helped Jerry was a method called "Focusing," developed by Eugene Gendlin, which is a way to identify feelings and resolve them. Jerry also did some journaling for neural integration, that is, he wrote about situations regarding his son in which he felt more emotional than seemed reasonable. It created awareness of unrecognized emotions and allowed him to discuss how earlier life experiences influenced his current emotional responses (see Siegel and Hartzell, 2003). We used eye movement desensitization and reprocessing (EMDR), developed by Francine Shapiro for trauma resolution and installing resources, to work through issues about how lost and incompetent he felt.

However, it seemed prudent to help Jerry learn and specifically apply some of the general principles that would help him to independently assess competence. Some examples of these principles that apply to many situations are:

- "Good enough is usually good enough."
- "No one can know how to do something without an opportunity to learn it."
- "When learning something new, find out who does it well and get input."

- "All people make mistakes while learning."
- "The process of all learning is progress, not perfection."
- "You will survive your mistakes."
- "In parenting, perfection is not only impossible but also not desirable."
- "Figure out what you can control now, what you can control later, and what you can never control."

Jerry's biggest concern was finding a parenting standard. We worked toward having him learn some rules of good parenting and follow them well—not perfectly. Discussing whose opinions to value, Jerry selected some parenting "gurus" whose books he could study. He had a couple of friends who seemed great at parenting and Jerry found they were delighted to talk about parenting when they got together socially. He figured out he would need to know things about how to parent as his son went through different stages of development, but he was able to relax and promise himself to learn about them later rather than try to figure out everything at once. This was a good use of the principle of deciding what one can control now and what one can control later!

Jerry also talked with his wife about their values system and found her willing to plan with him for how they would spend time with their son—whether they ate meals together, what kinds of routines they wanted for him, and so on. He could see that the way to measure his parenting was to look at whether he was living by his values, and that became an excellent anti-anxiety tool.

This time when Jerry terminated therapy, he felt he knew the difference between controlling the *process* of worry and the *content* of worry. And he had securely resolved the life triggers that had caused his anxiety to spiral out of control.

CONCLUDING COMMENTS

These clinical pearls are simple but profound. Putting them into practice will bring clients immeasurable relief and help therapists set the stage for more effective ongoing therapy. I hope that any therapist reading this chapter will be inspired to explore further for methods to provide hope and relief to their anxious clients.

BIBLIOGRAPHY

Gendlin, E. (1998). *Focusing-oriented psychotherapy*. New York: Guilford.

Shapiro, F. (2001). *Eye Movement Desensitization and Reprocessing: Basic Principles, Protocols, and Procedures* (2nd ed.). New York: Guilford.

Seigel, D., & Hartzell, M. (2003). *Parenting from the inside out*. New York: Putnam.

Wehrenberg, M. (2008). *The ten best-ever anxiety management techniques*. New York: Norton.

Wehrenberg, M., & Prinz, S. (2007). *The anxious brain: The neurobiological basis of anxiety disorders and how to effectively treat them*. New York: Norton.

BIOGRAPHY

Margaret Wehrenberg, PhD, is the author of two books on the neurobiology and treatment of anxiety. She has also written articles for magazines, including the award-winning *Psychotherapy Networker*. Wehrenberg earned her MA specializing in psychodrama and play therapy with children, and she had years of experience as a drug and alcoholism counselor before earning her PsyD and beginning a private practice as a licensed clinical psychologist in Illinois. Her private psychotherapy practice is located in Naperville, Illinois. More information about her work can be found at www.margaretwehrenberg.com.

Section Four:
Grief

Chapter 9
Grief, Illness, and Loss

Kenneth J. Doka, PhD

The mandate of the editor—to select from decades of clinical work three succinct techniques that qualify as "pearls"—is a daunting challenge, especially in an area as complex as counseling persons and families adapting to life-threatening illness and loss. Yet, as I critically reviewed my own work, I was able to identify three techniques or clinical focal points that seem to have some originality.

PEARLS

I have repeatedly used these pearls in my own clinical practice. I often teach the first two pearls in my classes and workshops. I teach the third, therapeutic ritual, in workshop and class settings but also have written more extensively about it (Martin & Doka, 2000; Doka, 2002a; 2008a).

Pearl #1. Explore the prehistory of relationships.

In assisting persons in dealing with loss, grief therapists generally explore the history of the relationship for clues toward understanding the nature of the attachment and consequent grief. For example, in assessing a grief reaction following the death of a spouse, it would be routine to begin by understanding how the couple met and then reviewing their courtship, wedding, and subsequent marriage. When a child dies, assessments often begin with the pregnancy.

I have found it useful to contextualize the relationship—that is, to begin before the beginning. Often this means getting a sense of the milieu that underlies the relationship. Many times this allows the therapist and client to gain an insight not always immediately apparent. For example, with spousal bereavement, I generally ask clients to tell me where they were 6 months before they met their mate.

When parents are grieving the death of a child, it is certainly important to review the period prior to the pregnancy. What was the birth order of the child? Was there anything especially significant in the circumstances of the pregnancy, birth, name, or gender? Was the pregnancy planned? Was the pregnancy especially difficult? However, I also like to go back even further. Most people, even prior to puberty, have images of the families they would like to have. Some may even have a fantasized idea of the age spacing, genders, and even names of the children they would one day hope to have. Examining these dreams can offer insight to the unique meaning of that child to the parent.

Even in the death of a parent, I ask the surviving children to recount the circumstances, as far as they know them, surrounding their own birth. In one illustrative case, the adult child recounted that his mother became pregnant prior to marriage, causing her to drop out of college and the father to secretly marry her as he completed his college education (their college did not allow married students at that time). Once the client acknowledged that reality, he understood the long-ambivalent relationship he had had with his parents—one that was not shared by his siblings.

Pearl #2. Help clients use their support systems well.

There are many circumstances in life where clients need the support of others. This can include individuals struggling with loss, caregiving, or illness. Many people have significant support systems but fail to use them effectively. I use an approach where clients assess the ways their support system most effectively supports them—an approach I have labeled DLR, for "Doers-Listeners-Respite." The DLR approach has two major benefits. First, it reaffirms to clients that they have a support system. Second, it allows clients to identify the most appropriate support members of their system.

This procedure should only be used when prior assessment has indicated that the client does, in fact, have a support system. For example, one of my clients was a 90-year-old woman struggling to take care of her equally aged husband. One of her three children had predeceased her. Another had a history of mental illness and was alienated from the family and possibly homeless. A third child was supportive but aging and ill herself and living over 1500 miles away. This client had outlived all of her siblings and friends. Someone so isolated would not be a good candidate for such a process, as it would only serve to highlight her isolation.

Assuming they are not so isolated, I assign clients homework of making a list of their support system. When the client returns with the list, I query as to completeness. Are there additional family and friends who ought to be included? Are there neighbors who should be on the list? Is the client involved in a faith community or other organizations? Are there persons from those organizations who should be included?

Once the list is complete, I ask clients to assign letters to each of the entries. "D" is for *doers*—these are the people you can count on to complete a promised task. "L" is for friends who are good *listeners*. "R" is used for persons who offer *respite*. I stress that grief (or caregiving, coping with illness, etc.) is hard work. Like any hard work, one needs time away. Respite people provide that. Their gift is that they generally do not focus on the problem. Rather, they offer a good time—a quiet dinner, companionship for a movie or concert, or perhaps a few laughs. Counselors should note that whereas multiple letters can be assigned to some individuals, respite persons are rarely assigned more than one letter.

This list is then processed between client and therapist. Often clients gain two insights. One is that they may not be using their support systems effectively. The second is that they have a renewed appreciation for those offering respite—persons once perceived as uncaring.

Pearl #3. Use therapeutic ritual.
Before history there were rituals. The tombs of prehistoric individuals

bear mute testimony to carefully performed rituals perhaps designed to send the dead to their afterlife. Rituals are powerful. Gennep (1960) described rituals as *liminal*, meaning they are transitional events that exist at the threshold between consciousness and unconsciousness. As a person goes through the steps of a particular ritual, strong feelings and reactions may emerge from the unconscious. For example, one may experience goose bumps or become tearful without being fully aware of what is creating these reactions.

The effect of rituals may be intrapsychic as well as psychosocial or social. Depending on the nature of the ritual, it may confer and reaffirm a changed state or status for the participants. For example, a boy leaves his bar mitzvah as a man, and two single people leave their wedding as a couple. Public rituals such as these have an additional social component—others who witness this transition are expected to affirm their support for it (Romanoff & Terenzio, 1998).

Because rituals are so beneficial, there is value in harnessing their power as a therapeutic tool. Much research indicates that funerals can be highly therapeutic (e.g., Bolton & Camp, 1987, 1989; Doka, 1984; Gross & Klass, 1997; Reeves & Boersma, 1990). Rituals can be developed for use as a therapeutic tool with individuals, families, or groups to facilitate the grieving process. Different rituals convey different meanings. Building on the work of Gennep (1960), Rando (1993), and Martin and Doka (2000), I delineate four kinds of rituals.

Rituals of continuity emphasize the continuing bond with the deceased. These can be quite simple. For example, a family might light a candle on the anniversary of the death or some other significant time to evoke the memory and continued bond with the deceased.

Rituals of transition mark some movement or change in the grieving process. For example, before the father of one of my clients, Jason, essentially abandoned his family, Jason had made a plaque in his middle-school ceramics class that said "Daddy's Garage." The divorce of his parents and subsequent paternal disinterest troubled Jason deeply. After a few months, he took the plaque down from the garage wall and carefully pulverized it. He proudly announced to his mother that it was no longer "Daddy's garage" and took over the space himself. Rituals of transition mark times of change.

Rituals of reconciliation tend to finish business—that is, they allow the grieving individual to express or receive forgiveness, or to offer a last message or simple farewell. For example, Joan, another client, lived much of her life struggling with her father's alcoholism. When her father developed cancer, he became and remained sober for the 2 years until his death as he struggled with his illness. In this period, she saw another side of her father. He was now an attentive and loving husband, father, and grandfather. When he died, Joan felt cheated. She experienced a loving father for only 2 years—had he been sober, she realized her life and her mother's life would have been very different. Eventually, she wrote her father a long letter conveying all her conflicted emotions, including her pride in his sobriety, her disappointment that he waited so long to recover, and her regret over the past. She read, and subsequently burned, the letter at her father's grave, witnessed by her own family, her siblings, and her mother. She was relieved that "she had said her piece."

Rituals of affirmation allow the bereaved person to thank the lost person for his or her presence and legacies. Ten-year-old Kieran and his father had often fished together—a sport they both loved. For a long time after his father's death, Kieran did not fish. When he decided to fish again, he reverently buried the first fish he caught near his father's grave, thanking his dad for teaching him the sport and promising that whenever he fished, he would remember his father and the special moments they shared.

A few principles should guide the creation of these therapeutic rituals. First, they should not be imposed but rather developed from the bereaved individual's own narrative of loss and grief. That narrative will suggest the appropriate kind of ritual and offer clues as to who should participate or witness it and what objects should be included. Rituals can be private or witnessed by small or even large audiences. The second principle is that rituals should include visual objects chosen for their symbolism. Third, rituals should be fully planned and carefully processed. Finally, rituals are likely to be more powerful if they include primal elements—for example, fire, water, music or chimes as wind, and flowers as earth. Because they are liminal, rituals can harness power in a therapeutic environment.

CASE EXAMPLE: MARION

Marion was a 43-year-old Caucasian woman who had been a fourth-grade teacher for 29 years. She first came to counseling as she was dealing with the illness of her husband, Jack. A year ago Jack had been diagnosed with ALS (amyotrophic lateral sclerosis), often known as Lou Gehrig's disease—a progressive, generally fatal motor-neuron disease. It was suggested that Marion seek counseling, as she was having a difficult time accepting Jack's diagnosis and prognosis. Marion had alternated between urging Jack to seek additional opinions and exhorting him to try alternative treatments such as herbal remedies, vitamin treatments, nutritional approaches, and even faith healers.

In counseling, **I began to explore the relationship between Jack and Marion, including its prehistory** (*pearl #1*). Her response to my question "Where were you 6 months before you met Jack?" was very revealing. She was engaged to a man she met at college. Unfortunately her fiancé had a problem with alcohol and was often verbally abusive. She was reluctant to go forth with the planned marriage but conflicted about ending the relationship. One night she and her fiancé were arguing in the parking lot of a bar. Her fiancé was very drunk but refused to surrender the car keys and was berating her loudly. Jack pulled up and offered to give her a ride home. Jack's size and obvious strength intimidated Marion's fiancé, and Marion accepted his offer.

She teased Jack about being her "knight in shining armor." She broke her engagement and began to date him. Although she loved him, she was reluctant to commit to marriage. Despite being a successful contractor, Jack had never attended college, and this troubled her. Within a year, though, they did marry. Their marriage was very happy and they had two sons, both now in college.

As we reviewed the relationship and explored its prehistory, Marion realized that she believed that Jack rescued her from a relationship she'd been highly ambivalent about. She understood that she had a need to "rescue" Jack. Whereas he used his strength and size to rescue her, she could use her intellect and research skills to save him. Once she gained this perspective, we could reframe her need as one to support Jack in the illness.

Marion continued counseling during the course of Jack's illness. As Jack deteriorated, caregiving became a burden. Previously strong and independent, Jack resented his increasing dependence, often exploding at Marion. Marion realized she now needed additional support. **Here we used the DLR list, labeling her support system as doers, listeners, or respite persons** (*pearl #2*). This exercise allowed Marion to use her support system more effectively. In addition, it led her to a new appreciation of her longstanding friendship with Phillip, an older gay man who originally had been her mentor when she began teaching and with whom she had worked for 25 years. Marion had been disappointed that Phillip, now retired, was not more present during the illness. Previously he had been a frequent visitor and godfather to one of her sons. His visits were now brief and he rarely asked Marion about Jack. Phillip was always willing to go to a movie or out for coffee but even then conversations remained light and superficial. Marion now recognized that Phillip's gift was respite. She also acknowledged that Phillip's own experience of having so many friends die in the early years of the AIDS epidemic was a factor in his inability to assist in other ways.

Marion also developed a nightly ritual of reconciliation with Jack. No matter how rough the day, each night, as they were in bed, they would hold hands so that their wedding rings touched and recite, once more, their wedding vows "in sickness and in health."

Marion terminated counseling after she resolved these caregiving issues. She asked to see me 6 years after Jack died. At this time, the presenting problem was that Marion now wished to begin dating but couldn't bring herself to take off her wedding ring. At every attempt, she would cry and return the ring to her finger. From her past history, I knew that Marion was a committed Catholic who took her vows seriously. **So we designed a new ritual—a ritual of transition** (*pearl #3*). Marion returned to the church where she and Jack married. After mass was finished, the priest called Marion to the altar. In front of her family and friends, the priest repeated the wedding vows, now in past tense. "Were you faithful in good times and in bad, in sickness and in health?" In the presence of her witnesses, Marion could affirm she was. The priest then asked for the ring. "It came off," Marion related, "as if by magic." We had already determined that the priest would keep the ring. It was later linked with Jack's ring (at the time of Jack's death, his ring no longer fit) and welded to the frame of their wedding photograph, symbolizing that her vow was now fulfilled.

CONCLUDING COMMENTS

Although these clinical pearls hopefully will be useful to counselors working with clients' illness, grief, and loss issues, counselors should be aware of the significant ways that grief theories have evolved in the last decades (Doka, 2007, 2008b). Grief counselors, for example, now consider the wide range of responses that individuals experience in illness and loss (Doka, 2008b; Martin and Doka, 2000; Rando, 2000). Reponses no longer focus exclusively on the emotional aspects of loss but recognize that grief is manifested cognitively, behaviorally, spiritually, and physically. This leads to one more brief clinical pearl—the value of questioning how clients *responded* or *reacted* after a loss rather than only assessing how they *felt*. Moreover, there has been an appreciation of the many contexts that generate grief (Doka, 2002b; Rando, 2000).

Second, there has been a move away from Freud's (1957) idea that the goal of grief therapy is to detach ego energy from the deceased and reinvest in others. New paradigms of grief stress the continuing bonds that are retained with the deceased (Klass, Siverman, & Nickman, 1996) even while acknowledging that not all ties may be beneficial (Stroebe, 2006). Hence words like *closure* and *recovery* may not be the best terms to describe outcomes in grief.

Finally, there has been a movement away from stage theories in grief (Kübler-Ross, 1969). Rather than look for universal stages, current grief theory stresses individual pathways. Theorists presently working in this field should acquaint themselves with such contemporary approaches as the dual-process theory (Stroebe & Schut, 1999), process and task approaches (Rando, 1993; Worden 2002), meaning reconstruction (Neimeyer, 2001), and transformative understandings of grief (Calhoun and Tedeschi, 2004; Doka, 2006; Prend, 1997).

BIBLIOGRAPHY

Bolton, C., & Camp, D. (1987). Funeral rituals and the facilitation of grief work. *Omega: The Journal of Death and Dying, 17*, 343–351.

Bolton, C., & Camp, D. (1989). The post-funeral ritual in bereavement counseling and grief work. *Journal of Gerontological Social Work, 13*, 49–59.

Calhoun, L. G., & Tedeschi, R. G. (2004). The foundations of post-traumatic growth: New considerations. *Psychological Inquiry, 15*, 93–102.

Doka, K. J. (1984). Expectation of death, participation in funeral rituals, and grief adjustment. *Omega: The Journal of Death and Dying, 15*, 119–130.

Doka, K. J. (2002a). The role of ritual in the treatment of disenfranchised grief. In K. Doka (Ed.), *Disenfranchised grief: New directions, challenges, and strategies for practice* (pp. 134–148). Champaign, IL: Research Press.

Doka, K. J. (Ed.). (2002b). *Disenfranchised grief: New directions, challenges, and strategies for practice*. Champaign, IL: Research Press.

Doka, K. J. (2006). Fulfillment as Sanders' sixth phase of bereavement: The unfinished work of Catherine Sanders. *Omega: Journal of Death and Dying, 52*, 141–149.

Doka, K. J. (2007). *Living with grief: Before and after death*. Washington, DC: The Hospice Foundation of America.

Doka, K. (2008a). The power of ritual: A gift for children and adolescents. In K. Doka & A. Tucci (Eds.), *Living with grief: Children and adolescents* (pp. 287–295). Washington, DC: The Hospice Foundation of America.

Doka, K. J. (2008b). *Counseling individuals with life-threatening illness*. New York: Springer.

Freud, S. (1957). Mourning and melancholia. In J. Strachley (Ed. & Trans.). *The standard edition of the complete psychological works of Sigmund Freud* (Vol. 14, pp. 237–260). London: Hogarth. (Originally published in 1917).

Gennep, A. (1960). *The rites of passage*. Chicago: University of Chicago Press.

Gross, R., & Klass, D. (1997). Tibetan Buddhism and the resolution of grief: The Bardo-Thodell for the living and the grieving. *Death Studies, 21,* 377–398.

Klass, D., Silverman, P., & Nickman, S. (Eds.). (1996). *Continuing bonds: New understandings of grief.* Washington, DC: Taylor & Frances.

Kübler-Ross, E. (1969). *On death and dying.* New York: Macmillan.

Martin, T., & Doka, K. (2000). *Men don't cry, women do: Transcending gender stereotypes of grief.* Philadelphia: Brunner/Mazel.

Neimeyer, R. A. (2001). *Meaning reconstruction and the meaning of loss.* Washington, DC: American Psychological Association.

Prend, A. (1997). *Transcending loss.* New York: Berkley Books.

Rando, T. A. (1993). *The treatment of complicated mourning.* Champaign, IL: Research Press.

Rando, T. A. (2000). *Clinical dimensions of anticipatory mourning: Theory and practice in working with the dying, their loved ones, and their caregivers.* Champaign, IL: Research Press.

Reeves, N., & Boersma, F. (1990). The therapeutic use of ritual in maladaptive grieving. *Omega: The Journal of Death and Dying, 20,* 281–291.

Romanoff, B., & Terenzio, M. (1998). Rituals and the grieving process. *Death Studies, 22,* 697–712.

Stroebe, M. (2006, April). *Continuing bonds in bereavement: Toward theoretical understanding.* Keynote presentation to the Association of Death Education and Counseling, Albuquerque, NM.

Stroebe, M., & Schut, H. (1999). The dual process model of coping with bereavement: Rationale and description. *Death Studies, 23,* 197–224.

Worden, J. W. (2002). *Grief counseling and grief therapy: A handbook for the mental health practitioner* (3rd ed.). New York: Springer.

BIOGRAPHY

Kenneth J. Doka, PhD, is a professor of gerontology at the Graduate School of the College of New Rochelle and a senior consultant to the Hospice Foundation of America. A prolific author, Doka has published

24 books and over 100 articles and book chapters. He is editor of both *Omega: The Journal of Death and Dying* and *Journeys: A Newsletter for the Bereaved*. Doka was elected president of the Association for Death Education and Counseling and chair of the International Work Group on Dying, Death and Bereavement. In 2006, he was grandfathered in as a mental health counselor under New York state's first licensure of counselors. He also is a Lutheran clergyman.

Chapter 10
Reconstructing Life Out of Loss: Reorganizing the Continuing Bond

Robert A. Neimeyer, PhD

My work with the bereaved and traumatized draws on the concepts and strategies of constructivist psychology (Neimeyer & Mahoney, 1995; Neimeyer & Raskin, 2000) to listen deeply and responsively to the stories clients tell themselves and others about their losses in order to foster new growth and coherence in those life stories.

PEARLS

I will anchor these three pearls, which have emerged from this constructivist work in my therapy, with one woman struggling with a complicated loss, and I will consider their fuller implications for helping people integrate bereavement into a self-narrative that retains, or even enhances, life's meaning.

Pearl #1. Use narrative methods, as well as concepts, in reauthoring lives disrupted.

As narrative psychologists of many orientations recognize, people live their lives in stories (Bruner, 1990; Hermans, 2002; McAdams, 2006). At the most obvious level, we seem neurologically "wired" (Rubin & Greenberg, 2003) to "package" our life experience as stories that have a meaningful beginning, middle, and end (Neimeyer, 2000). And when the stories of our lives are too anguished to be told to the conventional audience of friends and loved ones, or even to ourselves in private journals, we sometimes turn to psychotherapists who we hope can hear what others cannot, and who can help us find a way forward through a life narrative that has become unlivable.

In a constructivist perspective, grieving the death of a loved one entails reaffirming or reconstructing a world of meaning that has been challenged by loss (Neimeyer, 2002). Because our very sense of security and identity is braided together with others to whom we are intimately attached (Bowlby, 1980), separation from the key figures in our life can launch a quest to reorganize our self-narrative to accommodate the hard reality of our loss.

Evidence supports the positive effects of conceptualizing bereavement in narrative, meaning-making terms. For example, bereaved parents (Keesee, Currier, & Neimeyer, 2008) and those who lose a loved one through suicide, homicide, or a fatal accident (Currier, Holland, & Neimeyer, 2006) often enter a prolonged effort to find some meaning in a senseless loss. In both cases, success in making sense of the loss in spiritual, secular, or practical terms predicts the extent of the ability to surmount complicated, disabling grief symptomatology. Conversely, grievers with weaker beliefs in the meaningfulness of the world and lower perceptions of self-worth report greater distress symptoms than those who perceive the world and self in more positive terms (Currier, Holland, & Neimeyer, 2009), even when the losses are anticipated and normative ones through natural causes. It therefore makes sense to join our clients in sorting out the shattered or somber meanings with which they struggle in the wake of loss, in an attempt to help them integrate the reality of the death into their changed life story.

Pearl #2. Reconstruct, rather than relinquish, the relationship to the deceased.

In contrast to early psychodynamic understandings of grief as a process of "letting go of" the lost loved one, there is now a growing consensus that healthy grieving can continue rather than break bonds with the deceased (Attig, 2000; Klass, Silverman, & Nickman, 1996). Nonetheless, recent research has suggested that reorganizing an ongoing sense of attachment to the deceased can be difficult, requires time (Field &

Friedrichs, 2004), and can meet with all manner of clinical complexities (Rubin, Malkinson, & Witztum, 2003). In general, better bereavement outcomes are associated with forms of attachment that do not rely primarily on physical reminders of the loved one, that are uncontaminated by guilt and self-blame, and that are accompanied by high degrees of meaning-making regarding the loss. This kind of attachment permits survivors to retain a sense of connection to the deceased but nonetheless move forward with their lives (Neimeyer, Baldwin, & Gillies, 2006).

Pearl #3. Give voice to the unspeakable to track evolving meanings.

Although constructivist therapists emphasize the verbalization of experience, they also recognize that not only the core but also the "growing edges" of our meaning systems are difficult to formulate in public speech (Neimeyer, 2009). This implies that the deepest meanings with which our clients struggle, as well as fresh new possibilities for construing and doing life differently, are typically elusive and call for articulation in figurative rather than literal terms. Accordingly, constructivist therapists draw on a range of procedures for exploring the "felt sense" of evolving understanding, often first registered as a bodily, rather than cognitive, awareness (Gendlin, 1996). A keen attention to evolving meanings of this imagistic sort played an important role in my work with Deborah, the case to which I will now turn.

CASE EXAMPLE: DEBORAH

My first few seconds of contact with Deborah poignantly conveyed to me the severity of her suffering. In many respects it seemed that this 45-year-old single mother was entering her third *day* of bereavement, rather than her third *year*. Unable to continue in her work as a nursing assistant to the elderly and infirm, she now found herself struggling to function in daily life. I could not escape the feeling that it was as if her life effectively ended with her mother's. She described the 4 intensive years of caregiving to her mother as "lovely," because they permitted her to return some of the love that she felt she had received from the older woman. Now, the meaning of her own life seemed to slip out of focus, along with her life-sustaining bond with the person with whom she had always shared a home. How we could integrate the loss into the larger story of her life, and reconstruct the attachment to her mother that was sundered by her death, became compelling therapeutic priorities.

Toward the end of our first session, after listening to Deborah's labored and anguished account of what the hardest times were like for her, a spark of hope leapt up with a spontaneous comment: "I try to open whatever doors I can, and accept that she's gone. I *can* make decisions." With this expressed hope to get some footing back in life, and make it more as she wanted it to be, I proposed a narrative intervention as a "small and specific step that we could take in the direction of that hope." **In between sessions, Deborah was to write a letter to Mom, just as she had often written letters for Mom to other family members since her death as a continuation of her mother's role as the "family center point."** (*pearl #1: Use narrative methods, as well as concepts, in reauthoring lives disrupted by loss.*) To get her started, I elicited the first few lines of a heartfelt letter, converting statements from Deborah such as "I miss her" and "She always listened" into affirmations such as "I miss you" and "You always listened."

I handed Deborah the letter we had begun, and when I asked how it would be to continue it as therapeutic homework, she responded, "It would be scary, painful." This alerted me to the importance of structuring self-soothing activities that would give a temporary reprieve from the writing, such as listening to calming music, taking a walk, or scheduling a phone call to her adult daughter. Deborah suggested physical activity in the form of gardening. In closing, Deborah hoped that the letter might be a way to "reconnect" with her mother and with "her positive thoughts," something she tearfully realized that she greatly needed.

Deborah's appearance in the next session was markedly improved. In contrast to the disheveled hair and dark clothes of the first session, she was dressed in bright "business casual" attire with a smart pair of glasses and hair that clearly benefited from her attention; she also seemed to step more lightly, meeting my gaze and taking a seat, eager for our conversation to begin. Asked about her reaction to the first meeting, Deborah reported that the writing helped her realize that her mother "was in a better place," as well as to recognize that "her presence was within." Noticing that she saw signs of her mother's presence for the first time in the dishwashing gestures of her sister, and laughingly relating a story about how she blamed a recent stoppage of the sink on her mother, who often experienced a similar problem, Deborah was rediscovering her mother in these and other commonplace ways.

The writing also helped Deborah dispel some of the lingering resentment she harbored about having been neglected by her hardworking farming parents during her formative years, as it allowed her to draw her attention to how her mother had "been there" for her in important ways with the birth of her own daughter. Deborah reported that she was filled with "a new feeling of gratitude" for the belated but very welcome mothering she eventually had received.

At my invitation, Deborah slowly read aloud the letter she had drafted on elegant stationery, addressed to her mother by her pet name:

> *Dear Mom, my dearest Bertle:*
> *I miss you. It's hard without your guidance and encouragement,*
> *but I'm doing what you told me to do almost 26 years ago. I'm*
> *completing my associate's degree. I've also been supporting other*
> *members of our family as they deal with hard times, although it's*
> *very hard for me to function in this way when I am feeling down*
> *myself. . . . I pray to God I'm doing what I'm meant to do in this*
> *lifetime. How I miss your words of wisdom, and how you always*
> *told me to "keep up the good work." I know you're in a better place*
> *and I will see you again. I send you the biggest hug, and I'm*
> *trying to be the person you raised me to be. I pray that the blank-*
> *ness of thought I struggle with goes, and I am able to concentrate*
> *on the gift God gave me of having a mother like you for 43 years.*
> *I know you're keeping track of us, as your love lives in us all. I just*
> *wish that others in our family would have some of the faith, grace,*
> *and love you so patiently taught us.*
> > *Until we meet again, hugs and kisses,*
> > *Your daughter and friend,*
> > *Deborah*

Smiling broadly, I shared my appreciation of her "loving letter, filled with such gratitude in relation to Mom." It seemed to us both that some important kind of reconnection had begun.

Returning a Mother's Legacy to Her

Exploring the family issues hinted at toward the end of Deborah's letter a bit more, I soon learned that Deborah's identification with her mother's role was not limited to supporting family members on her behalf. Indeed, as she candidly acknowledged, "Since my mother's been gone I've been trying to be her replacement. And I don't think that's a good place for me to be, and it's something my family doesn't have acceptance of anyway. So I need to let that go, and let them be them."

"Let them be them," I echoed, adding, " . . . and let *you* be *you*, and not just Mom's placeholder in the family. . . . Do you think that your mom would approve of that, your relinquishing her role a little bit?" Deborah was uncertain. More relational renegotiation was needed for this necessary shift.

Based on feedback from Deborah, the second writing exercise was titled "Returning My Mother's Legacy to Her." She readily accepted my suggestion that she write on that theme as therapeutic homework, seeking her mother's permission to relinquish some of the overidentification with her advice-giving presence that had helped her maintain a (problematic) continuing bond with her mother but that clearly had been resisted by her adult siblings. We closed the session with her noting, "This sounds neat. I think I'm going to enjoy it. It's going to be a big milestone in my life."

Our third session of therapy took place 2 weeks later, following the "monthly anniversary" of Deborah's mother's death. Deborah opened by noting that she began "feeling down" on that day, but that when she started writing, "it was a kind of release."

"What was released with that writing?" I asked.

"Just the identification," she responded, "that I was trying to be my mother, and wasn't identifying with myself, doing what I wanted to do or needed to do. It was this obsession."

She went on to explain that she compulsively tried to perceive and meet the needs of everyone in the family, just as her mother had, but got a chilly reception in response. The writing, it seemed, led to an insight: "That's something I identified in the writing, that I was becoming this worry-wart of a person, and it was a very negative thing for me . . . because people didn't want it. I was trying to become Mom's replacement, and you really can't do that. It's almost like I was playing hide-and-seek with myself," she added thoughtfully.

"What an extraordinary image, playing hide-and-seek with yourself!" I said. "What were you hiding, and what were you seeking?"

Deborah answered that she was creating an identity that wasn't her own, and one that wasn't being asked for by others. She then accepted my invitation to read the remarkable letter in which so much had become clear:

> *Dear Mom,*
> *You were always the key-holder for our family's problems. You had an instinct about what to do in every situation, always made sure we felt loved and special. Since you've been gone from this world I've tried to be you within our family. I am returning your legacy to you. Our family has no acceptance, nor have they asked me to fill the hole that was made by your departure. You had one bad characteristic, and that was that you worried about us a lot. I picked up that characteristic, and this is something I've gone over-board with. . . . Most of all, I need to recognize that people are who they are, and I cannot make them into the person I want them to be. Mom, I am asking your permission to be me. I'm going to allow myself to be okay with who I am. I need to practice on my own individuality, and have faith that I'll be okay with myself. I have all the wonderful wisdom you taught me, and one of those things is the power of prayer.*
> > *Love, your daughter and friend,*
> > *Deborah*

Finishing the letter and commenting on her growing success in relinquishing her mother's role to the relief of her siblings, Deborah then shared with me a remarkable revelation: She had learned of a job at a foundation that provided toys to seriously ill children, and she uncharacteristically approached the prospective employer to ask that they consider her. "For that to come out of my mouth is really new!" she told me, laughing. She was offered an interview on the spot and was enthusiastic about the prospect of meaningful work that would let her "give back to society and to children who really need it." I affirmed this sign of growth and openness to possibility, suggesting, "In letting go of being Mom, you made room to become Deborah again, reaching back to who you had been, and reaching forward to who you want to become." She readily agreed, noting, "The door is starting to open. . . . Before, I felt like I was hitting my head on the wall, but I couldn't stop; it only grew greater and greater." Curious, I asked her what helped her break that pattern. She replied, "I really think it was that first letter, and then the other one. For the longest time, it's crazy, but it was like I was still expecting my mother to walk back through that door. . . . Writing to her helped me to face that reality, and I realized what I was doing—all this crazy stuff—and see it clearly. . . . And I could see there was a reason to her death. . . . People go on, and do different things. She's gone from this world, and doesn't need to be replaced, because I wasn't born to be her. I was born to be myself."

It seemed that Deborah, through her narrative work and its consolidation in our sessions, had begun to reconstruct, but not relinquish, her continuing bond with her mother (*pearl #2*), in a way that no longer required her to unconsciously attempt to "be" her mother in the context of her family. Instead, in ways that were keenly felt and clearly observable, she was winning back her sense of self and finding validation of this shift in the responses of others in the family and beyond it. Simultaneously, her mother's death seemed to be taking on a different meaning, one that did not require her physical presence in the world to leave a lasting legacy of love.

Dialogue With a Dead Mother

To further Deborah's reconstruction of her bond with her mother and to explore any relational impediment that could block this, I then suggested that we enter into a dialogue with her mother: "I wonder if we could have a conversation in here, in which I interview your mother, briefly, about the person her daughter, you, are becoming." Deborah chuckled a little nervously but agreed, so I immediately suggested that we switch chairs "to allow us to be someone else," and I began to interview her as her mother by her "public" name, Pat: "I've been having some conversations, Pat, with your daughter Deborah. . . . And one of the things she's been talking about is that she's looking for a way to let your legacy be yours, and for her to step back into being Deborah. And she's been a little bit worried as to how you feel about that. . . . What do you think of this move your daughter is trying to make . . . to make room for who she is as a person?"

Deborah, as Pat, affirmed that her daughter should be who she is, and especially should "erase" any negative traits she might have given her. Alerted to this incipient metaphor, I introduced the image of a "magic pencil," and with notepad in hand, I took notes as "Pat" listed traits she wanted Deborah to carry forward in her life and those she would give her daughter permission to erase or relinquish. Invited to share some "final words for this part of the conversation," "Pat" concluded that she hoped her daughter "would find total joy."

After we ended the conversation and we took our former chairs, I reread her "mother's" words aloud slowly and evocatively, as Deborah brushed away a tear. "I get caught up in the fact that she's not here, and I don't think she would want that." She paused and smiled.

"Of course not," I replied. "She wouldn't want to be banished, because she is here with you. When you invite her, she steps right back in."

Accepting the paper with my interview notes, Deborah remarked, "This is something I may type up, because they are words of wisdom. These are like words she could have said, and when I need her words, I can have them." She continued, unprompted: "Typing them will keep me in the positive swing that has been transforming my life the last couple of weeks. . . . It's funny when things start to roll in the right direction."

Encounter With the Unspeakable

Deborah returned for our fourth session in a positive mood. Elaborating on the theme of change, she acknowledged the need to "watch for the telltale signs" of sleep disruption, unwarranted anxiety, performance problems, and, most significantly, the "blankness" that she had experienced so frequently and disruptively over the last 2 years. Cuing on this term, I asked her what she thought this blankness meant. She answered that it was like a "void around her heart that wasn't filled." In response, I suggested we do a "body scan" to check on this feeling, in the wake of medical tests that had yielded no cause for concern. Inviting Deborah to relax, I then asked her to allow her attention to walk through her body, "looking for any tension, any sense, any feeling that feels significant, or related to the way you are holding the grief for your mother now. When you sense something, give me an indication of where it is and how it is for you."

With eyes closed, Deborah allowed her attention to settle and related that the void seemed to radiate over her head and shoulders like a dome. "It feels like a beacon, a beacon of light, like a warmth, that understanding *will* come, over time. . . . Almost like it's *embracing* me. . . . "

As we continued to bring awareness to sensations associated with the void—to give voice to the unspeakable—Deborah discovered that as she moved into the void, alongside grief, there was also joy. The meaning of her mother's absence was evolving (*pearl #3: Give voice to the unspeakable to track evolving meanings*). In processing the experience, Deborah affirmed, "It was really wonderful. You asked about my mom's presence, and I really didn't feel it until I felt that tickling. It was an electrical, staticky thing. I was reaching out for that humanistic feeling, but it was an energy thing. And that makes sense, because she's spirit now." We closed the session with a shared sense of the mother's accessible presence in Deborah's life (captured in Deborah's letters to her), her validation of Deborah's uniqueness (delivered in our dialogue with Pat), and her ongoing impact on the family (observable in myriad contexts of everyday life). Perhaps most vividly, as we moved beyond the tangible realm of public speech to invite and engage Deborah's most private meanings of the "void" she carried throughout her bereavement, we also encountered her mother's warmth and spiritual presence, rediscovered in imagery and bodily feeling. Significantly, the reconstruction of Deborah's continuing bond with her mother found strong expression in language, symbol, and lived experience, and it was consolidated in an exploration of her unconventional spirituality and a celebration of her revitalized life narrative in our remaining two sessions.

CONCLUDING COMMENTS

Like jazz improvisation, each "performance" of therapy is unique, as both (or in the case of couples, family, or group work, all) participants "riff" off of the offerings of the others in ways that cannot be specified in advance (Neimeyer, 2009). Constructivists recognize this innovative quality of all relationally responsive therapy, and accordingly view therapy as a process by which we join clients in articulating, symbolizing, and renegotiating those deeply personal meanings on which they rely to formulate their experience and action (Neimeyer, 1995). Nonetheless, certain abiding principles, if not strict rules (Levitt, Neimeyer, & Williams, 2005), can be discerned in constructivist practice, and my distillation and illustration of a few "pearls of wisdom" in this brief chapter represents one attempt to do so.

Although constructivism offers orientation to a vast range of human problems for which people seek therapy, I have focused here and elsewhere (Neimeyer, 2001, 2005, 2006a) on its special implications for grief counseling. I do so to emphasize its usefulness as a perspective from which to view the universal problem of loss—perhaps the only psychosocial/existential challenge that will be faced by every client we consult, and of course by every therapist as well. Often, as I have acknowledged, people cope with the death of those they love with remarkable and sometimes inspiring resilience—except when they don't, in which case they risk becoming immobilized in a world seemingly devoid of that one, compellingly essential attachment figure, unable to assimilate the apparent impossibility of the death into a life story now bleached of meaning by bereavement. Working with these impeded, shattered, or vitiated life stories using a variety of narrative concepts and methods has frequently helped me join clients in identifying the strands of continuity in their lives and in their relationship to the deceased, as well as in weaving a new fabric of connection that also accommodates threads of new possibility. Drawing on the rich vocabulary of words, meanings, emotions, and images with which each client engages in this task allows me to partner intimately with clients in reconstructing life out of loss, often reinventing themselves in the process. I hope that some of the ideas and illustrations I have offered in these pages provide encouragement for you as you undertake something similar in your own practice.

BIBLIOGRAPHY

Attig, T. (2000). *The heart of grief.* New York: Oxford.

Bonanno, G. A., Wortman, C. B., & Nesse, R. M. (2004). Prospective patterns of resilience and maladjustment during widowhood. *Psychology and Aging, 19,* 260–271.

Bowlby, J. (1980). *Attachment and loss: Loss, sadness and depression* (Vol. 3). New York: Basic.

Bruner, J. (1990). *Acts of meaning.* Cambridge, MA: Harvard University Press.

Currier, J., Holland, J., & Neimeyer, R. A. (2006). Sense making, grief and the experience of violent loss: Toward a mediational model. *Death Studies, 30,* 403–428.

Currier, J., Holland, J., & Neimeyer, R. A. (2009). Assumptive worldviews and problematic reactions to bereavement. *Journal of Loss and Trauma, 14,* 181–195.

Field, N. P., & Friedrichs, M. (2004). Continuing bonds in coping with the death of a husband. *Death Studies, 28,* 597–620.

Freud, S. (1957). Mourning and melancholia. In J. Strachey (Ed. & Trans.), *The standard edition of the complete psychological works of Sigmund Freud* (Vol. 14, pp. 152–170). London: Hogarth. (Original work published 1917)

Gendlin, E. T. (1996). *Focusing-oriented psychotherapy.* New York: Guilford.

Hermans, H. (2002). The person as a motivated storyteller. In R. A. Neimeyer & G. J. Neimeyer (Eds.), *Advances in personal construct psychology* (Vol. 5, pp. 3–38). Westport, CN: Praeger.

Keesee, N. J., Currier, J. M., & Neimeyer, R. A. (2008). Predictors of grief following the death of one's child: The contribution of finding meaning. *Journal of Clinical Psychology, 64,* 1145–1163.

Klass, D., Silverman, P. R., & Nickman, S. (1996). *Continuing bonds: New understandings of grief.* Washington, DC: Taylor & Francis.

Levitt, H. M., Neimeyer, R. A., & Williams, D. C. (2005). Rules versus principles in psychotherapy: Implications of the quest for universal guidelines in the movement for empirically supported treatments. *Journal of Contemporary Psychotherapy, 35,* 117–129.

Martin, J. (1994). *The construction and understanding of psychotherapeutic change.* New York: Teachers College Press.

McAdams, D. P. (2006). The problem of narrative coherence. *Journal of Constructivist Psychology, 19,* 109–125.

Neimeyer, R. A. (1995). An invitation to constructivist psychotherapies. In R. A. Neimeyer & M. J. Mahoney (Eds.), *Constructivism in psychotherapy* (pp. 1–8). Washington, DC: American Psychological Association.

Neimeyer, R. A. (2000). Narrative disruptions in the construction of self. In R. A. Neimeyer & J. D. Raskin (Eds.), *Constructions of disorder: Meaning making frameworks for psychotherapy* (pp. 207–241). Washington, D C: American Psychological Association.

Neimeyer, R. A. (Ed.). (2001). *Meaning reconstruction and the experience of loss.* Washington, DC: American Psychological Association.

Neimeyer, R. A. (2002). *Lessons of loss: A guide to coping* (1 ed.). Memphis, TN: Center for the Study of Loss and Transition.

Neimeyer, R. A. (2005). Growing through grief: Constructing coherence in accounts of loss. In D. Winter & L. L. Viney (Eds.), *Advances in personal construct psychotherapy.* London: Whurr.

Neimeyer, R. A. (2006a). Re-storying loss: Fostering growth in the posttraumatic narrative. In L. Calhoun & R. G. Tedeschi (Eds.), *Handbook of posttraumatic growth: Research and practice.* Mahwah, NJ: Lawrence Erlbaum.

Neimeyer, R. A. (2006b). Widowhood, grief and the quest for meaning: A narrative perspective on resilience. In D. Carr, R. M. Nesse, & C. B. Wortman (Eds.), *Spousal bereavement in late life* (pp. 227–252). New York: Springer.

Neimeyer, R. A. (2009). *Constructivist psychotherapy: Distinctive features.* New York: Routledge.

Neimeyer, R. A., Baldwin, S. A., & Gillies, J. (2006). Continuing bonds and reconstructing meaning: Mitigating complications in bereavement. *Death Studies, 30*, 715–738.

Neimeyer, R. A., & Mahoney, M. J. (1995). *Constructivism in psychotherapy*. Washington, DC: American Psychological Association.

Neimeyer, R. A., & Raskin, J. D. (Eds.). (2000). *Constructions of disorder: Meaning-making frameworks for psychotherapy*. Washington, DC: American Psychological Association.

Neimeyer, R. A., van Dyke, J. G., & Pennebaker, J. W. (2008). Narrative medicine: Writing through bereavement. In H. Chochinov & W. Breitbart (Eds.), *Handbook of psychiatry in palliative medicine*. New York: Oxford.

Prigerson, H. G., & Maciejewski, P. K. (2006). A call for sound empirical testing and evaluation of criteria for complicated grief proposed by the DSM V. *Omega, 52*, 9–19.

Rubin, D. C., & Greenberg, D. L. (2003). The role of narrative in recollection: A view from cognitive psychology and neuropsychology. In G. D. Fireman, T. E. McVay, & O. J. Flanagan (Eds.), *Narrative and consciousness* (pp. 53–85). New York: Oxford.

Rubin, S. S., Malkinson, R., & Witztum, E. (2003). Trauma and bereavement: Conceptual and clinical issues revolving around relationships. *Death Studies, 27*, 667–690.

BIOGRAPHY

Robert A. Neimeyer, PhD, is a professor of psychology at the University of Memphis, where he also maintains an active clinical practice. Neimeyer has published 24 books, including *Meaning Reconstruction and the Experience of Loss* and *The Art of Longing* and serves as editor of the journal *Death Studies*. The author of over 300 articles and book chapters and a frequent workshop presenter, he is currently working to advance a more adequate theory of grieving as a meaning-making process. For more information, visit web.mac.com/neimeyer/iWeb/Home/About%20Me.html.

● ○ ● ○ ● ○ ●

Chapter 11
Ascending the Spiral Staircase of Grief

Sameet Kumar, PhD

All of us at some time in our lives experience loss and the grief it brings. When clients come to therapy to cope with the grief of loss, they are often asking for help with the uncertainty of identity transition. In my practice, I have found that providing the bereaved with information about the grief process, techniques to endure the suffering of grief, and hope for attaining existential goals to be of tremendous help.

PEARLS
The following three pearls present concise tools for transforming the suffering of grief into a meaningful life transition.

Pearl #1. Grief is often nonlinear.
I am often referred people whose loved ones have died from cancer and have requested help with the journey through the labyrinth of grief. In these instances, the bereaved often have an unrealistic expectation of what the course of grief is going to be like. Many expect the intensity of death and loss to last a few weeks at the most and then dissipate gradually in a series of manageable and discrete stages until the person is back to "normal."

The stages of grief—disbelief, anger, bargaining, depression, and acceptance—were formulized by Elisabeth Kübler-Ross (1969) in a death-denying society that rarely acknowledged terminal illnesses to the patients who were suffering from them. Because of Kübler-Ross's pioneering work, the ability of patients and caregivers to anticipate and prepare for death has changed dramatically over the past 40 years.

A relatively recent study found that the stages of grief do indeed appear to be the norm for well-educated, affluent women who are neither depressed nor traumatized and whose loved ones died peacefully (Maciejewski et al., 2007). However, I have found that the stages for clinical populations seeking out or requiring psychotherapeutic assistance seem to follow a more nonlinear course. Rather than move in a relatively stable pattern over time, grief seems to follow a nonlinear sequence of powerful emotions, shuffling Kübler-Ross's stages in both order and intensity.

In clinical populations, the first year of grief is in many ways a "warmup lap" for how grief will fit into a full calendar year of holidays, anniversaries, and other milestones. The ebbs and flows of grief can often be tracked along these milestone dates of each year. Clients must be made aware of these ups and downs during the first session, while being reassured that the downs will likely become less intense and less frequent over time.

The year after a major loss can be understood to be a series of firsts. The first holidays without. The first New Year without. The first snowfall without. The first birthday without. Once clients have established an existential or spiritual context for experiencing these sometimes exhausting ups and downs, the path of grief can reveal itself to be like a spiral staircase, alternating in a natural cycle anchored by relevant dates that are peaks of intensity. The staircase metaphor is particularly useful because it connotes a sense of upward movement, or meaningful progression toward growth and potentially spiritual evolution.

Pearl #2. Normalize the universality of death in the human experience to facilitate acceptance of grief.

Most of us will see the dying process and death only a few times.

Having worked in a healthcare institution with hundreds of families experiencing the death of a loved one from cancer has taught me that the mystery of death often unfolds similarly across human experience. Teaching distress-tolerance skills and normalizing the experiences of caregivers often can have tremendous therapeutic benefit for bereaved family members who may be questioning the decisions and choices they make during this time.

But what is normal during the dying process? From an empirical perspective, we have a much better understanding of the physiological mechanics of the dying process than we do of the spiritual and psychological changes that accompany death and dying. Although there are some groundbreaking studies on near-death experiences, exactly what happens during actual death remains a mystery for most of us until we arrive at that point in our life span, as we all ultimately do. The world's spiritual and religious traditions are much more eloquent and speak with unverifiable certainty about what death brings. In many ways, they fill the gaps too difficult to bridge empirically.

Despite our cloudy understanding of the phenomenology of death from terminal illness, and near complete ignorance about the events of sudden death, some commonalities are evident in what is experienced at this time in people's lives (see Singh, 2000). Many become delirious in the final days, speaking about impending departures in allegorical language that describes going to the airport, train station, or bus stop, or getting ready for a cruise. People frequently talk about waiting for a ride to arrive, such as a taxi or a limousine. Just as often, it seems as though dying patients' minds have already journeyed elsewhere as they spend hours in a fixed, vacant gaze, indifferent to whether their eyes are open or closed.

One of the most common occurrences on the deathbed is the sense of being visited by deceased loved ones or "emissaries" from the afterlife. People will often feel tremendous relief about being reunited with beloved grandparents, parents, deceased children or pets, and siblings. Again, these visitations, whether believed to be real or imagined, are also indicators that death is near. While these visitations usually comfort the dying, the lucidity of conversations with invisible beings confuses loved ones.

Finally, the moment of death is sometimes shared, and sometimes not. Death can be difficult for the living to plan around and the dying will often wait for the arrival of a loved one before expiring. Alternately, the bereaved may feel guilty about the fact that despite keeping a near-constant death vigil, their loved ones died the moment they stepped out for a cup of coffee or a quick trip to the bathroom. In these cases, the survivor may ascribe intentionality on the part of the deceased to the circumstances of that final moment.

There are many other commonalities in the subjective experience of dying, but these three characteristics of the dying process are the ones that my bereaved clients bring up most often in therapy. Speaking with authority about how commonplace these features of the dying process are can often achieve the therapeutic goals of relieving confusion, frustration, and guilt in many grieving loved ones.

Pearl #3. Mindfulness is a transformative technique for facilitating meaning-making in times of grief and identity transition.

Grief does not always fit into our expectations, because it often involves the loss of a significant portion of the foundation upon which we build our identities. What we do and what we have may be large parts of who we are, but when the fragility of our existence is revealed through death or another major loss, most of us find that our identities consist primarily of the relationships we have. We are all brothers, sisters, sons, daughters, friends, colleagues, mothers, fathers, husbands, wives, girlfriends, boyfriends, or strangers, depending on the connections we have or do not have with others. When a significant person in our lives dies or leaves us in another way, our identity is changed. Although the connection may be severed, the relationship will sometimes continue as the identity of the bereaved struggles to establish a new equilibrium.

The grief process is one of intense emotions that can quite easily become disorienting. In grief, the mind engages intensely in reflecting on past moments, and in distressing anticipation of an uncertain future. Mindfulness practice helps the bereaved to take a step back from intense thoughts and feelings to find islands of present-centered self-care and acceptance. The process of setting meaningful goals in grief is about using these islands to shape the identity emerging from this most painful period. This process of mindfully making choices of who we want to be can not only alleviate some of the distress of grief, but also help give the nonlinear ups and downs direction and life-promoting context.

Using mindfulness meditation and mindfulness-promoting exercises with the bereaved often helps them to return to the here-and-now by facilitating distress tolerance. Using this acceptance-based approach, the bereaved are often able to endure the twists and turns of the spiral staircase of grief by validating their capacity to feel pleasant and unpleasant emotions. I encourage people to set meaningful goals for channeling the unfolding of their emotions. By accepting the fact that grief can be a time of tremendous ambiguity regarding one's place in the world, we can use this ambiguity as an opening to establish existential goals about the desired meaning of one's life.

Grieving mindfully can become a transformative experience, despite the fluctuating presence of emotional pain and existential uncertainty. Frequently, once people have mastered basic mindfulness skills during the grief process, they are able to identify and pursue pro-social, life-affirming goals. Movement toward these goals not only helps to contextualize grief as a meaningful experience, but also helps to steer the direction of that meaning.

CASE EXAMPLE: CINDY

Cindy was a married 53-year-old who requested my services because of the difficulty she was having coping with the recent death of her mother, Dorothy, from an inoperable pancreatic cancer 5 weeks prior to our appointment. After completing a psychiatric diagnostic screening and history, and assessing her social support, we discussed the history of the relationship between Cindy and her mother, and the events of the last year that led to both Dorothy's death and Cindy's grief. Given the recent nature of Cindy's loss, I devoted particular attention to the circumstances around the last few weeks of her mother's life to help clarify how she had experienced the transition from caregiver to bereaved.

Cindy reported that their relationship was difficult for most of her adult life. Although she described them as having been close when she was a child, she said that their relationship became distant and often argumentative after Cindy left for college. Although Cindy returned to the area near her childhood home after college, married, and had her own children, who were now away at college, Dorothy played no active or significant role in her daily life. They lived just 20 minutes apart but only saw each other on holidays, with minimal contact otherwise.

Once Dorothy was diagnosed with an aggressive, terminal illness, the distance between them disappeared almost overnight. During the brief and rapid decline of her mother's health, Cindy was a compassionate and attentive caregiver. She went to every medical appointment and, as verified by the healthcare team, improved Dorothy's quality of life for the last few months of her 84 years of life. Although they never communicated explicitly about their years of disconnection, to outside observers it was as if they had no need to.

Toward the final weeks of Dorothy's illness, she was hospitalized due to uncontrollable vomiting and ultimately liver failure. During her final days of life, she was either delirious or sleeping. She began to talk to her husband, Cindy's father, who had died suddenly of a heart attack when Cindy was a child. Dorothy died comfortably one Thursday morning in between nursing shifts in the oncology unit in the hospital.

Cindy discussed with great remorse the fact that, although she had been a nearly ideal caregiver for the last few months of Dorothy's life, she had not been present at the moment of her mother's death. Prior to the last two nights of her mother's life, Cindy spent nearly every night on a cot in the hospital by her side. However, the dying process was much more difficult for her to observe than she had anticipated, especially after 2 weeks of sleepless nights. She was exhausted physically and emotionally. She went home and slept soundly, returning in the morning. Keeping vigil all day, she again returned home to sleep. When she awoke on that fateful Thursday morning, she received a call to get to the hospital immediately. By the time she arrived, her mother had died. Cindy felt that she needed help with her grieving process because of the constant guilt she felt for leaving the death vigil to go home and get some rest

After the initial rush of out-of-town guests and arranging her mother's affairs had dissipated, Cindy found herself ruminating and feeling guilty about sleeping at home while her mother was taking her last breaths. She found herself constantly wondering, *Did I do the right thing?* She wanted to remember happier moments with her mother and focus on the fact that although they had had a difficult relationship, they had been able to make amends and even become friends for the last few months.

However, the feelings she was experiencing were not what she was expecting from grief. **Rather than experiencing the feelings that characterize stage theory, such as denial or bargaining, Cindy was feeling the heavy weight of guilt for not being with her mother at the moment of her death, and also guilt for feeling relief that her mother was no longer suffering** (*pearl #1: Grief is often nonlinear*). Cindy felt that because of her feelings, she was not grieving in a healthy way along the prescribed stages, and would therefore be caught in a web of suffering and distress, perhaps for the rest of her life.

I asked her to share with me the last memory she had of her mother while she was still alive. Cindy told me that by the time she left Dorothy's bedside, her mother no longer recognized her and mostly stared into a corner of the room with vacant, glazed eyes. Dorothy sounded more and more congested, a common symptom of imminent death frequently referred to as the "death rattle." Probing further, I asked Cindy if she had ever seen anyone at the moment of that person's death, or been near someone right after his or her death. She replied that she had not, despite having had many occasions to do so with several elderly family members. When I asked about how she had always been able to extricate herself from these situations, Cindy replied that being present at death "would have destroyed me." She had been an excellent caregiver, bathing and cleaning her mother, driving her to appointments, administering medication as prescribed, and taking over household tasks. At the end, Cindy's own instinct for self-preservation had kicked in, and, as often happens, the death of her mother seemed to wait for the moment that her child left the room.

I shared with Cindy the fact that it is common for a dying patient to become nonresponsive and delirious, and die during a moment when the caregiver is not present. Similarly, it was not unusual that her mother had felt that she was being reunited with her deceased husband. In fact, these experiences were quite normal. **Normalizing these experiences communicated to Cindy that the death of her mother unfolded naturally** (*pearl #2*), even in a hospital, and that Cindy's absence during the very end of the process did not negate her tremendous contributions to her mother's care.

I hypothesized with Cindy that, from her mother's perspective, her passing away while Cindy was not there may have been intentional— a way to spare her daughter the moment of her death. I also made it clear that any hypotheses about the circumstances of the moment of her mother's death were unverifiable and therefore open to a wide range of interpretations. This uncertainty, rather than fueling distress, allows us tremendous freedom in developing hypotheses that can alleviate our suffering in grief. For Cindy, this freedom helped her to stop asking herself *Why did it happen this way?* and *How could it have happened this way?* and start accepting the way this death had happened. In doing so, Cindy was asked to accept the uniqueness of her own grief, with all of its ups and downs that spoke to the relationship she had with her mother, rather than force herself to conform to stages that she felt did not reflect her own experiences. She was now given permission to experience her grief rather than focus on the circumstances of her mother's death.

The fact that Cindy and her mother had been estranged for so long led me to consider that her guilt about not being present for her mother's death was perhaps misplaced from the years lost between them. After considering this hypothesis, Cindy stated that she had thought about this herself but did not feel it to be true. She said she had very few feelings of guilt about the years spent apart. Over the months of her mother's illness, Cindy reported that both she and her mother seemed to have come to an unspoken agreement that what mattered most was that they were together when they were. They were unable to tolerate each other in health, but grew closer in illness. Cindy felt that both her caregiving and her mother's humiliation at having to be cared for was their mutual atonement for the roles they had played in each other's lives. The lack of guilt about the years between them was verified in future appointments.

The order by which the initial session was organized, beginning with diagnostic screening and background information, then moving to normalizing the details surrounding the death of her mother, and addressing the seeds of guilt or unfinished business that Cindy was experiencing in her grief, allowed us to now explore Cindy's future goals. This transition began with the question, "Who do you want to be as you grieve?"

Articulating an answer to this question sets up the central existential task of the grief process. For Cindy, the answer was to become closer to her own adult children. Although they already enjoyed a good relationship with each other, in many ways in mindful contrast to Cindy's relationship to her own mother, Cindy felt that reinvesting in her remaining family was her central task in grief. Additionally, she reported that for years she and her husband had been dreaming of relocating to another state, but their plans had stagnated due to the busy nature of their lives. Running out of our allotted time, I devoted the final 10 minutes of the initial session to teaching Cindy the basics of diaphragmatic breathing to help her tolerate the emotional roller-coaster that she was going to continue to experience. I also gave her a quick tutorial and a handout on the basics of mindfulness meditation, encouraging her to experiment with the breathing and counting of exhalations central to the practice. Mindfulness instruction also provided a resilience-based context for introducing the metaphor of the spiral staircase of grief.

We met again 2 weeks later. Cindy reported that not only had she shared the contents of our session with her husband, but that they also had agreed to place their house on the market. Additionally, they had looked for new jobs in the area of the country that had long held their interest. Cindy's goals for her grief had become to attain the life goals she had been putting off for many years. Although for many people such drastic life changes shortly after the death of a loved one may not be recommended, Cindy and her husband had been researching moving for a long time.

Furthermore, Cindy had been able to practice diaphragmatic breathing during moments of peak distress and had a new confidence in her capacity for resilience. Her guilt had disappeared. She not only was able to accept the circumstances of her mother's death but also felt satisfied regarding her contributions as a caregiver (*pearl #3: Mindfulness is a transformative technique for facilitating meaning-making in times of grief and identity transition*).

In this second session, we explored Cindy's mindfulness practice in a bit more detail, as the other areas of her life seemed to be better. I discussed the importance of twice-daily mindfulness practice. She had never meditated before, but because it helped her ride through the spiral staircase of grief and also seemed to help her sleep better, committing to a regular practice required minimal effort on her part. We practiced together for 5 minutes and then returned to discussing the grief process.

Two weeks later, at our third session, Cindy's improvement appeared to be sustained. She continued to develop an even closer bond with her own children. Because we were experiencing a local real-estate boom at that time, her house already had several potential buyers. Her husband's company agreed to transfer him to the location they had picked out. Cindy still had moments of intense sadness, including crying periodically, but she was hopeful and empowered about her future. She was grieving mindfully, having escaped the path of complicated grief. I felt that our work was done, but she insisted on scheduling a follow-up appointment, which she later cancelled. Six months later, she stopped by my office for a brief, unscheduled visit. She was going to be moving the following week. She had come to tell me, with tears in her eyes, "You helped me. Thank you."

CONCLUDING COMMENTS

In reading Cindy's case, the effects of mindfulness may not be readily apparent. First and foremost among these is the mindful presence of the therapist, which has a profound impact on the process. Sustained mindfulness practice for both client and therapist is central to doing mindfulness-based therapies. In my own life, I casually meditated for 10 years before I committed to the idea of daily practice after attending a ceremony with the Dalai Lama. Almost immediately, I realized that utilizing this therapeutic dose was radically different from casual practice. I also noticed that clients were sensitive to mindful presence, especially in a healthcare setting such as an oncology ward or cancer center.

Facilitating the process of grieving mindfully does not rely solely on the client's practice; it includes the involvement of the therapist, who can model mindful acceptance and compassion in session, especially with the intense affect that so often accompanies grief. This does not mean a cold stoicism, but rather an informed empathy that allows the unfolding of affect to a depth that the client may not be able to reach on his or her own. Having cultivated mindfulness skills in our own lives, we as therapists can model distress tolerance in session. The goal is to allow this distress tolerance to be internalized by clients with their own mindfulness practice. When we utilize these skills, the spiral staircase of grief unfolds with acceptance and meaning that can promote resilience in the face of distress. Although therapist and client may not know the precise outcomes of the grief process or each mindfulness session, mindfulness practice can serve as an anchor to help steer and stabilize identities in transition.

Within the context of existential therapy that is well suited to grief work, the central tenets of autonomy, agency, and responsibility have a powerful synergy with mindfulness practice. By stripping away the secondary emotional process—feelings about feelings—mindfulness practitioners are left with the responsibility of witnessing and steering the direction of their own emotions. Having established therapeutic goals in session, practitioners are mindful of how their choices affect the unfolding of their lives during the course of their grief.

The lessons of grieving mindfully are not limited to grief from death and dying. Grief enters our lives in myriad ways, such as through divorce or unemployment. Additionally, not all griefs are straightforward. In the case of complicated grief, goals may need to be revisited and reestablished as events unfold. The issue of termination is also one that requires flexibility in grief cases. Generally, in the beginning of grief work, appointments are scheduled with regularity. As the nonlinear spiral of grief progresses, appointments may follow along in response to or anticipation of periods of acute distress.

Ultimately, grief and mindfulness share common ground: the awareness of the fragility and preciousness of life and all of its fleeting moments, as well as of the importance of choosing wisely the direction and meaning we seek to create in life.

BIBLIOGRAPHY

Kübler-Ross, E. (1969). *On death and dying*. New York: MacMillan.

Kumar, S. (2005). *Grieving mindfully: A compassionate and spiritual guide to coping with loss*. Oakland, CA: New Harbinger.

Maciejewski, P. M., Zhang, B., Block, S., & Prigerson, H. (2007). An empirical examination of the stage theory of grief. *Journal of the American Medical Association, 297*, 7.

Singh, K. (2000). *The grace in dying*. New York: HarperOne.

BIOGRAPHY

Sameet Kumar, PhD, is a staff psychologist at the Mount Sinai Comprehensive Cancer Center in Miami Beach and Aventura. In addition to being a clinical psychologist, he has also studied with numerous Hindu and Buddhist teachers as part of his training. His professional interests include Buddhist spirituality, palliative care, hypnosis, meditation, and grief and bereavement. He is the author of *Grieving Mindfully: A Compassionate and Spiritual Approach to Coping with Loss* and *The Mindful Path Through Worry and Rumination*. He lives in south Florida with his wife and two sons. He can be followed at twitter.com/sameetkumar or you can read his blog at sameetkumar.blogspot.com.

Section Five:
Couples

Chapter 12
Emotionally Focused Couple Therapy: It's All About Emotion and Connection

Sue Johnson, EdD

Pearls form as a result of an irritant becoming trapped in the soft tissue of a living creature as this creature attempts to grasp the nutrients needed to sustain life. One way of dealing with this irritant can result in something precious and beautiful. This image reflects one of the basic truths about adult love. Loss of safe emotional connection is a powerful irritant in a love relationship. Distressed partners often become trapped in negative ways of dealing with threats to their attachment bond, which only exacerbates the pain and irritation. Emotionally focused therapy (EFT) offers a structured guide to effective dependency where partners can respond to such moments of disconnection in a way that ensures that a relationship will become a secure bond, a treasure—a pearl of great value.

The outcome data on EFT are very positive (Johnson, Hunsley, Greenberg, & Schindler, 1999). Studies show that 70–75% of couples recover from distress by the end of therapy and that EFT has significant effects on other key variables such as trust and depression. There are also data on the stability of these effects and on outcomes for key issues, such as the forgiveness of injuries (Makinen & Johnson, 2006).

PEARLS
The pearls of wisdom at the heart of EFT reside in its central focus on

emotion and the ongoing attachment drama of connection and disconnection in a love relationship. The EFT therapist attempts to follow the innate, wired-in pathways of emotional experiencing and connection with others to help clients shape this engagement with self and other—to turn "irritants" into pearls.

Pearl #1. Emotion really is the heart of the matter, so it's best to follow it.

I have learned from my clients and from the perspective offered by the new science of emotion and adult attachment that there really is nothing haphazard or illogical about emotions in love relationships. They orient us like a compass, tell us clearly what matters to us, and move our feet in the dance with our partner. Emotion and emotional signals are the music of the dance between intimates.

The power of these signals is astounding. I have learned that a flash of emotion, encoded by a listening partner before the more cognitive part of the other's brain has even formulated the message being sent, can instantly shift the listener's physiology, emotional reality, cognitive processing, and responses. If, as a therapist, I do not actively work with this power, it easily derails other interventions. In addition, the emotional signals—that is, the attachment responses that make for lasting change in relationships, increased accessibility and responsiveness, and compassionate and loving attention—are tied inextricably to how each partner regulates his or her emotion. Working with emotion is often the only route to the changes that really matter.

Science is now confirming much of what I have learned from my clients. For example, those we are attached to are the hidden regulators of our physiology. The touch of a trusted partner's hand can literally calm jittery neurons in our brains when we are threatened (Coan, Schaefer, & Davidson, 2006). Perceived disconnection from an attachment figure seems to elicit a "primal panic," a very special kind of fear that compels primates to struggle to regain access to a loved one (Panksepp, 1998). Six core emotions (joy, shame, anger, sadness, curiosity, and fear) are instantly recognizable by all humans on this planet regardless of culture (Ekman, 2003). Without access to our emotions we cannot make decisions because we do not know what it is we need (Damascio, 1994). The suppression of emotion is a fragile strategy that often creates more arousal and also is picked up by inter-actional partners, causing tension in them (Gross, 2001). Hurt feelings are best understood as a mixture of anger, sadness, and the fear of being abandoned or rejected and so losing connection with a valued other (Feeney, 2005). Furthermore, in EFT, research into the process of change tells us that key events in therapy—where the therapist helps clients experience and organize deeper emotions into new, more positive signals in enactments—predict recovery from distress and lasting change (Johnson & Greenberg, 1988).

As an EFT therapist I have learned to step past the myriad of content issues that a couple brings to therapy and stay with the core emotions just mentioned, observing how they trigger the partners' reactions. Partners often come in expressing reactive surface feelings, such as frustrated anger or a numbing of emotion. The EFT therapist will create a safe environment, slow the process down, and unfold these feelings to help partners connect with deeper emotions such as fear of abandonment or rejection.

Pearl #2. It's all about attachment, so focus on it.

More specifically, the drama of distress is all about the emotional star-vation and anxiety that arises when a partner's need for safe connection is not met. The key factor in any relationship may well be how moments of disconnection are handled. Such moments are inevitable even in the best of relationships. They are coded by the brain as danger, just as safe-haven moments—when the question "Are you there for me?" is answered positively—are coded as safety. Experiences of rejec-tion and abandonment are, in fact, coded in the same parts of the brain as physical pain is (Eisenberger, Lieberman, & Williams, 2004). Attach-ment offers a framework for understanding the nature and intensity of the emotional responses between partners; demanding, critical partners nearly always access deep feelings of aloneness, helplessness, and fear at perceived abandonment, whereas withdrawers most often access fears of being rejected or never being good enough and shame at having failed to please. This perspective also helps me find the logic behind behaviors that perpetuate emotional disconnection, so that I can empathize with my clients and reframe their responses. When Lois gets caustic and hostile with Ken, I remind myself that she is very afraid of his apparent ability to shut her out, and so she protests by attacking him. In attachment terms, any response is better than none.

I have learned to listen for attachment emotions and moves rather than getting sucked down the content tube of a couple's issues and pragmatic differences. If partners are securely attached they can protest disconnection and be heard, and they are not easily threatened by differences with their partner. The conflicts that define a relationship are always about emotional accessibility and responsiveness—that is, about the security of the bond between partners (Mikulincer & Shaver, 2007). Secure partners can tune into their loss of felt security, tolerate it, articulate their need, and risk reaching for their partner. This maximizes the partner's ability to respond. This is what I want partners to be able to do at the end of EFT. Conflict containment or a more friendly relationship is not enough. An understanding of attachment tells me what is necessary and sufficient to move couples from distress to satisfaction.

In attachment relationships, when we do not have a sense of felt security with a loved one, there are really only two options open to us. One is to ramp up attempts to influence the other in order to get a response and to become ever more vigilant for cues of separation. The other is to dismiss one's own attachment needs, numb out, and focus on tasks in an attempt to become impervious to negative responses from those we depend on. These ways of dealing with disconnection from a loved one often become habitual and problematic, pushing loved ones away from us rather than bringing them close. This formulation helps me grasp the negative cycles in distressed relationships and support the partners who use these strategies. As partners make sense of the inner emotional chaos and the evolving drama of their relationship, their image of the other partner becomes less narrow and absolute and they slowly develop a new language for their needs and fears, a language that can be shared. The attachment framework keeps me focused in session and across sessions, giving me (and the couple) a roadmap for change. When in doubt, I come back to emotional cues and dilemmas and place them in the context of attachment.

Pearl #3. To create a new positive pattern, you have to dance it, enact it.

In key change events in the second stage of EFT, withdrawers move toward openness and emotional engagement and blamers soften their stance and are able to ask for their needs to be met from a position of vulnerability. This does not result in some form of enmeshment or codependency, but rather in both partners becoming more flexible in their responses, better regulators of their own emotions, and stronger and more confident in themselves. The couple therapist works in a context where a person's most basic fears, coping strategies, and needs are enacted with a loved other. This is a powerful arena for change, but change requires that new responses not only be encoded cognitively and emotionally, but also enacted.

Beginning therapists in EFT often omit enactments. They are more comfortable getting clients to talk about their relationship, preferably to the therapist. An expert EFT therapist, on the other hand, knows how to set up, process, and expand key attachment-focused interactions, as well as how to catch the bullets that sometimes fly when such enactments go wrong (Bradley & Furrow, 2004). When shaping enactments, especially in the "restructuring" stage of EFT, the therapist encourages partners, moment by moment, to move toward the responses typical of securely attached partners—toward what I call a "hold me tight" conversation (Johnson, 2008). These conversations are pivotal moments of change and healing where a positive pattern of reaching and compassionate responding begins.

The expert EFT therapist does everything to maximize each partner's engagement in these interactions. Therapists speak slowly, repeat messages and cues, soothe and validate, help partners clarify messages, and encourage partners to face each other and respond in simple, direct, and specific ways. Recent brain research on mirror neurons suggests that in this kind of face-to-face interaction, these neurons mimic the movement and responses of the other so that we feel these in our own bodies. This literally creates a tuning into the other and an increase in empathy. This kind of enactment also allows for structured risk-taking and thus creates a "safe emergency," which is the factor that Perls (1973) suggested is at the heart of significant change. Once partners can do this, at first in the session guided by the therapist and then at home, they can create their own safe haven and secure base and deal with moments of disconnection constructively.

Thirty years of working with couples leaves me absolutely persuaded that these enactments are the power behind the large effect sizes found in EFT outcome studies. They speak to our deepest longings and move us in a profound way. In these enactments, expressions of vulnerability, when respected and responded to by another, are natural bonding experiences. This is the time in EFT when you and the couple are hitting all the notes and a new dance takes shape in front of your eyes. The therapist heightens emotional signals, blocks exits, guides partners into new moves, validates new steps, helps partners to respond in new ways, and then has the enormous satisfaction of watching the couple naturally move together into a dance of loving connection that is the birthright of us all.

CASE EXAMPLE: LOIS AND KEN

Ken and Lois had been together for 20 years. They had very busy lives with three kids and a pharmacy they ran together. They also were great sports and adventure buffs. They were a great "team," but 3 years ago Ken had had an affair with a colleague. He ended the affair when Lois found out, but it increased his awareness of the emotional emptiness he felt in his marriage. Both Ken and Lois remembered the first years of their marriage as happy, but neither could remember any secure attachments as children. Lois was the caretaker for her chaotic family and Ken was the task-focused, high achiever who constantly fought with his judgmental father. Both agreed that the intimacy between them had eroded over the years. According to Ken, in the period before the affair, he and Lois had experienced a few very volatile "power struggles." After the affair, he attempted to improve the relationship by cooking for her, asking for lovemaking, and rebuilding the house. Lois did not get the message; she felt used in sex and withdrew further into mothering and running their business. The affair was a wakeup call for both of them.

When they arrived in my office, Ken said that he was "flat" emotionally and did not feel "moved" by Lois. He moved away from any affection or touch and did not respond to her sadness in the session. Lois was now pursuing him, alternating between angry remarks and withdrawal into grief when he did not respond.

During the first stage of EFT, negative-cycle deescalation, Ken told his wife that he was sorry about the affair but that long before this occurred he had "lost all his feelings" for her. He had, he said, a "PhD in 'don't give a damn,'" and so he stayed in withdrawal. I find that with clients like Ken who deny emotion, it helps to remind myself that attachment emotions are wired into our brains. Even in numbed-out or untrusting clients, the hurts, fears, longings, and needs are still there. All we get to choose is how to handle them.

As an EFT therapist, I began by reflecting on the pattern of inter-actions and their effect on Ken and Lois's sense of emotional connec-tion and security. Ken said that he stayed distant and went "flat and still" in personal interactions with his wife. Lois, understandably, felt "shut out." They were able to see how this pattern of rigid demand and withdraw defined their relationship. We were also able to focus on the emotions—the music of their dance. Ken's way of coping with his emotions slipped a little when, in a fight about helping in the kitchen, his face and voice changed and he angrily told his wife that she used to " slice him open" when he tried to help and please her by cooking. His eyes then filled with tears as he touched his "hurt place" that was usually compartmentalized and hidden even from himself.

I reflected on this scene in the kitchen, and helped Ken unfold the elements in his emotional response. **In response to my focusing on the moment and asking evocative questions, Ken was able to tell me that Lois's "critical" tone of voice was a trigger for this hurt. His stomach knotted when he heard it and it reminded him of his withholding and hostile father** (*pearl #1: Emotion really is the heart of the matter, so it's best to follow it*). He then told himself, "I will not be hurt like this. You can't get to me," and numbed out. As he coherently walked through this experience and ordered it, I invited him to tune into the deeper emotions expressed by his tears. He was able to tell Lois, "It's auto-matic. I listen for the tone in your voice and numb out. I thought this was just me or the way it was. Now I get that I am actively doing this. I tell myself that I won't let you hurt me again. The way he did. So I shut down. Now I don't know how to do anything else." This was very different from his initial "I have just lost my love for her and feel nothing" stance.

With my help, Ken was also able to see that as he shut Lois out, her "desperate panic"—that natural wired-in response to an attachment figure's stonewalling—was expressed as irritation. I validated Lois's angry "digs" and her attempts to "hammer" Ken into responding. **They began to see this cycle of demand and withdraw as the enemy that defeated them both and kept them both in what Ken now called "killer isolation." They also saw how their ways of dealing with their "softer" attachment emotions were a key part of this negative cycle** (*pearl #2: Focus on attachment*). The first stage of EFT was on track.

In the second stage of EFT, the goal is to guide partners into being able to access and share their deeper fears and needs in ways that help their partner respond to them. Partners then help each other create a felt sense of security. Rather than staying cool and distant, Ken could tell his wife, "I do shut down. I put up a wall. I never saw how it hurt you. I just couldn't deal with your criticism and I didn't know how to ask for closeness, so part of me said that the only way out was not to care. Now I am scared to let you in." He talked about how his fear of rejection particularly came up around physical closeness and he was able to explore with Lois how rejected he had felt in their sexual life. Lois was able to comfort and reassure him.

Also, when Ken became obsessed with how his past efforts were "spurned" by his wife, I could tell him, "When you were trying to be a good husband, to get reassurance and closeness from Lois, you tried to do it through lots of problem-solving and performance of tasks. But your signal wasn't clear. She didn't understand. And she just got angrier because she wanted you, your emotional presence, not your problem-solving." Ken then looked at his wife and repeated with increasing levels of feeling, "You wanted *me!*"

Lois was also able to share her hurts, fears, and needs with her husband. She told him, "I thought you wanted a strong, independent woman. So I did that. I was scared to show you how much I needed you. So I got into being the fierce, coping taskmaster. But I am so scared, so scared of you going flat and still on me. I lose you a hundred times a day. I need your reassurance, your comfort." Ken reached out to hold her hand. These kinds of moments of mutual accessibility and responsiveness transform an attachment relationship. They also provide the safety for the couple to work through difficult issues, such as the hurt of the affair in Ken and Lois's case.

The key elements in this second stage of EFT are the enactments where "hot" attachment fears and longings are shared. Partners do not always want to risk this level of emotional engagement with their lover. Lois told me, "He is sitting there. He's heard me talking about how I feel ashamed of my needs and get afraid that he doesn't want a needy person. It's too scary to go to that level. He knows that already." **But I insisted that she turn her chair toward Ken and tell him this herself** (*pearl #3: To create a new positive pattern, you have to dance it— enact it*). We started from where she was, not where I wanted her to be. I asked, "So can you tell him, 'It is so hard for me to show you, to tell you about my needs, to get past my shame, to risk sharing my soft places with you'?" Ken was able to tell Lois that he felt safer and closer to her when she talked like this. He asked how he could make this less risky for her. I then encouraged Lois to tune into her own experience, and to formulate and share her own attachment fears and longing for connection. The couple then moved into a new level of secure emotional connection.

Ken and Lois successfully completed the last stage of EFT: shaping a consistent, integrated story of their relationship distress and recovery, creating attachment rituals to promote a felt sense of daily connection for each of them, and solving pragmatic problems together. When they checked in some 5 months later, they and their relationship were on track and going well.

CONCLUDING COMMENTS

Not every couple can reach the point in therapy where they can find their way into accessible and responsive loving interactions, but the insights that have emerged in the last 15 years regarding our understanding of adult love and how to shape its emotional realities are more than cause for hope. These insights are part of a new science of relationships, a science that is already ushering in a new era for couple therapy. If we are beginning to know how to turn loneliness and the irritant of frustration into love and connection, that is indeed a pearl of great value.

BIBLIOGRAPHY

Bradley, B., & Furrow, J. (2004). Toward a mini-theory of the blamer softening events. *Journal of Marital and Family Therapy, 30,* 233–246.

Coan, J., Schaefer, H., & Davidson, R. (2006). Lending a hand: Social regulation of the neural response to threat. *Psychological Science, 17,* 1–8.

Damascio, A. R. (1994). Descartes' error: Emotion, reason, and the human brain. New York: Putnam.

Eisenberger, N. I., Lieberman, M. D., & Williams, K. (2004). Why rejection hurts: A common neural alarm system for physical and social pain. *Trends in Cognitive Science, 8,* 294–300.

Ekman, P. (2003) *Emotions revealed.* New York: Henry Holt.

Feeney, J. (2005). Hurt feelings in couple relationships. *Personal Relationships, 12,* 253–271.

Gross, J. (2001). Emotion regulation in adulthood: Timing is everything. *Current Directions in Psychological Science, 10,* 214–219.

Johnson, S. (2004). *The practice of emotionally focused couples therapy: Creating connection.* New York: Brunner/Routledge.

Johnson, S. (2008). *Hold me tight: Seven conversations for a lifetime of love.* New York: Little, Brown.

Johnson, S., & Greenberg, L. (1988). Relating process to outcome in marital therapy. *Journal of Marital and Family Therapy, 14,* 175–183.

Johnson, S., Hunsley, J., Greenberg, L., & Schindler, D. (1999). Emotionally focused couples therapy: Status and challenges. *Clinical Psychology, Science and Practice, 6,* 67–79.

Makinen, J., & Johnson, S. M. (2006). Resolving attachment injuries in couples using emotionally focused therapy: Steps towards forgiveness and reconciliation. *Journal of Consulting and Clinical Psychology, 74,* 1005–1064.

Mikulincer, M., & Shaver, P. (2007). *Attachment in adulthood: Structure, dynamics and change.* New York: Guilford.

Panksepp, J. (1998). *Affective neuroscience: The foundations of human and animal emotions*. Oxford: Oxford University Press.

Perls, F. (1973). *The gestalt approach and eye-witness to therapy*. Palo Alto, CA: Science and Behavior Books.

BIOGRAPHY

Sue Johnson, EdD, is a professor of psychology and psychiatry at the University of Ottawa. She is a practicing clinical psychologist, the director of the Ottawa Couple and Family Institute, and one of the originators of emotionally focused couples therapy. This approach is supported by 15 years of empirical research and is now taught in graduate schools internationally. Johnson has received the American Association of Marriage and Family Therapy Award for Outstanding Contribution to the Field. She is well-known as a prolific author and as a dynamic and engaging teacher. Her latest book is *Hold Me Tight: Seven Conversations for a Lifetime of Love*. Her combination of clinical, academic, and teaching skills makes her one of the leading figures in the expanding field of couples therapy. For more information about Sue Johnson, visit www.eft.ca.

●●●●●●●

Chapter 13
Dialing Down Distress:
Affect Regulation in Intimate Relationships

Carolyn Daitch, PhD

All people in committed relationships grapple with conflict. In my experience, conflict itself is rarely the problem; rather, it is the knee-jerk, unrestrained escalation of discord that tends to undermine trust and intimacy. The three pearls discussed in this chapter help clients respond more intentionally in the face of interpersonal triggers.

Used together, these pearls can make the difference between over-reacting in an intense interpersonal encounter and responding with a measure of calm, consciousness, and even wisdom. I have found these strategies to be vital not only for diffusing relational tension but also for helping partners rediscover and strengthen a genuinely loving connection.

PEARLS

Pearl #1. Take a time-out to interrupt overreactions.

When I see couples who are vulnerable to conflict escalation, my first order of business is to teach them to take immediate, interruptive breaks that cut short the beginning of a destructive reaction. I encourage clients to get into the habit of taking "time-outs" as soon as they notice they are upset, thereby giving themselves quiet moments to calm their inner turmoil, gain perspective, and plan appropriate dialogue with their partner.

I begin by training partners to quickly catch the warning signs—somatic, emotional, and cognitive—that indicate the need for a time-out. It might be a tightness in the throat, a sudden chill of fear, or a thought such as "You're not getting away with that!" I encourage my clients to welcome these responses and observe them without judgment: "Here you are again. Come on in. Let's take some time out to calm down."

Then, I teach partners a variety of self-soothing techniques, including slowed-down breathing, calming imagery, self-hypnotic induction, and autogenics, a technique in which individuals create a sense of warmth and heaviness in their bodies. All of these tools help to calm the body and mind, and in the process create a sense of inner safety and comfort. (See Daitch, 2007, for more detailed accounts of these and other self-quieting interventions.)

Once partners have mastered the processes of interrupting reactivity and initiating self-soothing, they are in a better position to observe their reactions in a more dispassionate way, own their part in the relational power struggle, and rehearse more productive responses. I have found that with time and faithful practice, individuals can begin to change entrenched patterns of reactivity and reduce their overall level of arousal.

Pearl #2. Access more mature parts of the self.

Once clients have learned to take a "time-out," they can learn to access parts of themselves that are less reactive and more mature, even while they are in an emotionally triggered state. In the first part of this practice, clients are encouraged to get in touch with the wisest part of their being—the part that is most loving, nurturing, and mature. For clients who have a spiritual or religious practice, it may be helpful to suggest contacting the "higher" or more spiritual part of the self. Then clients are encouraged to hold onto that more compassionate part of the self, and to connect with the thoughts, images, and bodily sensations associated with that part. Finally, clients learn to visualize interacting with a partner from that more mature part of the self.

With further guidance, clients learn that they can experience and hold two conflicting responses at the same time—both a highly reactive one and a calm, compassionate one. The client is encouraged to reflect on what is endearing in his or her partner, even while one is feeling angry, hurt, or frustrated. Getting in touch with valued qualities in a partner helps a couple to amplify and maintain the positive affect that is so vital to sustaining close relationships. The process tends to elicit a kind of openhearted curiosity about the partner, rather than a headlong rush to judgment.

Pearl #3. Practice makes permanent: rehearse and transfer new relationship skills.

Although it is relatively easy for clients to learn and rehearse intentional responses in the therapy office, it can be extremely challenging to transfer them to "real life" when individuals are hijacked by sudden, strong emotions. Because the hard-wired neural processes of the brain have evolved to help us survive, we are instinctively ready to react to threat with an angry offense or a fearful defense, rather than with measured reason. Not surprisingly, research has validated the difficulty of making enduring changes in problematic interpersonal patterns (Jacobson & Addis, 1993).

As clinicians, then, we must not only teach our clients to interrupt overreactive responses and learn more intentional ones, but also help them to permanently integrate these new mechanisms into their everyday response repertoires. Successfully combating and overriding ingrained behaviors and reactive styles requires practice—and lots of it. It is our job as therapists to guide clients through explicit processes that facilitate skill transfer for the long haul.

First, during each therapy session, I help clients visualize themselves engaging in their newly learned behaviors. For example, I might recommend rehearsing the use of positive-self statements paired with deep breathing to help a client remain calm and centered in the face of criticism from the partner. This rehearsal process allows the client to practice more intentional responses, as well as to experience desired feelings toward both self and partner. The exercise also helps clients to anticipate the kinds of relational encounters that typically trigger overreaction, so that they'll be prepared to put their new tools into action as soon as the moment demands it.

Following these in-office rehearsal sessions, I introduce a variety of specific practice sessions that clients will do at home. I explicitly ask clients to practice these exercises each day. Via daily practice, clients begin to experience that their success in regulating emotions depends not on quick tips picked up in the therapy hour, but rather on committing themselves to a regular, enduring discipline that will reap benefits over time.

CASE EXAMPLE: ANDREA AND DENNIS

On the face of it, Andrea and Dennis seemed an unlikely couple. Having achieved both an MD and a PhD, Andrea served on the faculty of a major university and managed a busy internal medicine practice as well. At our first meeting, she proudly described herself as a "high achiever, driven to pursue excellence and be recognized in my field." By contrast, Dennis had more modest worldly aims. He worked as a hospital-supplies salesman and was frequently able to complete his assignments by mid-afternoon. He often spent the rest of the day watching television or puttering around the yard.

When they married 14 years ago, each had been recently divorced, and they found their obvious differences—Dennis's laid-back approach to life and Andrea's whirlwind of activity—admirable and intriguing. But the honeymoon had ended long ago. "Dennis is a truly nice and decent guy," Andrea said in our first joint session. "But his lack of ambition is driving me crazy!" With an impatient gesture, she swept her long, dark hair out of her eyes. "It's not just that he's not making much of a living, but he doesn't push himself in other areas of his life, either. When we get together with my friends, he gets all withdrawn when the conversation shifts from sports to anything remotely intellectual." She let out a loud, frustrated sigh.

Turning to Dennis, I asked him to describe his marriage. A sturdy-bodied, square-jawed man, he took some time to respond. Finally, he said softly, "I still find Andrea to be amazing. She's beautiful, brilliant, and accomplished. But she works so hard in her profession that she's constantly tired, pressured, and irritable." An exasperated note crept into his voice. "I swear, the only time she seems peaceful is when she's sleeping."

Shaking his head in discouragement, Dennis went on: "I try to do everything I can to make her life go smoother. I pick up around the house, pay the bills, get her car washed, et cetera, but she never seems satisfied. She criticizes me constantly for the least little things." Now he looked directly at Andrea and said in a low, tight voice: "I'm sorry I don't make more money. You're far from perfect yourself, you know. And if you wanted an intellectual for a partner, you should have stayed with your first husband!"

When I asked Dennis how he typically reacted to Andrea's criticism, he replied that he felt hurt and went on the defensive—as he just had demonstrated. "If she keeps at me long enough," he admitted, "I sometimes just swear at her and walk out of the room." Here, Andrea interrupted again—but this time to make a small concession. "I know I can be way too critical of Dennis," she said. "But it's really hard to look at our problems when he just shuts down on me. I feel like there's nowhere to go!"

Assessment and Treatment Plan

From this initial assessment interview, it was clear to me that Andrea was a highly ambitious and goal-directed woman. However, her fundamental sense of self-worth seemed to be quite fragile, driving her to strive for constant career accomplishments, status, and validation from others. When stressed or anxious, she often became vehemently critical of Dennis, which appeared to be a projection of her own fear that she was never quite "enough."

Although Dennis seemed to be the more easygoing of the two, he was very sensitive to criticism—especially from his wife. When he felt attacked by Andrea, he typically reacted by becoming distant, resentful, and even sullen. Sometimes he responded with passive aggressiveness, becoming unwilling to engage with his wife for periods of time or presenting vague obstacles to agreed-upon plans. At times, by his own account, he felt "locked in inertia."

Clearly, Dennis and Andrea displayed all of the hazardous relational behaviors that marriage researcher John Gottman (1999) has described as the "four horsemen of the apocalypse": criticism, defensiveness, contempt, and stonewalling. Andrea was chronically critical and contemptuous of Dennis, implying that she was superior to him. He, in turn, launched defensive counterattacks and withdrew into stony silences. I feared that if this couple couldn't learn new ways to respond to each other under stress, their marriage might not survive their mutual, escalating dance of reactivity.

In my view, their most immediate need was to learn simple tools to soothe themselves in the midst of relational stress. I believed that if they could learn to quickly and reliably calm themselves, Andrea and Dennis would be ready to learn how to access their positive feelings for each other even while in the grip of strong negative emotions. In addition, I felt that Dennis needed to rehearse more assertive and proactive behavior with his spouse. Andrea, for her part, would benefit from learning to view herself as "enough" without having to pile up new accomplishments. If Andrea and Dennis could make these significant shifts, they would be able to better manage conflict and—crucially—rediscover some of the pleasure in each other that had brought them together in the first place.

Breaking the Circuit

In their second session, the couple had barely sat down in my office when Andrea turned angrily to Dennis. "I can't believe the way you acted this weekend!" she snapped. Before Dennis could respond, Andrea whirled toward me and reported that on Sunday they'd visited some of her friends, a couple that Dennis had never met before. She accused Dennis of being too quiet, even unfriendly, animated only with the other couple's golden retriever. "I was so embarrassed," she said, her voice edged with bitterness. "These are people who really matter to me—and he couldn't care less."

"Well, I happened to like the dog more than your friends," Dennis countered. "You knew I didn't want to go. I wanted to stay home and watch the tennis match, but no, we had to see friends of yours who aren't even interested in me." His face had become a tight, miserable mask. "Do you ever really care about how I want to spend a weekend?"

This dance of criticism followed by defensiveness was a perfect moment to introduce a lesson on taking a time-out. **Without commenting on their emotion-charged exchange, I simply asked the couple to close their eyes and begin to attend to their breath** (*pearl #1*). After a few moments of quiet, focused breathing, I asked them to continue the process while saying to themselves, "With each new breath, I breathe in soothing comfort. With each breath out, I release frustration and judgments."

After several more moments, I asked them to open their eyes and notice if they felt any differently. Andrea said she felt "slowed down—something I'm not used to." Dennis simply said he felt a little "more in control."

Now that both partners were in a calmer state, I began to give them some feedback on their communication style. I pointed out to Andrea that when she treated Dennis with contempt, his knee-jerk reaction was to become defensive. I encouraged her to take solitary time-outs before bringing up resentments to Dennis, so that she could prepare to clearly identify and express her complaints without resorting to attack. I encouraged Dennis to take time-outs as well, so that he could prepare to hear Andrea's grievances with curiosity instead of defensiveness and to take ownership of his role in their differences.

We spent the remainder of the session on the initial concern that Andrea had raised about Dennis's behavior with her friends. The couple made a conscious effort to maintain a respectful dialogue, with some inevitable slips on this first try. They were quick studies; the question was, would they be able to adhere to these tools? I knew that the capacity to use these time-outs effectively, under duress, would require a genuine commitment of time and effort—at bottom, a commitment to the relationship itself.

Contacting Wisdom

Once Andrea and Dennis were able to reliably self-soothe under stress, **I taught them the next step: accessing the part of themselves that could pause and reflect on their initial reactions** (*pearl #2*). After guiding them into a relaxed state, I asked them to visualize and elicit the part of themselves that was most mature, nonreactive, and compassionate. In this state, I told them, they could determine whether it was reasonable to react at all, and if so, how they might most effectively express their feelings to the other.

For Andrea, it was important that she disengage from her critical side and access the part of her that knew both she and Dennis were "enough." This was a part of her that could individuate from her husband and not expect him to be a replica of her. Meanwhile, Dennis needed to contact a side of himself that was strong and centered, so that he felt entitled to assert himself when he felt unfairly criticized. I also encouraged him to access a more resilient part of himself that was less affected by criticism.

However, in the next session, Andrea reported that she was having difficulty with the process. "Whenever I get irritated with Dennis, I just disconnect from the parts of him that I do love—like his humor and generosity," she said. Dennis nodded, adding, "I have a hard time feeling positively about her, too, especially when she's coming at me with one more thing she wants me to change."

To help the couple contact and hold onto their positive feelings for each other, even in the face of conflict, I taught them a technique called "alternating hands." This process provides a kinesthetic experience of merging negative and positive feelings. After guiding the couple into a relaxed state, I directed Andrea and Dennis to focus their attention on one of their hands, and as they did so to imagine placing into that hand a quality in their partner that caused them pain. Then, I directed them to focus on the other hand, placing into that hand the part of the partner that they found endearing.

"Now, rub those two hands together, and bring them to your chest, over your heart," I said. "As you blend those two sets of feelings, perhaps you can experience that they can coexist." Slowly, almost imperceptibly, I felt the energy in the room begin to shift. When they opened their eyes, Andrea and Dennis looked at each other, smiling tentatively. Dennis took Andrea's hand in his.

Practice—and Practice Some More

As mentioned earlier, habitual, highly reactive interpersonal interactions can be very challenging to change. Practice is essential. Therefore, at the end of each session **I spent time allowing Andrea and Dennis to practice the tools they had learned thus far** (*pearl #3: Practice makes permanent: rehearse and transfer new relationship skills*). As I guided them through time-out sessions, I encouraged them to scan their bodies for tension when they felt triggered by the other, and then to direct their attention to the thoughts and emotions that accompanied that somatic tension. I reminded them that whenever they felt "hijacked," they would need to take a short time away from each other to calm down. Once they reached a more relaxed state, they could then contact more positive feelings toward their partner, and rehearse an appropriate response.

Finally, I asked Andrea and Dennis to spend time each day "practicing the practice." At my request, each made a commitment to create a daily quiet time to practice self-soothing and to contact more mature, loving parts of themselves. In the following session, Andrea reported that she had initiated a daily, 20-minute practice of mindfully attending to her breath. She found not only that she was becoming less critical of Dennis, but also that the daily self-soothing was creating more capacity to reflect on her life overall.

Dennis reported that in addition to daily practice, he was now able to initiate time-outs almost at the very moment he felt judged or criticized by Andrea. During these self-soothing sessions, he said he was more able to contact a compassionate side of himself that could nurture his wife when she seemed stressed rather than automatically disconnect from her. Both partners acknowledged how much they depended on their regular, daily practice of self-soothing, shifting gears, and rehearsal to help them to make these relational shifts. They recommitted themselves to these daily practices.

Five months later, at our final therapy session, Dennis and Andrea exuded palpable energy and hope. They admitted that they still got reactive with each other—plenty of times—but now found themselves able to dial down their distress more quickly and reliably. In the face of conflict, Dennis was more able to calmly stand up for himself rather than disappear into resentment. Andrea, meanwhile, found herself more interested in changes she might make in her own behavior, rather than in her husband's. "I can see how daily practice makes the difference," she said. "It's easy to forget that I have all this quiet inside me."

She also had pared down her workload somewhat, which freed the couple to spend more time together on activities they both loved, such as mountain biking and cooking. As Andrea leaned toward her husband, smiling, Dennis said, "I think we're on our way." There were no guarantees, and they knew it. But they were clearly proud of their patient, steady progress toward handling conflict with more self-awareness and mutual respect. They were hopeful. So was I.

CONCLUDING COMMENTS

Helping couples navigate the tumultuous waters of relationships, where we all meet our dark sides, has been deeply satisfying for me. It has also been an extended, exciting process of learning. The strategies I've developed and discussed in this chapter have evolved out of nearly three decades of working with couples. Over the years, I've witnessed just how easy it can be to focus on a partner's weaknesses. I've seen how tempting it is to cling to the illusion that winning an argument is somehow a victory. I have seen just how challenging and painful it can be to accept that one's partner is a truly separate person, and to embrace—or at least learn to tolerate—inevitable differences.

In the course of trying to help couples make these challenging shifts, I have discovered over and over again that insight takes people only so far. Goodwill takes people only so far. I have learned that to help relationships improve, it is vital to offer clients concrete, reliable strategies for self-soothing, switching emotional gears, and rehearsing new behaviors. Couples must not only learn these skills but also be prepared to practice them for a lifetime.

In developing my approach to affect regulation, I have been profoundly influenced by my training in clinical hypnosis. I have seen how simple self-hypnosis tools give clients enormous power to pause, buy time, and form more intentional responses. In shaping my approach with couples, specifically, I've also been deeply influenced by my training in Imago relationship therapy, developed by Harville Hendrix, and by the groundbreaking work of marriage researcher John Gottman.

On a personal note, I want to acknowledge how much I have learned from the clients I am honored to treat. As I worked with Andrea and Dennis, for example, I found myself sometimes identifying with Andrea. Like her, I can become overly busy with my own work challenges, prone to forgetting that just "being" can be more sustaining than perpetually "doing." I know, too, how easy it is to judge the people I love most. But, as I advised Dennis and Andrea, I try to spend time each day in stillness, so that I can pause, observe, and connect with what is best in me. It is a discipline that requires much patience and diligence, but it yields rewards that continue to grow and deepen.

BIBLIOGRAPHY

Daitch, C. (2007). *Affect regulation toolbox: Practical and effective hypnotic interventions for the over-reactive client.* New York: Norton.

Daitch, C. (2008, September/October). Practice makes perfect. *Psychotherapy Networker,* 48–52.

Frederick, C. (2005). Selected topics in ego state therapy. *The International Journal of Clinical and Experimental Hypnosis,* 53(4), 339–429.

Gottman, J. M. (1999). *The marriage clinic: A scientifically based marital therapy.* New York: Norton.

Hendrix, H. (1988). *Getting the love you want: A guide for couples.* New York: Harper.

Jacobson, N.S. & Addis, M.E. (1993). Research on couple therapy: What do we know? Where are we going? *Journal of Consulting and Clinical Psychology,* 61(1), 85–93.

BIOGRAPHY

Carolyn Daitch, PhD, is the director of the Center for the Treatment of Anxiety Disorders in Farmington Hills, Michigan. She is a certified and approved consultant and fellow with the American Society of Clinical Hypnosis and a certified Imago therapist. She routinely trains and presents to practitioners in the U.S. and abroad. She is also a consultant with the University of Michigan Department of Integrative Medicine.

Daitch is the author of *The Affect Regulation Toolbox: Practical and Effective Hypnotic Interventions for the Over-reactive Client* (W. W. Norton, 2007). The Society of Clinical and Experimental Hypnosis recently awarded her book the Arthur Shapiro "Best Hypnosis Book." Daitch is currently writing two additional books: *Anxiety: The Go-to Guide for Therapists and Clients* and *The Hypnotherapy Toolkit.*

●○●●●●●○

Chapter 14
Respectful Curiosity, Collaborative Ritual-Making, Speaking the Unspeakable: A Multi-Contextual Therapy of Love and Loss

Evan Imber-Black, PhD

The task to extract three "pearls of wisdom" that underpin my work is daunting. Thirty-five years of teaching, writing, and practicing family therapy have taught me a particular humility, for every time I experience sureness I am blessed to meet a family who challenges my beliefs. I am old enough to have lived through the crowning of many models as "ultimate truth." And I am young enough to eschew cynicism and instead embrace the continual search for new ways to ameliorate relational suffering. I am pleased to offer my current three pearls, secure in the knowledge that they will undoubtedly evolve.

PEARLS

Pearl #1. Bring a stance of respectful curiosity.

Whether as a therapist, teacher, supervisor, or scholarly journal editor, I bring a stance of respectful curiosity to my work. Before methods, models, theories, or techniques I place my commitment to walk alongside, offering what I may know while anchored in the belief that others—family members, trainees, authors—have special knowledge of their own. I am eternally curious about what others believe, not because I hold a solipsistic "all ideas are equal" position, but because this is the starting place for dialogue. I believe this stance subtly communicates an overarching premise: When people initially experience that what they have to offer, no matter how rough-edged, has value, they are more likely to begin a process of questioning and development.

It is my job to fashion thoughtful questions, to offer ideas, and to take direct positions that reflect my beliefs and points of view while carefully observing and responding to feedback. I must be alert to small opportunities for change and facilitate these. I see my role as being in the service of expanding the capacity to hold and express difference and enabling the relational complexity so necessary to solve problems and recover resiliencies. I have no interest in a family confirming a theory, or a student exhibiting cloneship. When a trainee leaves a workshop telling me "You have made me believe I can do this work," I know I have succeeded. When prior students who have become colleagues describe my mentoring as what ultimately made a symmetrical shift respectfully encompassing where we align and where we may delightfully differ, I know I am the teacher I most want to be. When manuscript authors who have received a major revision letter from me with 25 requests for changes write to tell me I understood their work and helped them to bring it to a richer, deeper focus, I know I am the journal editor I most aspire to be. And when families at the close of therapy comment that the room felt just safe enough but not too safe, that they were simultaneously acknowledged and challenged and— most of all—witnessed, I know I am the therapist I most hope to be.

Pearl #2. Collaboratively create rituals.

Some of my most moving experiences as a family therapist have been in the domain of rituals. Marking life's transitions—whether the seemingly ordinary ones of daily life such as parting and reconnecting, meals or bedtime; the annual or seasonal, such as birthdays, anniversaries, holidays, and vacations; or the profound signposts on life's journey, including birth and death, and all of the individual and family life-cycle changes such as adolescence, leaving home, and making committed relationships—allows us to hold and express complex and often contradictory meanings and emotions. A single ritual may concurrently heal and celebrate, bind an unresolved family-of-origin wound while opening a contemporary connection. Rituals alter and outline the shapes of relationships, frame beliefs, paint new identities, help heal losses, and celebrate what it means to be alive (Imber-Black & Roberts, 1998).

No other aspect of human interaction captures and reveals the required duality of our existence—anchoring us in the past, in our multigenerational families of origin, our culture, ethnicity, and religion while simultaneously pointing the way to a transformed future. Continuity and change are enabled through rituals large and small.

Comprising symbols, symbolic actions, special times, special places, structured aspects, and open aspects, rituals differ markedly from tasks in therapy. With tasks, the therapist expects certain outcomes. With rituals, the therapist expects the unexpected. Tasks rely primarily on the therapist's directions; the rituals I have in mind are a cocreated phenomenon.

When the family therapy field first became interested in rituals in the early 1980s, the clinical literature focused on rituals as strategic technique (Selvini-Palazzoli, Boscolo, Cecchin, & Prata, 1977). The therapist "invented" rituals; the family "performed" them. At the same time, family researchers began to look at existing family rituals as potentially holding mental-health protective qualities (Wolin, Bennett, & Jacobs, 2003). Starting at this time with my colleagues Janine Roberts and Richard Whiting (Imber-Black, Roberts, & Whiting, 2003), I began what became a three-decade-long exploration of the power of collaborative ritual-making with families.

In order to wrest rituals from mere technique, we focused on the naturally occurring rituals in families. In order to do this, a much larger frame was needed. This work is embedded in foundational theory—multiple interacting systemic contexts, including the social, cultural, and political, family-larger system relationships (Imber-Black, 1988), multigenerational genograms (McGoldrick, Gerson, & Petry, 2008), household interactions, and family and individual beliefs and themes (Papp & Imber-Black, 1996); the family life cycle in all of its varied cultural permutations (Carter & McGoldrick, 2005); and circularity. Within this theoretical container, rituals became a potent therapeutic element. Learning about a family's existing rituals allows entry into the world of relationships, emotions, and values. When a family is frozen, alienating silences, stereotypical and repetitive painful arguments without resolution, conflict with families of origin, and unmourned and unhealed losses may be revealed through the prism of rituals. A husband and wife repeat the same aching *pas de deux* every holiday— she wants to celebrate joyfully as her family in the Dominican Republic always did, while he hides in the bedroom, sullen, sad, and angry. A simple use of the genogram to trace each one's experiences with holidays might reveal an unspoken secret: When the husband was a young boy in Puerto Rico, his father became drunk on every holiday and beat him with a belt until he bled, while his mother hid in the kitchen. This side-by-side examination of each one's experience of holiday rituals could lead to a question to this husband: "How might this coming Christmas be different?" Within half an hour the couple and therapist could collaborate to fashion a new ritual. "When I first wake up on Christmas morning, put on salsa music—loud! Take my hand and dance with me. This will tell me today is different from all those other Christmases." Thus begins a new ritual, one unmoored from the memories of abuse and capable of beginning a path of healing.

Collaborative ritual-making starts with the discernment of major themes in a couple or family. I interview with an ear for meanings and offer metaphors. I search for rituals and wonder aloud whether or not they promote well-being. We join in an anthropological journey exploring their cultures and their mini-cultures. Missing rituals—no protected time for a family meal because Dad is at the computer, a 5-year-old who puts herself to bed because Mother is sick with cancer and the family is in chaos, minimized holidays because of unaddressed religious difference—signal opportunity for relationship-building anew. Rituals gone flat like an airless balloon because they have not made evolutions required by new family membership, developmental shifts, divorce, or death may stand as allegories for necessary relationship change. As we work together to alter old rituals and create new ones, unanticipated personal and relational fortuities emerge.

Pearl #3. Speak the unspeakable.

The therapy room is frequently a vessel capable of holding the never-before-spoken, the taboo, the secret. The family-therapy consulting room is replete with secrets and silences, but until the 1990s, the field either ignored the topic or split it into a "never tell/always tell" polarity (Imber-Black, 1993) inadequate to embrace complexities. My own focus is on the particularity of each secret, embedded in contexts of multiple interacting systems. Some families hold a central secret, often putting more and more topics off-limits for conversation, whereas other families erect barriers of language, eroding cognitive and emotional connections. Family violence, sexual abuse, addictions, extramarital affairs, adoption, infertility, life-shortening illness—all require theory and practice capable of helping individuals and families to examine their silences and make decisions regarding when, whether, and to whom to speak. Socially generated shame attached to abortion, paternity, mental and physical illness, sexual orientation and gender variance, skin-color differences, immigration, and social class status all require a therapy able to lift fear and dissolve humiliation. I must help families to draw distinctions between troubling secrecy and healthy privacy. Choices regarding whom to tell must be steeped in age appropriateness, potential healing, and a sense of future well-being, not in "tell-all" talk-show ethics (Imber-Black, 1998). When secrets emerge, I must distinguish historical toxic secrets where slow consideration is possible and immediately dangerous secrets where acute action is necessary. Not all secrets require revelation. I believe it is my responsibility to shape a therapy context where the benefits and risks to persons and relationships regarding secrecy and openness can be thoroughly examined.

My commitment to theory and practice-building in the realm of secrets arose first from work with a family whose painful predicaments did not fit the models *du jour*. Focused solely on an intractable phobic symptom in a 75-year-old woman, this multigenerational family and all who had treated them in many hospitals and clinics were tied in unyielding knots. Suggested interventions in the various larger systems were growing punitive. Relationships within the family and with helpers were at once alienated and engulfing. Grown children and grandchildren formed and re-formed alliances and splits. Energy for life's unfolding in new directions was sapped.

When our therapy began, thinking in the field held that secrets did not need to be opened (Haley, 1978). Only the relational process of secret-keeping required our attention (Boscolo, Cecchin, Hoffman, & Penn, 1987). When this woman's aching 50-year secret of the before-marriage birth of her two older daughters finally opened in a therapy session, rapid individual and family-relationship changes followed. Secret upon secret tumbled open. When I first met this family, the woman had not touched another person for a decade. At the close of the session in which she opened her secret to her daughters, she folded my two hands in hers. My commitment to aiding families and their helpers to speak the unspeakable began.

CASE EXAMPLE: FINDING A ROOM WHERE OPENESS DWELLS—A THERAPY OF RECOVERED LOVE AMID LOOMING LOSS

A referral came to me at the Center for Families and Health, which I direct at the Ackerman Institute for the Family. Bill, age 48, had stage-four colon cancer, metastasized to his brain and liver. He and his wife of 20 years, Annie, age 47, wanted couples therapy. They had one child, Jeremy, age 12.

As I prepared to meet this couple, I imagined an initial session focused on Bill's illness and what this now meant to the couple and family. I was wrong. In our first meeting, the couple told me they had come to "work on their marriage." Cancer was not the subject of interest. When I gently inquired about Bill's health, they changed the subject. When we started their genograms, I learned that each had a father who died in midlife of cancer, and each came from family where the rule was "the less said about illness and death, the better."

In keeping with my stance of respectful curiosity (*pearl #1*), I listened. I heard stories that day of a marriage filled with disappointments, underpinned by a stereotypical pattern of Annie "nagging" and Bill "withdrawing" that cut across every imaginable topic—parenting, money, housework, and especially Bill's career. I searched for daily rituals, points of meaningful connection, but found none. Rather, their arguments were the electric current between them.

Referring only obliquely to just how sick Bill was, Annie spoke about his need to "establish his legacy." Each was in show business. Both agreed that Bill was the more talented and Annie the more successful, mirroring in the outside world their overfunctioning/underfunctioning dance. With no mention that Bill was obviously close to death, Annie expressed deep anxiety about his musical career not being secured for future generations. Bill responded with stony silence. Symbolic of their alienation, they told me they no longer slept in the same room, and had not done so for years.

During our first three sessions, I remained close to their request to work on their marriage. Small signs of mutual caring emerged as I asked about memories of better, earlier times. There continued to be no mention of cancer until our fourth session, when Annie referenced an episode at home. A friend had urged her to buy a book about hospice care. She did so secretly and was reading it behind a closed door when Bill came upon her weeping. I took this as my signal to begin our journey to speak the unspeakable. I inquired about sadness, and each spoke of hiding deeper feelings of fear and sorrow from the other.

After this session, Bill had a severe medical emergency. At first he refused to go to the hospital. Their "nag/withdraw" pattern returned with a vengeance. Only when a friend arrived at 2 A.M. did Bill agree to go to the emergency room. He required a colostomy. Annie came alone to the next session to tell me what happened. She cried, "I'm always the bitch, I'm always the hard one—I'm sick of it!" It was the first time she had revealed to me (and to herself) how scared she was at the prospect of losing Bill. I asked her to start to consider ways she might respond differently. She spoke poignantly of knowing a softer self.

This therapy was emotionally risky for each partner. Opening their hearts to one another meant facing looming loss. With my encouragement, this couple, who had spent the better part of two decades locked in distracting bickering, finally decided to put this nonsense away and take tentative steps toward each other. As their relationship grew, meaningful rituals entered. They began to share meals and quiet conversation. Annie surprised Bill by gathering all of their friends to honor him, play and sing his music, and make a CD. All seemed to know that this was an opportunity to celebrate his life while he was still alive.

Following Bill's medical emergency, our work turned to secrets. They had not told their son of Bill's colostomy. When I asked about this decision, each emphatically told me "it's private." New professionals were in and out of their apartment to teach them to deal with the colostomy bag. Jeremy hid in his room. Bill remarked that he had overheard Jeremy telling a friend that his dad no longer had cancer. Neither parent had corrected his misconception. I invited them to bring Jeremy to the next session, but they expressed uncertainty and said they would think it over.

We also spoke that day of the upcoming Thanksgiving holiday, as they were struggling over whether to stay home or join their extended families for what, they now acknowledged for the first time, might be Bill's last Thanksgiving. We traced this ritual in the history of their marriage and their mutual families. Thanksgiving had historically been a significant holiday, one marked by warmth, touch, laughter, and loving.

Through our conversation, they decided to join the whole family for this holiday. As I find often happens, following this meaningful ritual, they decided to open a secret. When families participate in authentic rituals, greater openness often follows. They told Jeremy of Bill's colostomy. He responded, "Well, I knew that. I was just waiting for you to tell me." This, in turn, led to their decision to bring Jeremy to a therapy session where Bill had an opportunity to tell him several previously unspoken truths: "I still have cancer and I have it all over my body," and "I am so proud of you—do you have any idea how proud I am?" and "Jeremy, I love you so much."

Jeremy and I also spoke privately. He told me how much he loved to use a video camera. I took him behind the one-way mirror to see our camera. He quietly confided how scared he was to lose his dad. **I asked him if he might want to interview both his mom and dad about their lives and their careers and put this on tape, thereby enabling a ritual of parent-child storytelling that might remain with Jeremy long after his father's death** (*pearl #2: Collaboratively create rituals*).

Whenever I work with families with illness, I ask for the diagnosis story. Bill's initial story when I met him was flat, short, and linear. "I had colitis for 15 years. I got colon cancer 2 years ago." Further inquiries were blocked, while Annie looked away. In a session near the end of our therapy, however, a much more complex story replete with secrets, guilt, and shame emerged. Bill began a session praising Annie for taking care of him. **She immediately stopped him, declaring that she did not deserve to be put on a pedestal. I inquired** (*pearl #3: Speak the unspeakable*). In tears, Annie avowed that Bill's advanced and incurable cancer was, in good measure, her fault. Eight years before I met them, during one of their many "nag/withdraw" episodes, Annie pushed Bill to change doctors, to go to a doctor who treated famous people. This "doctor to the stars" misdiagnosed Bill's cancer. When it was properly diagnosed, it was too late to cure. Hearing Annie state this for the first time, Bill took her hand, wept, and told her he never knew she believed this and that he did not hold her responsible. In turn, Bill spoke of his own responsibility as he lived a life trying to please authorities and never asking necessary questions. Annie responded, "I'm just so grateful you don't do that here with Evan." I also felt gratitude that together we had shaped a place sufficient to hold anything each needed to say. Following a deeper discussion of these painful revelations, Bill declared for the first time where he truly saw himself: "For these last many weeks, I'm dying. We don't speak of this and we must. I am dying."

The couple reached for each other as we spoke of their pending loss. I raised the natural asymmetry attendant to their situation. From moment to moment, each was in a place different from the other. Just as Bill was imagining his death, Annie was fielding calls from his oncologist and thinking he should fight more to stay alive. Within the same hour that Annie was silently planning her future without him, Bill was growing optimistic about the possibility of more brain surgery. In keeping with our therapy of "talk about it, talk about it, talk about it," I encouraged them to let each know their innermost thoughts, "no matter how wild and crazy these might seem."

Soon, Bill could no longer walk. He came to our session in a wheelchair. They told me they had shared a bed for the first time in years, "just to be close and warm." We spent the session mostly reminiscing about their lives, their careers, their relationship, their family. When we spoke of Bill's wishes, he told Annie he wanted all of his friends and family to come to say good-bye. Near the end, I asked, "What worked for you in this therapy?" Annie responded, "Here in this room, we are more open than anywhere else in our lives." Bill added, "It's getting to be like that at home, too."

A few days later, Bill entered the hospital for the last time. I spoke with Annie and told her I wanted to come. When I arrived, I found that Annie had honored Bill's wish with a final ritual, a vigil. In the visitors' room next to Bill's room were perhaps 50 friends and family members. Candles were lit, Bill's music played quietly, and stories of Bill filled the air. Annie was a sentry, moving people in and out of Bill's room to say good-bye. She immediately ushered me in, along with Jeremy. Bill told me Jeremy had been in a play the night before, and friends had videotaped it for him, enabling him a glimpse of his legacy. I told them how moved I was to walk alongside them. Annie gently stroked Bill's arm and told him he no longer needed to fight. The vigil continued for 6 more days, when Bill died with Annie at his side.

This couple clearly knew what they needed when they had told me 5 months earlier, "We are here to work on our marriage." Our therapy became the crucible for shattering years of deadening silence, healing the wounds of alienation, and allowing a death enveloped by life.

CONCLUDING COMMENTS

I have been extremely fortunate in my career. From the very beginning as a graduate student, I had mentors who believed deeply in my abilities, who saw talents in me before I saw them, and who refused to allow me to indulge self-doubt. I took it as my responsibility to both live up to their expectations and play it forward with my trainees.

I have not invented a model. Nor have I attached myself to one central theory. Rather, my three major bodies of work—families and larger systems (Imber-Black, 1988), rituals (Imber-Black & Roberts, 1998; Imber-Black, Roberts, & Whiting, 2003), and secrets (Imber-Black, 1993; Imber-Black, 1998)—have intentionally cut across models of practice with the hope that others will find new meanings and fashion new directions.

I have been blessed with my husband, Lascelles Black, a family therapist committed to the most difficult problems in the public sector, and colleagues from among the many fields of thought in family therapy whose rich conversations and writings have contributed to my own sense of inquisitiveness, creativity, and aliveness.

I have purposely spent my work life in multiple contexts—universities, academic medicine, psychiatry, family therapy training institutes—as doing so has allowed me to continually question emerging certainties and search for multidisciplinary applications of thought and practice. I have been able to create a work life braiding a couple and family therapy practice, teaching locally, nationally, and internationally, consulting to larger systems, theory-building, and writing. Serving as editor of the scholarly journal *Family Process*, whose unique niche brings readers quantitative and qualitative research, clinical theory, and practice, has contributed to my own kaleidoscopic vision. This delicious variety continues to nourish my appreciation that there are many ways to be in the world.

BIBLIOGRAPHY

Boscolo, L., Cecchin, G., Hoffman, L., and Penn, P. (1987). *Milan systemic family therapy: Conversations in theory and practice*. New York: Basic Books.

Carter, B., & McGoldrick, M. (Eds.). (2005). *The expanded family life cycle* (3rd ed.). Boston: Allyn and Bacon.

Haley, J. (1978). *Problem-solving therapy*. San Francisco: Jossey-Bass.

Imber-Black, E. (1988). *Families and larger systems: A therapist's guide through the labyrinth*. New York: Guilford.

Imber-Black, E. (Ed.). (1993). *Secrets in families and family therapy*. New York: Norton.

Imber-Black, E. (1998). *The secret life of families: Truth-telling, privacy and reconciliation in a tell-all society*. New York: Bantam.

Imber-Black, E., & Roberts, J. (1998). *Rituals for our times: Celebrating, healing and changing our lives and our relationships*. Northvale, NJ: Jason Aronson.

Imber-Black, E., Roberts, J., & Whiting, R. (Eds.). (2003). *Rituals in families and family therapy* (Rev. ed.). New York: Norton.

McGoldrick, M., Gerson, R., & Petry, S. (2008). *Genograms: Assessment and intervention*. New York: Norton.

Papp, P., & Imber-Black, E. (1996). Family themes: Transmission and transformation. *Family Process,35*(1), 5--20.

Selvini-Palazolli, M., Boscolo, L., Cecchin, G., & Prata, G. (1977). Family rituals: A powerful tool in family therapy. *Family Process, 16*(4), 445–454.

Wolin, S. J., Bennett, L. A., & Jacobs, J. S. (2003). Assessing family rituals in alcoholic families. In E. Imber-Black, J. Roberts, & R. Whiting (Eds.), *Rituals in families and family therapy*. New York: Norton.

BIOGRAPHY

Evan Imber-Black, PhD, is the director of the Center for Families and Health, a senior faculty member at the Ackerman Institute for the Family in New York City, and the acting program director of the Marriage and Family Therapy Masters Program at Mercy College. She is a professor in the Department of Psychiatry at the Albert Einstein College of Medicine in the Bronx, New York. She maintains a private practice in couple and family therapy in New York City and Westchester County. She is the editor of *Family Process*, the major scholarly journal in family-systems research and family therapy. Imber-Black is a past president of the American Family Therapy Academy, recipient of the 1990 American Family Therapy Academy Award for Distinguished Contribution to Family Therapy Theory and Practice, and the 1999 recipient of the American Association for Marriage and Family Therapy Cumulative Contribution to Marriage and Family Therapy. She is the author of over 50 original papers and several books.

Section Six:
Children

Chapter 15

Attachment-Focused Treatment for Children

Dan Hughes, PhD

Through our understanding of infant research on attachment and intersubjectivity, we have become aware of the central importance of the reciprocal, contingent, nonverbal (bodily) communications between parent and child in facilitating optimal human development. Such dialogues, happening long before verbal communication, enable the young child to discover who he or she is, the nature of the social/emotional world, and how to have an impact on that world. As children mature, these nonverbal communications gradually include words as well and become shared conversations with the parents and others. Children discover who they are—including the vast, diverse qualities of thought, emotions, perceptions, memories, and intentions that constitute their inner lives—through their experience of their parents' experience of them. The research and theories of Colwyn Trevarthen and Daniel Stern greatly influenced my awareness of these important developmental factors (Trevarthen, 2001; Trevarthen & Aitken, 2001; Stern, 1985, 1998).

PEARLS

The following three interventions are based on these theories of attachment and intersubjectivity, both of which are central features in human development, being crucial for both safety and exploration.

Pearl #1. Match or lead the expression of affect.

When an adult matches a child's nonverbal affective expression of his or her underlying emotion, the child often is able to experience the adult's empathy for his or her experience and better regulate the underlying emotion. The adult's affective communication of his or her experience of the child's emerging experience enables the child to become aware of—and deepen—his or her own experience.

When children (and probably adults as well) give expression to their inner lives, they do so with an expression of affect that reflects both the information and energy that characterize the focus of their attention. The particular emotion associated with an event that they are describing is conveyed with a unique facial expression, voice prosody, and gestures and movements that best convey the particular meaning of that event for the child. The rhythm and intensity of the nonverbal expression conveys "how" and "how much" the event affected the child. When the adult matches that affective expression (often without feeling the child's underlying emotion), the adult is able to convey that he or she "gets it," and the child feels "felt." In other words, the child experiences the adult's experience of empathy for him or her in a way that words would never communicate alone. For example, if a child screams "I *hate* my dad!" in a therapy session, and the therapist replies, with the same intensity and rhythm as the child's expressions, "*You* are *really angry* with your *dad* right now!" the child is likely to feel that the therapist does "get" his experience. If, however, the therapist says "you are really angry with your dad right now" in a flat tone of voice, the child is not likely to experience the therapist as "getting it."

Along with conveying empathy for the child's experiences, matching the affect also helps the child to regulate his or her experience. When a child experiences intense anger, that expression of anger is demonstrated by an intense affective expression in his or her voice, face, and gestures. If the child does not experience a similar response from an adult, the intensity is likely to escalate, as the child may struggle to regulate the emotion. If the child lacks general affect-regulation skills, any increase in intensity only increases the risk of dysregulation. By matching the intensity and rhythm of the affective expression (and remaining regulated him- or herself), the adult is able to help the child to remain regulated. By finding the adult with him or her in the intense experience, and communicating with the adult about it, the child often finds him- or herself becoming less distressed and agitated.

Children may have trouble identifying an experience because it is new. They may be uncertain how to communicate it or worry that maybe they should not have it. This is especially true of children raised in circumstances where aspects of their inner lives are not seen or encouraged or when they have experienced traumatic events. In those situations, if a therapist is able to make sense of the child's experience and take the lead in its nonverbal affective expression, the child is often able to experience it more deeply and communicate it more fully him- or herself.

Pearl #2. Be curious about the child's inner life.

When curiosity is directed toward the child's experiences—rather than toward the factual events of his or her life—and when it is conveyed with both affective and reflective features, the child is likely to go with the therapist very deeply into his or her life's story, coregulating any emotions that are associated with what is being explored and cocreating the meaning of the events.

Curiosity, used in this sense, is not a barren or intrusive exploration into the recent or remote past, but rather is an act of discovery—an experience of fascination—with who this child is and how his or her life has unfolded, along with the impact of that history on his or her sense of self. The facts themselves are not as important as the meaning of these events on the child's developing narrative. Through nonjudgmental, "not-knowing" curiosity, the therapist is often able to assist the child in deepening the experience of the event, along with reorganizing it and integrating it into his or her narrative. A word of caution: If the child experiences the adult's interest as suggesting what he or she *should* have thought, felt, or wanted, the child is likely to begin losing interest in the process and may actively conceal his or her inner life from the adult.

For curiosity to go deeply into the child's life story, it must contain not only a reflective but also an affective component. It must not be a detached, professional, observer's interest, but rather the experience of someone who is truly deeply interested in the inner life of the other. While exploring the child's narrative, the therapist needs to be affected by what they are experiencing together through the act of discovery. In his or her wondering—his or her deep interest—the therapist is likely to express him- or herself in deeply affective manner, such as: "Wow! Do you think that maybe . . . ?!" or "*Wait* a second, wait a second . . . I wonder if . . . ?!" or "*Yes*, I think I get what you are saying! *It's* like . . . !" or "So *that's* what made it so hard for you! Now I get it, now I get it. You had always thought . . . !" The therapist's enthusiasm for the process of discovery, or his or her compassion and empathy for what they are discovering together, helps the child to experience his or her inner life as being very important and meaningful, and the process of discovery as being safe. What the child thinks, feels, remembers, and makes sense of in his or her life is completely accepted by the therapist. Further, this joint exploration "touches" the therapist. What they discover together gradually elicits less shame or fear. The child now is much more able to begin to establish a coherent narrative.

Pearl #3. "Talk for" and "talk about" the child.

Children who manifest various psychological problems often have gaps in both their affective and reflective skills. They often have difficulty regulating, identifying, and communicating their inner lives to others. Giving them the safety to "find the words" can often be a slow and unproductive process—they truly do not "find" them. Utilizing metaphor to express their inner lives is often insufficient for empowering them to be able to integrate and communicate their narrative. Taking the lead in assisting them to give voice to the events of the past often also greatly assists them in organizing these events into a coherent narrative.

When a therapist "talks for" a child, he or she tries to replicate the child's own speech and voice prosody and speaks in the first person as if he or she were the child. The therapist's words are embedded in nonverbal affective expressions. The child is then able to "try out" the therapist's expressions as if they were his or her own. The child often then makes use of the expressions that resonate with the wordless experience of his or her inner life, which frequently leads to a spontaneous elaboration of it, or a modification that best describes that unique experience. The therapist's guesses that do not resonate with the child's inner life tend to be quickly discarded and forgotten. Throughout this process the therapist is clear that when he or she speaks for the child, he or she is guessing what the child might want to say if he or she had the words. The therapist is clear that he or she always accepts the child's statement as to whether or not the guess is accurate. If the child tells the therapist *not* to guess, the therapist always complies with those wishes. When the therapist *is* able to take the lead in finding the words to describe an experience of an event in the child's life, frequently the child begins a process of being able to identify and communicate an aspect of his or her inner life that previously had been unknown, nameless, and often frightening and chaotic. This process also often leads the child to begin to deepen and integrate his or her emotional experience of the event. The nonverbal affective expressions of the therapist, associated with the verbal content, often lead the child into an emotional experience that is congruent with the expressed affect. We tend to forget that this same process occurs countless times in the intersubjective activities that exist between parent and infant.

"Talking about" a child is often a valuable complement to the affective meaning-making that is often facilitated by "talking for" a child. Talking about a child involves turning to his or her caregiver and reflecting something that just happened with the child, often connecting it to a deeper or more comprehensive aspect of the child's narrative. This reflection always conveys a positive, accepting tone. This intervention can also be used by talking to a poster, stuffed animal, or even oneself by "thinking out loud" about the therapist's experience of the child's strengths and vulnerabilities. This process tends to lower the affective tone of the discussion and help the child to move into a calmer, more reflective stance. Such a stance enables the child to stay regulated while exploring stressful events from the past. It gives him or her a break from the affect generated by the explorations. At the same time, it enables the child to step back and reflect upon what he or she and the therapist (and possibly the parents or other significant people in his or her life) have just experienced together. During the affective exploration, the child experiences unique events in his or her narrative, and through the reflection the child is able to take a more distant and integrative perspective. When the therapist talks about the child rather than to him or her, the implied message is that the child does not have to respond, and he or she often more fully listens to what is being said without being distracted by having to prepare a response. Children also often more fully accept what is being said about them because they are less likely to experience the words as trying to influence them.

CASE EXAMPLE: ROBBIE

Robbie was a 10-year-old boy who was adopted at the age of 8 by Jane and David. He had been physically abused by his father and exposed to domestic violence while residing with his biological parents until he was placed in foster care at the age of 5. After two foster placements and no efforts by his parents to resolve their problems, he was free to be adopted. Jane and David were very committed to Robbie; they also had a strong marriage and no unresolved issues from their own childhoods.

Robbie's behavior in foster care and with his adoptive parents was characterized by habitual oppositional-defiant features as well as verbal and physical aggression primarily directed toward Jane. He often reacted with anger to routine discussions or discipline, and this was quickly followed by his withdrawal and resentment. His extreme reluctance to explore his abusive past as well as his current symptoms appeared to represent a mixture of both fear and shame. He also had great difficulty giving expression to his inner life, which appeared to reflect a poor ability to identify and express his thoughts, emotions, and intentions.

Our first joint session included Robbie, Jane, and David. (I had previously met with the parents to understand their concerns as well as to give suggestions regarding how I would like them to respond to Robbie during our conversations in therapy. Such suggestions—and the parents' ability to understand and follow them—are crucial if the sessions with their child are to be effective.) Robbie sat between his parents on the couch and I sat in a chair near them. After an initial discussion of Robbie's interest in basketball, I turned our attention to the fact that he had again hit his mother over the weekend when she would not allow him to ride his bike until his dad returned from the store and could go with him. (Robbie was not allowed to ride on his own because he was impulsive and disregarded the rules of riding his bike.) As I began to explore this with him, he yelled, *"They* are *so stupid! They treat me like a baby!"*

In order to match Robbie's nonverbal affect, I used the same intensity and rhythm that he had. **"You think that they treat you like a baby! And you're 10! No wonder you get mad if you think that!"** (*pearl #1*).

"They do!" Robbie said.

"That is *certainly* how it seems to you! If you're right—why *would* they do that? *Why would they?"* I asked.

"I don't know!"

"Let's figure that *out!"* I said. "*Let's understand* why if they do treat you like a baby, *why it could be?* What could it be? Wait! *Wait! . . .* Maybe *they worry about you!* Maybe they don't want *you* to get hurt!"

"I won't!" Robbie said.

"So you think that they have no reason to worry! But if they do . . . *why would they worry about you? . . .* Maybe . . . *maybe . . .* they don't want you to get hurt . . . *because they love you!"*

"That's stupid!" Robbie said.

"That they *love you?"* I asked.

"Sometimes I wish they didn't!" Robbie said.

"You wish they didn't! *Wow!* **Not love you!** *What's that about?"* I asked (*pearl #2: Be curious about the child's inner life*).

"I don't need their love!" Robbie said.

"Ah!" I said. "I wonder if you're saying that sometimes you don't want their love."

"I don't!" Robbie said.

"Can you tell your parents that?" I asked. "Can you tell them that sometimes you don't want their love?"

"No!" Robbie said. "That's stupid!"

"**Would you let me say it for you, if that's want you think and feel sometimes?**" **I suggested** (*pearl #3: "Talk for" and "talk about" the child*).

"I don't care," Robbie said quietly.

"If I get it wrong and say anything that you don't think or feel, just tell me and I'll change it the way you want me to," I reassured him. "Or you can say it yourself if you want. Okay?"

Robbie looked down and whispered, "Yeah."

I moved my chair closer to Robbie, put my hand on his arm, and spoke to his parents as if I were him. "Mom, Dad," I said, "sometimes I don't **want** you to love me! I just *don't*! Sometimes I just want you to stop *worrying* about me, stop *caring* for me!"

Jane conveyed compassion for her son as she leaned toward him and quietly said, "Robbie, I'm so *sorry* that you sometimes don't want our love. We love you *so much* and want you to be our son and be glad that you are!"

Speaking for Robbie again, I replied, "Why *would* I be glad? You *never* let me do what I want!"

"I know that we say 'no' a lot, Robbie, and I know that you get angry about that!"

"If you really loved me you'd let me do what I want!" I said.

Jane squeezed Robbie's hand as she said, "I still love you when I say 'no' Robbie. I'm sorry that it's hard to believe that!"

"It *is* hard for me to believe that you love me," I replied. "Why *would* you, anyway?" As I said this, I was watching Robbie to see if he was listening, engaged, and seemed to be accepting what I was saying for him. Robbie was quiet and attentive, with no signs of anger or distress, so I continued to deepen the possible meaning of the discussion for Robbie.

"Because you are *so special* to us!" Jane said. "Because you have *not given up*! Because you want a better life for yourself and we want to help you to get it!"

Robbie was still quietly attentive, so I continued to speak for him: "But I don't feel that! I don't think that I'm so special! And I don't think you do either when I hit you!"

"I do get angry when you hit me, Robbie, but I still love you and hope to be able to make it easier for you someday to be able to accept my 'no' and my love."

"I think you might give up first!" I said. At this, Robbie anxiously glanced at his mother.

"That's not going to happen!" Jane said. Her eyes began to well up with tears. "I will never stop loving you!"

At this point I softened my voice and said quietly and sadly, "But my first parents gave up. They didn't seem to think that I was so special. I don't think I was worth much to them."

Jane choked back more tears. "I don't know why they didn't take better care of you, Robbie. But I'm so sad that you didn't think that you were special to them. That must have been so hard for you. You must have felt so alone."

"I did," I said in a whisper. "And I never want to feel that again." I glanced again at Robbie, who looked very sad as he sat on the couch between his parents.

"I hope that you someday will not feel so alone with us, Robbie," Jane said. "I hope that someday you will want our love and not feel so alone."

"Do you feel the same way that Mom does, Dad?" I asked.

"I do, son, I really do," David said. "You are my boy and you always will be!"

"You must hate me, Dad, for hitting Mom," I said.

"I don't want you to hit your mom, son, and I get angry about it, but I don't hate you when you do."

Suddenly Robbie looked quickly at his dad and spoke up, with panic in his voice: "I don't want to hit Mom, Dad! Sometimes I just can't stop myself—I get so mad."

"I believe you, son, I really do!" At this point Robbie became tearful, and David did as well. He leaned over and put his arm around Robbie, pulling him to him. "We'll help you, son. We'll help you because we love you."

After a few minutes of quietly hugging his dad, Robbie turned quickly to his mom. "I'm sorry, Mom, I'm sorry that I hit you!"

Jane moved toward her son, stroking his hair. "I know, son, I know. We'll get through this. Yes, we will. And we'll still be loving you!"

After sitting in silence with the family for a few minutes, I began to quietly talk about Robbie to his parents. I spoke in a rhythmic, almost singsong voice that usually works to elicit a receptive openness to what is being said and often leads to an increased reflective stance toward the immediate experience as well as the bigger picture of the narrative. For Robbie, a similar process of intersubjective exploration occurred in future sessions around the aspects of his narrative associated with abuse and neglect.

I saw Robbie and his parents for 25 additional sessions over the following 9 months. As progress was made in facilitating his attachment security with his parents, he became increasingly able to rely on them for the comfort and support that he needed to begin addressing his history of abuse and neglect and moving toward their resolution and integration into his narrative. Jane and David's support in his trauma treatment facilitated his attachment with them and vice versa.

CONCLUDING COMMENTS

As I discovered how intersubjective experiences with attachment figures propel the young child's development of his or her inner life, I have become convinced that such experiences should be the central feature in the therapeutic alliance developed with the child. The more traditional therapeutic stance tended to create ambiguity in how children experienced their therapist's experience of them. Such a stance valued providing safety for the children so that they could resolve distress and organize their inner life mostly on their own, without depending on the therapist to do it with them. Another intention of this stance was to facilitate the "transference" of the child's implicit relational knowledge onto the therapist.

Over time, it became evident that many children did not have the inner resources to identify, regulate, and organize their inner lives without the active intersubjective participation of the therapist in the process. These children often experienced intrafamilial trauma and manifested disorganized attachment patterns. They also tended to demonstrate a history that lacked the very intersubjective experiences they so needed to be able to develop a coherent narrative. A new stance appeared to be necessary. In this new affective/reflective stance, the therapist makes his or her experience of the child very explicit. As the therapist becomes more explicit regarding the positive impact the child has on him or her, the child experiences felt safety more quickly and deeply. Nonverbal communications regarding the impact that the child has on the therapist are exaggerated—much like parents exaggerate their responses when with their baby. In taking such a stance, the therapist becomes responsible for ensuring that the child has a positive impact upon him or her. The therapist is able to explore, with nonjudgmental, active curiosity, the child's inner life that exists under the problems, defenses, or symptoms. He or she is able to discover the child's strengths and vulnerabilities lying within and then respond to these discoveries with empathy and deep appreciation. The therapist experiences the child's courage, honesty, persistence, and various other qualities that the child might not have been aware of him- or herself. Affected by the child's inner qualities, the therapist is then able to intersubjectively have an impact on the child.

The three interventions described in this chapter have all been very effective in facilitating the coregulation of affect and cocreation of new meanings that are the hallmark of effective therapy. Matched affective expression is often the starting point of intersubjective experience (described as attunement by Dan Stern and synrhythmia by Colwyn Trevarthen). Without losing this affective engagement, the therapist's active, not-knowing, nonjudgmental curiosity leads the child into his or her inner life, where he or she can begin the process of addressing the many traumatic or confusing events of his or her life and developing them into integrative experiences that will evolve into a coherent narrative. Because many children lack sufficient reflective skills to take the lead in this process, the therapist must be ready to facilitate the flow of the affective/reflective conversation by offering to guess about the child's inner life. Such guesses constitute "talking for" the child, and later "talking about" the child, and these dialogues often enable the child to develop his communication skills about his inner life. These initiatives activate greater affective resonance within the dialogue than would occur if the therapist simply talked to the child. Such "talking for" communications become unnecessary as the child develops his or her own reflective and communication skills, spontaneously—and creatively—taking the lead in the process of weaving the tapestry of his or her inner life.

BIBLIOGRAPHY

Hughes, D. (2004). An attachment-based treatment of maltreated children and young people. *Attachment & Human Development, 6,* 263-278.

Hughes, D. (2006). *Building the bonds of attachment: Awakening love in deeply troubled children* (2nd ed.). Northvale, NJ: Jason Aronson.

Hughes, D. (2007). *Attachment-focused family therapy.* New York: Norton.

Hughes, D. (2009). *Attachment-focused parenting.* New York: Norton.

Hughes, D. (2009). Principles of attachment and intersubjectivity: still relevant in relating with adolescents. In *Teenagers and attachment: helping adolescents engage with life and learning.* Perry, A. (Ed.). London: Worth Publishing Co.

Stern, D. (1985). *The interpersonal world of the infant.* New York: Basic.

Stern, D. (1998). The process of therapeutic change involving implicit knowledge: Some implications of developmental observations for adult psychotherapy. *Infant Mental Health Journal, 19,* 300–308.

Trevarthen, C. (2001). Intrinsic motives for companionship in understanding: Their origin, development, and significance for infant mental health. *Infant Mental Health Journal, 22,* 95–131.

Trevarthen, C., & Aitken, K. J. (2001). Infant intersubjectivity: Research, theory, and clinical applications. *Journal of Child Psychology and Psychiatry, 42,* 3–48.

BIOGRAPHY

Dan Hughes is a clinical psychologist who resides in Lebanon, Pennsylvania. After receiving his PhD in clinical psychology from Ohio University, he specialized in the treatment of children and youth who had experienced abuse and neglect. He developed an attachment-focused treatment and parenting model that relies heavily on the theories and research of attachment and intersubjectivity, and he gradually expanded the model to make it applicable for all families.

Hughes provides training and consultations to professionals throughout the U.S., Canada, U.K., and Australia and provides regular training courses in Maine, Pennsylvania, London, and Glasgow. More information about Hughes's work can be found at www.daniel hughes.org.

●●●●●●●

Chapter 16

Traumatized, Terrorized, and Frightened Children

Lenore C. Terr, MD

After completing two intensive studies of trauma in 26 children kidnapped from their California schoolbus, I have followed up with a number of observational studies of natural healing from trauma and of how psychotherapy works with traumatized kids. At first, I was struck by how useful it was to help children discover modes of prevention (such as taping quarters inside their shoes to pay for phone calls to the police) and to elicit their ideas for correction (such as bringing in the toy armed forces to combat the evil dinosaurs). Later, I observed that children also became relieved of trauma by giving names to their feelings and by telling or playing out the emotions that were connected to their traumatic events. Finally, I came to realize that when a child forms a perspective on a personal trauma—seeing it in context with other situations in life and in the world at large—he or she is better able to regain a sense of normalcy. In summary, then, I found that there were three essentials to any successful psychological treatment of trauma in children. They boil down to working with the child's emotions, thought, and actions.

PEARLS

Pearl #1. Help the child patient abreact.

Abreaction is the full expression of feelings brought on by an unexpected, overwhelming experience. These emotions usually include severe fright, sadness, anger, and confusion. Many times the mix of post-traumatic emotions feels more upsetting to a youngster than having one feeling alone. The helplessness brought on by a sudden threatening event makes children feel less autonomous, and thus humiliated or embarrassed by the public or private exposure. In addition to these difficult feelings, certain traumas evince almost uncontrollable sexual or aggressive excitement in children. Others bring on utter disgust or despair. Young people who have been repeatedly abused or neglected can look unremittingly sad, or they may develop a distance from all human feelings. Whatever the subjective emotional experiences connected to terrible events in a child's life, they must eventually be reexperienced and fully dealt with as part of the youngster's psychotherapy.

Traumatized children often need to be taught the various names for their feelings before they can express them. This can be done with therapeutic doll play in which the doll's emotions are defined as various pretend scenarios take place. Frightened children also need to learn and express gradations of feelings before they can fully abreact. For example, they benefit from knowing the differences between "furious," "mad," "irritated," and "annoyed." It helps to understand that whereas their teacher "irks" them, their abuser "enraged" them. It may also help to realize that "horrified" and "uneasy" are not at all the same.

It is important for our child patients (or clients) to tell us their stories in their own voices, in their own ways. Even if they remember just a shard of the complete occurrence, that piece must be expressed. Sometimes it is helpful for us to ask to hear the tale "once more with feeling." After abreaction has taken place, however, it is not necessary to evoke these feelings again, again, and again. One full abreactive moment for a child goes a long way.

Pearl #2. Assist the child patient in finding a context for the experience.

Finding a *context* is the act of forming helpful perspectives on traumatic events. It includes putting a meaning to the event, gaining an understanding of the event, or seeing how the event fits in with the child's past, present, and future life. While evaluating traumatized or terrorized youngsters, it is crucial to glean whether the child has already formed a perspective on the event. These early meanings and understandings may underlie the child's symptoms and signs as well as the child's altered psychology. The young person's contexts may be discovered in his or her play and art. They may emerge in therapeutic conversation. The clinician's task is to work with these contexts through education, clarification, interpretation, and intervention (in play or art). It is sometimes important to offer ideas to frightened children about history (where their trauma fits with other such events) or geography (where else these things have happened). Religion, politics, philosophy, and science are also helpful contexts. Sometimes it is useful to talk with children about why people (or puppets and dolls) *do* such things or how other children have also suffered—and, perhaps, prevailed. Contexts can be found at times in simple rhythms, a song, a poem, or a picture.

It is important for a traumatized child to voice his or her own concepts regarding a trauma. Then we—as therapists—offer new pieces of information about "life." We must then receive words and signs back that indicate that the child's context has become organized or reorganized in a helpful way. This feedback may come to us in the guise of play, art, or a child-initiated narrative. It may come in the form of a dialogue or a pretend scenario. Most important, the clinician must try to perceive whether or not the child's new or fuller context is serving a useful purpose in the youngster's recovery.

Pearl #3. Lead the child patient toward discovering a correction.

Correction is the act of putting a new ending to a terrible event or setting up a new prevention for other such events. The correction may be real or fantasized. It may be personal or an action for the community at large. When a youngster comes up with a correction, he or she is offering a personally meaningful way to master the ordeal, even if only in retrospect. What can be done? How can we stop this kind of thing? What would one say? Or do? What would Superman say? What would Hannah Montana do?

In our pragmatic, action-minded society, correction is not particularly difficult for young people to consider. But we, as therapists, must often make sure that the correction is miniaturized—acted out in play, art, or stories. On the small-scale canvases of our office rugs and tables, villains can be put to justice, tsunamis can be properly predicted, and terrorist attacks warded off by effective police departments.

If a traumatized child thinks of real ways to help other young victims, this, of course, becomes a powerful route toward healing. It is important, however, not to feed too many corrections to our young patients. They must try to find them for themselves.

In general, then, my three "pearls" are equally important and may occur in any order during the psychological treatment of childhood traumas, terrors, or brushes with terrifying events. To check for a completed treatment, one should be able to recognize that all three processes have occurred. They do not have to be conscious on the child's part, but they should be conscious on the therapist's part. Of course, traumatized children may be successfully treated with medications or cognitive-behavioral therapy. This does not, however, eliminate the need for *abreaction*, *context*, and *correction* in order to complete a thorough posttraumatic treatment plan.

CASE EXAMPLE: TAMMY

Tammy was 5 years old when I first met her. The second child of an older set of parents (a biologist father and school-psychologist mom), she lived in a midsized town 3 hours north of San Francisco, where she had moved when she was 31 months old. When Tammy was 27 months of age, she was placed for 4 months in a daycare program run by a woman named Yvette. At that time Tammy began acting "different" but her parents could not identify a particular problem. Then they moved to their new home and new town, trying to adjust to their surrounds and work. They noticed that Tammy had become irritable and angry, often hitting the family dog in the face with a stick. But they did nothing about it, even after they learned—when Tammy was 4—that Yvette's 20-year-old son, Pierre, had been arrested and convicted of sexually assaulting children at her daycare center. "Lucky," they agreed, "we escaped just in time."

One day the kindergarten-aged Tammy asked to see a scrapbook made while she was a toddler. "I want to find pictures of me unhappy," she said.

Her mother was puzzled. "Where would you find those?"

"When I was at a lady's—'Eve' or something's—house." It was Yvette.

"Why?"

"There was a guy there named 'Pear' [Pierre]. He put a palm tree in my face. He hid us in another room and made us pretend we were asleep. He hit us. He poked us with a stick in our mouth, eyes, and stomach." Within days, Tammy began acting meaner than she had ever acted before. Her dog (because of her frequent assaults on his head) began avoiding her. She slapped her mother full in the face. She was having trouble with her older brother and her kindergarten peers. The family brought her to San Francisco. I would be allowed to see Tammy once a month.

On evaluation Tammy was a pretty, bright little girl, eager to tell me about her school and neighborhood. Her drawings, however, had a different story to tell. She drew a "child chimney sweep" covered in filth. She drew a baby, all alone in a room—"the dirtiest baby in the world," she said. In talking about a cookie, which had turned into a fish, she said, "I bend on the floor and it hurts me. Then I say 'Hah!' when I get hurt. I don't cry. I sure am brave!" Tammy feared burglars and had repeated dreams about them. She was terrified about driving in a car "with no one in the front seat." There were nightmares about that, too. The worst thing that had ever happened in Tammy's life had been "Pear," she said. But she could only remember being taken "one kid at a time" and hit with Pierre's stick all over her body. Tammy realized, she said, that the time she spent at Eve's house (Yvette's daycare) had made her frightened and angry. She was willing, though uncomfortable about it, to come to my office whenever her parents could bring her. That, however, was relatively infrequent for the serious problem she had. My diagnosis was posttraumatic stress disorder (PTSD). I encouraged Tammy's family to go ahead with a civil lawsuit on their daughter's behalf. I also encouraged them to report Yvette to the licensing agency of our state. These moves might eventually help provide a reality *correction* for the entire family.

The Pearls Applied

Tammy's emotions—despite her frequent plays at bravery—were right on the surface. We looked at her drawings and then considered what she had said about the filthy baby. "How did he feel?" I asked. "Angry, disgusting," she answered. In talking about this "baby," Tammy could express her own feelings without fully realizing it. (If she had not yet had sufficient vocabulary to verbalize emotions, I might have had to define words for the full gamut of feelings for Tammy, but that was not the case.)

It was important to let Tammy lead me. I said that she had told her mom a few curious things about the guy named "Pear" and a palm tree. She said that she was embarrassed about Pear. "I just couldn't tell it [the story] back then," she said. She felt angry at everyone—"for having me there," "for not knowing," "for letting Pear hurt us." She was still terribly angry and scared. Her bad dreams of burglars haunted her by day and completely upset her nights. She also showed me excitement, especially by humping her hand under her little body as she spoke of Pierre's big stick ("with moss on it, I think"). I wondered aloud if Pierre's stick and its hurts had excited her in addition to frightening her. She nodded solemnly. **We identified all the separate feelings—her anger, fright, disgust, excitement, and embarrassment—and then agreed that the mix of so many of them had upset her even more than if she had felt one at a time** (*pearl #1: Help the child client to abreact*).

For a few sessions we discussed Tammy's new, ongoing series of drawings largely in terms of the young animals' (always victims) feelings. Then we were able to leave abreaction almost entirely. Tammy had expressed herself well. Her fear of robbers disappeared in about 8 months: "I moved to a new house. And I realized that robbers are nice guys, too." But her sexual excitement continued (she would ask her father to show her his penis; he would refuse), as did her anger (explaining a drawing to me: "The mother knows the baby is climbing an apple tree and is in danger. But she lets him. I feel angry at the mother. She shouldn't have let him. He is only 2.").

After a number of drawings and playtimes about dirt, goo, and slime on animals' or babies' faces, I felt it was time to tie the situation together for 6-year-old Tammy in terms of context. She needed an explanation of sex, including the penis and vagina, the issue of erections and seminal fluid, and the absolute essential, adult "love." I asked her parents for permission to tell Tammy about sex. I said that when adults love each other and feel very serious romantic feelings, they want to kiss and touch each other a lot. Eventually, in fact, they might feel like becoming almost like one instead of two. In that case, the grownup's penis fits into the other grownup's vagina and they make love. It feels good. Babies are started this way and the adults know that can happen when they do this.

I went on to say to Tammy that I wasn't absolutely sure what had been done to her, but her worries indicated that Pierre had probably ejaculated on or near her face, making her feel like a "filthy baby." Also, because there had been no adult love between her and Pierre, whatever he had done had felt yucky, not wonderful, to her. Furthermore, I explained, trusting adults, like Tammy's parents, believed that the son of a licensed daycare director would behave himself with children. What Pierre did, I said, was almost beyond belief. Over the next few sessions, I showed Tammy her 5-year-old drawings. **We talked about how the "sick sex" she had been subjected to was Pierre's problem, not hers. She would be able to have wonderful adult sex when the right time and the right person came along** (*pearl #2: Assist the child client in finding a context for the experience*).

Once the context had been established through our brief conversations about sex, Tammy found her own corrections. Her behavior had improved so much that her appointments were cut back to every 2 to 3 months. In second grade (at age 7), she led a game called "Rabbits and Hunters" with several other girls ("we've been playing for months and months"). The rabbits ran from the hunters, who were invisible (several boys had wanted to play, but Tammy refused them). Each time a rabbit (a child victim) was caught, it escaped. It was caught again. It ultimately escaped, however. Rabbits were never hurt. Invisible hunters (Pierre and the other baby molesters) were. I eventually interpreted Tammy's game as a way of practicing at defeating bad people, like Pierre. **It was a way to end Tammy's mental misery by deciding what to do if such things ever happened again** (*pearl #3: Lead the children toward discovering a correction*). She smiled, and stopped the game within weeks. She went on to play "Princess," "Zombie," "Witches," and "Vampire"—nontraumatic games—out on the playground. I could tell they were nontraumatic because they were not repeated endlessly and because they reflected common pop-culture, playground themes.

Tammy's eventual termination of treatment came at age 8. Her behavior and attitudes were developmentally normal by then. "I've talked enough about Pierre," she declared to her mother, father, and me. She received a daily allowance, at my suggestion, but only for fine all-around attitudes and behavior. She also had spontaneously made a poster, titled "Pets Are Are [*sic*] Friends," that explained never to be cruel to any animal. This final correction for her old mean behaviors signaled for me an end to Tammy's treatment.

Follow-up

Tammy came back to my office for three visits, along with one phone appointment, in her second year of college. She had tried a number of advanced sexual experiments with a boyfriend—all of which had been pleasurable. But for relatively minor things, like holding hands and deep kissing, she felt disgusted and looked for ways to escape. Now Tammy needed a more grown-up context than I'd been able to bring up when she was young. She had been sexually assaulted in the face, I discussed with her. In fact, I thought that her hands had been held down as Pierre forced himself on her. She had been raped in the mouth. It was something for Tammy to explain to an intimate partner so that they could work on the problem together. She agreed. Tammy received quick-acting benzodiazepine tranquilizers that year at school. She also saw a counselor weekly at her university health service. I hope that the new, more adult context helped. I did not see Tammy again.

CONCLUDING COMMENTS

Because of my lifelong research into childhood trauma, I have been fortunate enough to treat many patients who were traumatized as children. Over the years, I have found that the three most important factors in their psychotherapies were *abreaction, context,* and *correction.* In individual treatment, there are many other factors that come into play, including handling deep grief and mourning, personality problems, dissociation, and withdrawal from relationships or life itself. In most traumatic situations, however, the three "pearls" will be helpful and will move the patient in a positive direction.

BIBLIOGRAPHY

Cohen, J. A., Berliner, L., & Mannarino, A. P. (2000). Treatment of traumatized children: A review and synthesis. *Journal of Trauma, Violence, and Abuse, 1,* 29–46.

Gardner, R. (1971). *Therapeutic communication with children: The mutual storytelling technique.* New York: Science House.

Levy, D. (1939). Release therapy. *American Journal of Orthopsychiatry, 9,* 713–736.

Pynoos, R. S., Nader, K., & March, J. (1991). Post-traumatic stress disorder in children and adolescents. In J. Weiner (Ed.), *Comprehensive textbook of child and adolescent psychiatry* (pp. 339–348). Washington, DC: American Psychiatric Press.

Terr, L. (1990). *Too scared to cry.* New York: Harper & Row. (Paperback, 1992, New York: Basic)

Terr, L. (1994). *Unchained memories.* New York: Basic.

Terr, L. (1999). *Beyond love and work: Why adults need to play.* New York: Scribner. (Paperback, 2000, New York: Touchstone)

Terr, L. (2003). "Wild child": How three principles of healing organized 12 years of psychotherapy. *Journal of the American Academy of Child and Adolescent Psychiatry, 41,* 1401–1409.

Terr, L. (2008). *Magical moments of change: How psychotherapy turns kids around.* New York: Norton.

Terr, L. (2009a). Using context to treat traumatized children. *Psychoanalytic Study of the Child, 64.*

Terr, L. (2009b). Individual psychotherapy. In M. Dulcan (Ed.), *Dulcan's textbook of child and adolescent psychiatry.* Washington DC: American Psychiatric Press.

BIOGRAPHY

Lenore Terr, MD, is known—because of her Chowchilla, Challenger, and Columbine studies—as one of the leading child and adolescent psychiatrists in the U.S. The recipient of three of the major research prizes in American psychiatry, she teaches at the University of California San Francisco and treats patients in her downtown office. Donna Shalala, then Secretary of Health and Human Services, named her as a "Hero of Medicine." Terr's chief interest in recent years has been "what makes child psychotherapy work." Play, art, storytelling, and metaphor are her fortes. Psychic trauma is her area of expertise.

●●●●●●●

Chapter 17

Riding Up and Down the Worry Hill: Engaging Children in OCD Treatment

Aureen Wagner, PhD

Obsessive-compulsive disorder (OCD) affects 1% to 3% of children and can be quite debilitating. However, OCD in youngsters can be successfully treated with the cognitive-behavioral therapy (CBT) techniques of exposure and response prevention (ERP). ERP involves gradually facing one's fears to test their reality while refraining from rituals. It helps people with OCD realize that their obsessive fears do not come true even when they resist rituals, and that the anxiety they experience subsides as a result of autonomic habituation.

CBT is widely considered the treatment of choice for children with OCD, with a 65% to 80% success rate. However, effectiveness is contingent on overcoming a formidable obstacle: the child's intuitive reluctance to engage in ERP because he thinks that facing his fears without performing rituals will simply be too frightening. The child's disinclination can be challenging for the therapist, who must find ways to engage the child and obtain participation.

My focus in treating OCD in children and adolescents has been on making empirically proven CBT user-friendly for children, parents, and therapists in everyday clinical practice. ERP works; getting children (and sometimes parents) to understand it, believe it, and do it—therein lies the challenge that calls for creativity, flexibility, and clinical artistry in implementation.

PEARLS

Through my early years of less-than-desirable success in treating young-sters with OCD, I asked myself, "How can I get a child to buy into the treatment? How can I bridge the gap between hearing, believing, and doing? What can I do to engage children and families to stay in treatment without dropping out prematurely?" These questions shaped the evolution of the following clinical concepts and applications.

Pearl #1. Cultivate treatment readiness.

Families seeking help for a child's OCD frequently present with a sense of urgency when children are unable to function and parents are at their wits' end. The therapist who is faced with the child and family's suffering usually wants to help as quickly as possible. In this context, it is easy to unwittingly launch into ERP prematurely, before the child is equipped with the proper understanding or tools to cope with the initial rise in anxiety with ERP. Rushing into ERP almost always backfires, because neither the child nor the family is ready for what ERP entails. When initial attempts at ERP are unsuccessful, children, parents, and even therapists may be inclined to abandon treatment because it is "not working."

Treatment readiness is therefore a vital precursor to ERP. Carefully and thoughtfully preparing the child and family for treatment is an important front-end investment with huge dividends. Cultivated actively and systematically, readiness involves four steps: stabilization, communication, persuasion, and collaboration.

Stabilization

A child who is overwhelmed and struggling to function each day simply may not have the wherewithal to consider CBT. Stabilization involves first calming the crisis, so that the child and family can optimize their resources for CBT. It begins with providing support, validation, and perspective with compassion. Educating children about OCD as a neurobehavioral disorder that affects about 1 million children in America provides the relief of knowing that they are not alone. A "no blame, no shame" approach helps reduce hostility and guilt in the family. Stabilization also involves providing the child with respite through flexible expectations and temporary accommodations at home and at school. I encourage families to function in "survival mode," to set priorities, and to cut back on discretionary commitments in order to conserve time and energy for treatment. In some instances, the child may need medication to reduce the severity of symptoms prior to engaging in ERP. When the crisis has abated, it is time to proceed to the next step.

Communication

A critical part of building readiness is effectively communicating the key CBT concepts of *exposure, habituation,* and *anticipatory anxiety.* OCD is overcome by confronting fears (exposure) to learn that they are false alarms, getting used to the anxiety, much like getting used to cold water in the swimming pool (habituation), and realizing that *thinking* about confronting fears may be harder than actually *doing* it (anticipatory anxiety).

A child's success in treatment might hinge on this understanding, yet these are not intuitive concepts. Most children (and their parents) are not aware that the body is designed to habituate naturally to anxiety. This lack of awareness and inability to tolerate increasing anxiety often leads them to give in to rituals to escape anxiety.

I developed the metaphor of riding a bicycle up and down the Worry Hill™ (Wagner, 2002, 2003, 2004, 2007) to convey CBT concepts in child-friendly language. A bell-shaped graph illustrates how anxiety rises with exposure until it reaches a peak, at which point it automatically begins to decline if the child persists in resisting rituals. When children understand the metaphor of the Worry Hill, it is often an "aha!" experience that makes them more willing to tolerate the initial anxiety experienced during ERP, because they know it will eventually subside.

Persuasion

Persuasion involves helping children see the necessity for change, the possibility for change, and their innate power to change. Understanding both the costs of OCD to themselves and the benefits of overcoming it convinces children that change is necessary. Many children do not even know that it is possible to overcome OCD. Educating them about treatment success rates gives them hope and optimism. When they want to know how hard ERP will be, I tell them that it is probably no harder than their life currently is with OCD; however, the effort of ERP may result in improvement whereas the effort they put into rituals only makes OCD worse. When I tell stories of other youngsters who have ridden up the Worry Hill, successfully overcoming OCD, children begin to believe that they have the power to do the same.

Collaboration

Collaboration makes the child a vital partner in treatment. The child, parent, and therapist have different but complementary roles to play in treatment. The therapist's role is to *guide* the child's treatment, the child's role is to *ride* up the Worry Hill, and the parents are empowered to *rally* for the child. Proactively defining each of these roles *before* treatment begins can expedite progress by preempting the conflict and frustration that can ensue from misunderstanding. It also corrects the misattribution of power to the therapist. The child and family need to know that the therapist is not the one who will "fix" the child's OCD—it is the child who holds the power.

Pearl #2. Clarify the right versus the wrong goal of treatment.

It is natural for youngsters (and adults) with OCD to approach treatment with the goal of never having OCD thoughts again. However, surveys have indicated that about 80% to 88% of people *without* OCD experience fears and bad thoughts similar to those of people with OCD (Rachman & de Silva, 1978; Salkovskis, 1980). Thus, it is unrealistic to be completely free of fears and thoughts, because they are normal, prevalent, and recurrent.

When people with OCD unknowingly approach treatment with the wrong goal—to make the thoughts go away and never return—they are disillusioned when the thoughts recur, and they conclude that the treatment does not work. Therapists may also inadvertently subscribe to the wrong goal in treatment in their desire to help relieve their clients' distress.

It is therefore critical to establish and agree to the right goal *before* embarking on ERP. I inform children and their families that fears about germs, disease, accidents, death of a loved one, wishing harm on others, bad luck, and even violence are normal and common and that most people have them at some time or another. The credibility of the research surveys brings both surprise and relief to youngsters and their families.

The *right* goal of treatment is to tolerate the worries in the same way that those without OCD do, and to understand the difference between *liking* and *tolerating*. No one *likes* having disturbing thoughts; the goal is to learn to *tolerate* them and habituate to the anxiety, rather than get rid of them (which is not possible). Having realistic expectations prepares children and families for the waxing and waning course of OCD, which can be seen as normal "bumps in the road" rather than failure.

When readiness-building is completed, I deliberately do not begin ERP until the child voluntarily expresses willingness to proceed, the child and parents have agreed to their roles in treatment, and all understand the right goal of treatment. I assure my child clients that I will not force them to face their fears, and that they and I will together plan exposures when they are ready. Most children relax and are more willing to participate when they do not have to be on guard. I test readiness in older children and adolescents by giving them the freedom to decide if they want to go ahead—with no coercion from their parents or me. I tell them that I do not want an answer immediately and give them my telephone number to call with their response.

I have rarely had children refuse to participate in treatment when they understand what it entails and are given the choice. When a child declines to participate despite proper preparation, it may be a good indicator that the child is truly not ready for CBT and therefore unlikely to benefit from it. The reasons for treatment reluctance must be examined, and other therapy options may need to be considered. For some children, CBT may have to be deferred temporarily and attempted later when they are older, more mature, or more willing.

Pearl #3. Take the RIDE up and down the Worry Hill.

Once the child has agreed to participate in ERP and understands the right goal of treatment, it is time for him or her to experience the relationship between gradual exposure and habituation. All the preparation that has occurred will now come to fruition when the child puts ERP into action.

I developed the four-step RIDE acronym (Wagner, 2002, 2003, 2007) to help children successfully tackle the Worry Hill. The RIDE breaks down ERP into four concrete steps—*r*ename the thought; *i*nsist that *you* are in charge, *d*efy OCD (do the opposite); and *e*njoy your victory (reward yourself). These steps tell children exactly what to do and what to expect during ERP. The process includes cognitive elements such as externalizing (rename) and taking control of OCD thoughts (insist that you are in charge). It also includes behavioral elements such as ERP (defy OCD), and self-reinforcement (enjoy).

The RIDE steps help youngsters focus on the process of exposure and tolerate anxiety until habituation takes place. The combination of the acronym, logical steps, and visual features of the RIDE make the ERP process easy to grasp and recall, even in the midst of anxiety. Children who are well prepared for the RIDE and the Worry Hill often find that ERP is somewhat of an anticlimax—it is simply not as "scary" to face their fears as they imagined. ERP shows them that if they can wait it out without doing rituals, their fears do not actually come true, and anxiety dissipates naturally. This experiential learning provides the child with powerful tangible feedback about the process whereby fears can be extinguished.

CASE EXAMPLE: DANNY

Danny was 12 when he began to fear that electronic and magnetic waves were injuring his muscles. He avoided being near cell phones, battery chargers, and remote-control devices. What initially seemed like a little extra caution soon grew into a web of terror: Danny could not be in the same room when the TV was on and panicked if family members used cell phones or video games in his presence. He repeatedly sought reassurance, asking his parents if they thought his muscles might atrophy. He had to verify several times a day that his muscles were still strong by running in the yard for 20 minutes and flexing his limbs. It didn't matter if it was freezing outside or if he was at school—if Danny couldn't run and check, he would panic.

Stabilization

Danny was embarrassed as his parents described his symptoms and their futile struggle to get him to see reason. "I know it's too much," he said quietly, "but I can't stop worrying."

"What should we do?" asked his desperate parents. "Should we just point the remote control at him to show him that nothing bad will happen to him?"

"No," I replied, "He's not ready for that yet. For now, you will need to help him just get through each day." I encouraged them to be flexible in their expectations, accommodate Danny temporarily, and cut back on discretionary commitments to reduce his stress level. Danny sighed with relief. He was ready to listen.

In the first session, I focused on helping them understand OCD. "Everyone has worries, Danny. But when you have OCD, your brain sends you a lot of worry messages that get stuck in your mind, even when there's no reason to be worried. It's like a false alarm—it warns you of danger even when there really isn't any. The false alarms are 'obsessions,' and the things you do over and over again to make the obsessions go away are called 'compulsions' or 'rituals.'"

To alleviate blame and shame and build an alliance with the family, I clarified, "Having OCD isn't your fault. It's not your parents' fault either. It's like having allergies or asthma—it happens to you because you're more sensitive to it. There may be others in your family who are also sensitive and have OCD. Your family may think that you're just being stubborn or annoying. It's hard for them to understand that you don't want to do it, but you don't know how to stop." Danny and his parents were surprised to hear how many children have OCD and relieved to hear that he wasn't alone.

Communication

I described the Worry Hill to Danny and his parents, using a bell-shaped curve to visually depict it. "Learning how to face your fears and stop your rituals is like riding your bicycle up and down a hill. At first, it's tough. You have to work very hard to huff and puff up a hill, but if you keep going, you can get to the top of the hill. Once you get to the top, it's easy and fun to coast down the hill. You can only coast down the hill if you first get to the top. Likewise, if you face your fears and stick it out, the bad feeling will go away and you will see that your fears do not come true. But if you give in to the rituals, it's like rolling back down the hill. You don't give yourself a chance to find out that your fears will not come true even when you don't do rituals." Danny and his parents were surprised to learn that anxiety habituates naturally.

Persuasion

I helped Danny understand how OCD was interfering with the things he enjoyed. He was a star athlete but was late to practices because he was checking his muscles. Danny was shocked to hear that it was possible to overcome OCD and that success rates were as high as 80%. He was even more surprised to learn that he had the power to take charge of OCD, instead of letting it control him. Until then, Danny had thought he was destined to be a helpless victim of OCD.

Collaboration

I assured Danny that we would work together as a team. "I won't force you to face your fears," I reiterated. "You and I will discuss together what you'll do when you're ready. I will guide you and your parents will support you, but no one can ride a bicycle for you, so you'll have to do it for yourself. **We'll take one step at a time, so that it will never be too scary." (This was the first step in *pearl #1: Cultivate treatment readiness*.)**

Danny clearly understood the Worry Hill. The realization that he could exercise control over his OCD appeared to be liberating. I gave Danny my telephone number to call within the next week and let me know if he would like to ride the Worry Hill. He called the next day. "Okay, I'm going to try it. I'm ready to beat my OCD! " I applauded his decision and reiterated that we would work as a team to help him master OCD, with no pressure from his parents or me.

The key to CBT for Danny's fears was accepting the difference between unpleasant and dangerous. Danny needed to learn that although he didn't like feeling scared, using household electronic items was not calamitous or life-threatening. In any case, he would never be able to completely avoid interacting with electronics or magnets, as they are everywhere. He needed to learn to live with the unpleasant feeling.

"Danny, you may not *like* the feeling," I explained. "No one likes having worries. But even if we don't like them, we have to learn to handle them. When you touch electronic items but don't check your muscles, you'll get used to the feeling. You will ride up and down the Worry Hill and learn that your fear of getting injured won't come true." Danny listened thoughtfully, cringing at the mention of touching electronic items, but then nodded to indicate he understood.

Danny then asked if he was always going to have his worries. I replied, "The thoughts may come and go. However, when you learn how to handle them, your brain will get used to them, and you won't notice them as much." Danny nodded. **He understood the right goal of treatment** (*pearl #2*).

Danny and I together made a list of all the things he was afraid to do because of his OCD, and all the rituals he employed to deal with his fears. Using a 10-point scale called a *fearmometer*, Danny then rated how "scary" it would be to face each fear on the list. We then created an exposure hierarchy, or *fear ladder*, placing the fears in order from least to most scary.

Toward the bottom of Danny's fear ladder were being near someone using a cell phone and sitting within 5 feet of one. In the middle of the ladder were items such as holding the cell phone to his ear while it was off, holding it in his hands, and turning it on. Pointing the cell phone at his body and making a call were at the top of Danny's fear ladder.

Now it was time to begin the ride up and down the Worry Hill (*pearl #3*). Danny chose to start with being near someone using a cell phone. He used the RIDE steps with courage, determination, and trust. "It's not me, it's my OCD," he said, renaming his thoughts to prepare himself for this challenge. "I'm in charge. I'm going to do what I want to do, not what OCD tells me to do!"

As Danny cautiously looked at the cell phone in my hand, I used the fearmometer to help him actively and tangibly experience the initial rise and peak in anxiety, followed by the onset of habituation. "What's your feeling temperature now?" I asked.

"It's a 5," he replied. "I'm nervous."

"Good, it's going up!" I said. "That means you're riding up the Worry Hill, just as we expected."

I dialed a number and held the phone up to my ear. "How does it feel now?" I asked.

Danny looked apprehensive. "It's an 8, but I'm going to defy OCD and ride the Worry Hill. I'm going to stick it out until the bad feeling goes away," he replied. Minutes later, he exclaimed, "Oh, wow! My fear temperature is 2! I went up to an 8 and now it's a 2, and it only took a few minutes."

Afterwards, I asked Danny to compare his expectations with his experience, and I reiterated, "See how your anxiety went up before it went down? Did your fears come true? How hard was it to do it?" Danny beamed with pride. He had done it, and it had been easier than he expected.

We repeated this exercise three more times to promote practice and habituation. Danny agreed to practice daily at home until his feeling temperature was down to 2. I reminded Danny and his parents to stay with the assigned task and not get ahead of themselves until we collaboratively agreed to proceed to the next step.

Danny was ready for the next ERP exercise on the hierarchy. We reviewed his previous ERP experience to prime him for the upcoming one. He was able to sit close to the cell phone and experienced the same process of anxiety rising and then subsiding. During the next four sessions, Danny slowly but surely tackled each ERP step on his fear ladder—holding the cell phone to his ear while it was off, and turning it on in his hands. The tasks got progressively harder. Although he struggled at times, Danny persisted and always made it up and down the Worry Hill. I helped Danny through the tougher exposures by reminding him of his previous successes, continually encouraging his efforts and urging him to "stick it out." With repeated practice, difficult exposures became easier. Each exercise was also practiced at home, with support from Danny's parents.

The hardest exposure for Danny was pointing the cell phone at his body. I pointed the cell phone at myself first and then suggested that he try letting me point it at him for the count of 1. He agreed and was surprised to find that he survived it. He smiled and asked me to keep counting up to 10, and then up to 30. Before the time was up, he announced triumphantly that he was ready to point the cell phone at himself.

After eight weekly sessions of CBT, Danny was able to ride the Worry Hill confidently and successfully, with 80% improvement in his symptoms. Danny's obsessions were now passing thoughts rather than paralyzing fears.

CONCLUDING COMMENTS

The effective implementation of CBT with children calls for familiarity with developmental issues, a sound therapeutic relationship with the child and the family, and facility in adapting and customizing treatment protocols. A key issue is cultivating readiness before rushing into ERP.

Why is readiness so crucial to treatment? It is because CBT involves actively learning and using a new set of skills to overcome OCD. It is similar to learning any other new skill such as riding a bicycle—no one can ride a bicycle for a child. Adults can help the child get started, but eventually the child must learn to ride for him- or herself, and he or she will do it when ready. Likewise, children need to face their fears for themselves to learn that they are unwarranted. No one else can do it for them. They will only do it when they're ready. Ironically, when they feel pressured, they are less likely to be ready. Rather than slow treatment down, building treatment readiness makes ERP proceed faster.

Youngsters can be very successful at mastery of OCD, and it is gratifying to watch them take back their lives and fulfill their potential. However, unless they understand the right goal in treatment, they can set themselves up for failure. Realistic expectations from the start can spare them from unnecessary disillusionment.

The Worry Hill is a universal and cross-cultural metaphor because children as young as 4, adolescents, and adults across most cultures can relate to the idea of riding a bicycle up a hill. Parents, siblings, and teachers find the metaphor equally helpful in understanding how CBT works. The easy acronym, logical steps, and visual features of the Worry Hill and the RIDE process are simple to grasp, remember, and recall, even in the midst of anxiety, reducing chances of premature termination of exposure.

BIBLIOGRAPHY

Rachman, S., & de Silva, P. (1978). Abnormal and normal obsessions. *Behaviour Research and Therapy, 16,* 233–248.

Salkovskis, P. M. (1985). Obsessional compulsive problems: A cognitive-behavioural analysis. *Behaviour Research and Therapy, 23,* 571–583.

Wagner, A. P. (2002). *What to do when your child has obsessive-compulsive disorder: Strategies and solutions.* Rochester, NY: Lighthouse Press.

Wagner, A. P. (2003). Cognitive-behavioral therapy for children and adolescents with obsessive-compulsive disorder. *Brief Treatment and Crisis Intervention, 3*(2), 291–306.

Wagner, A. P. (2004). *Up and down the Worry Hill: A children's book about obsessive-compulsive disorder and its treatment* (2nd ed.). Rochester, NY: Lighthouse Press.

Wagner, A. P. (2007). *Treatment of OCD in children and adolescents: A professional's kit* (2nd ed.). Rochester, NY: Lighthouse Press.

Worry Hill™ is registered in the U.S. Patent and Trademark Office.

BIOGRAPHY

Aureen Pinto Wagner, PhD, is a clinical associate professor of neurology at the University of Rochester School of Medicine and Dentistry and a member of the Scientific Advisory Board of the Obsessive-Compulsive Foundation. As a clinical child psychologist, she is internationally recog-

nized for her unique Worry Hill approach to making cognitive-behav-
ioral therapy accessible to youngsters. Wagner has also written several
books for professionals, including *Treatment of OCD in Children and
Adolescents: A Cognitive-Behavioral Therapy Manual, Worried No
More: Help and Hope for Anxious Children, Up and Down the Worry
Hill: A Children's Book about Obsessive-Compulsive Disorder and Its
Treatment,* and *What to Do When Your Child Has Obsessive-Compul-
sive Disorder: Strategies and Solutions.*

Section Seven:
Adolescents

Chapter 18

Avoiding the Trap of Trying Too Hard: Appreciating the Influence of Natural Law in Adolescent Therapy

Janet Sasson Edgette, PsyD

Despite our communal anxiety about keeping adolescents in check, our culture still seems to like its teens a little coltish and unruly. You see this in parents' bemused tolerance for their kids' antics, and in the charity afforded them when rude or irresponsible; "typical teenage behavior" it's called, which is unfortunate. Teenagers can do better, and they know it, but why wouldn't they capitalize, en masse, on this romanticized vision of adolescence? This way, moms and dads start second-guessing themselves left and right, leaving all kinds of room for their kids to take advantage of the parents' anxiety over scholastic achievement, their desire to avoid conflict, and their wish to see their children be happy and successful. This is why it's so easy for kids to get their parents to shoulder the responsibility for everything from making sure assignments are in on time to making sure there are clean socks in the morning for their 17-year-old's job interview.

Therapists know all about this clever use by teens of the principle of "least want"—whoever is less invested in the outcome is the one with more power. Charged with providing services to kids who never asked to be in our offices in the first place, we learn early in our careers about the quick judgments and deft footwork teens can exhibit regarding issues of power and control. It's easy to find oneself trying too hard to make a connection, to get therapy off the ground.

PEARLS

My three pearls all have to do with the ways in which therapists and adolescents engage with one another, or don't, and the relationships fashioned out of the initial contact. In my experience, I've found that how therapists present themselves and their work in the beginning accounts in large measure for whether or not therapy will be successful.

Pearl # 1. Establishing credibility with adolescent clients is more important for the relationship than establishing rapport, per se; it serves as the foundation upon which a strong rapport is built.

By no coincidence, we therapists are a compassionate lot. Sitting in front of troubled kids, commissioned to help them feel or do better, most of us try from the outset to communicate our genuine wish to be of service. But in the trying, we become something different. Probably the most compromising example of this is when, in the spirit of demonstrating support and understanding, a therapist will allow a teenager's inappropriate remarks or behaviors to go uncontested— something that person wouldn't sit silent for in any other setting.

Ironically, this response communicates little of the therapist's compassion, and only his or her willingness to accept less than what real relationships require for the sake of keeping the peace. This is disarming to kids, not comforting. They have enough people in their lives who sacrifice authenticity for the illusion of intimacy. What they don't have are people who are willing to hold them to a just standard of relating without forcing it upon them.

Pearl #2. Teenage clients should know that in future sessions, they are not obligated to report on progress, return to a prior conversation, or even show the same degree of concern or commitment regarding a problem they brought up in a prior session; every contact is allowed its own definition and purpose.

Locking a kid into something he or she earlier showed intent for or interest in is not going to move the therapy forward. It's more likely that it will only make the client reluctant to speak freely in the future. Additionally, clients lose faith when their therapists try to control the therapy by controlling its content. But when we disconnect *doing something* about a problem from *talking* about a problem, we make it easier for kids to look at some of the things that are holding them back, if only because they can do it in piecemeal fashion. Without the ability to retreat, reconsider, and even change one's mind, therapy will feel like too big a buy-in up-front for most teens. If "in or out" is the only option, most kids are going to play a conservative game.

This brings up the matter of treatment goals, which, for kids who don't want treatment, can be tricky. I think it's fair to argue that talking about goals with kids who claim adamantly to have none is disrespectful to them; we've just steamrolled over their message: *I'm not interested/I don't need this/I may want help but can't say it out loud yet*. The other problem with predetermined goals for involuntary clients is that progress is determined by specific outcomes, and therapists are forced to watch for a prescribed set of changes. What's lost is therapist's freedom to observe the impact of their work in unexpected or more organic ways. Granted, working with minor clients who run away, cut, or contemplate suicide means that we are often pressed to identify very concrete treatment objectives—she's stopped cutting, he's had two negative drug screens, she hasn't snuck out of the house for the past 3 weeks. These objectives aren't controversial; it's just that they're not the only ways to evaluate the effectiveness of therapy. Some adolescents will get better only if they can keep scaring the bejesus out of the adults around them.

Pearl #3. Holding teen clients accountable for the impact of their behavior on others, while remaining emotionally warm and available, is a very powerful intervention.

Often, therapists who see their role primarily as being advocacy-based are tempted to only empathize with their young clients' plights and avoid issues of accountability altogether. Concerned that a teenager will see them as "not on her side," they become apprehensive about asking the client to account for her role in some of her problems.

Appealing to clients in this way is the sort of thing that makes sense on paper, but not under the scrutiny of "natural law"—those intrinsic, ever-present, universal forces governing human relationships. Natural law tells us through our senses what's okay and what's, well, *weird*; we corrupt therapist-client relationships by thinking that just because they develop due to external forces, these laws don't apply. I believe instead that unless a therapist communicates an easy, forgiving, and unapologetic willingness to view a client's actions as a function of the choices he or she is making, there will be no real connection, and no real change. That therapist's quiet, understated refusal to go along with the party line (she can't help it, he didn't mean it, it was just a joke), without being critical or demanding that the client explain or do anything different in the future, is a very compelling stance.

I think of *this* as being the important role of accountability in adolescent therapy—its ability to disillusion the teen without directly confronting her. It's not a matter of "getting" the adolescent to own up to problems or agree to work on them. The disillusionment rests in the teenager's realization that people throughout his or her life will adopt their own perspective on the teen's person and actions, irrespective of his or her wishes; it's not something the teen can control. However, in the context of therapy, teenage clients can learn that being defined differently than how you want to be defined is not such a deal breaker for relationships after all.

CASE EXAMPLE: KATY

Miserly and aloof, 15-year-old Katy sat reluctantly in my office, next to her parents. Though recently divorced, both Katy's mother and father wanted to come to this first session, agreeing to keep their personal business out of it. Katy's younger brother, Eric, also attended the session. Katy had chosen not to speak, so it was her parents who told me why they had come: concerns about Katy's declining grades, volatile moods, and avoidance of family, for starters. In the manner of many parents befuddled by and feeling sorry for their sad or troubled child, Katy's parents, wishing not to create more stress around the house, had simply stopped pressing her on such matters as homework, household chores, and manners.

Katy's habit of withholding information made it easy for others to fall into the trap of trying hard to get her to speak. Her father was a prime example of this, asking her question after question in the initial session, to which his daughter only shrugged or shook her head no.

The more Katy ignored him, the more solicitous he became. And the more solicitous he became, the more patronizing she was toward him.

It was Eric who finally handed me my lead. "She gets away with everything," he mumbled, looking down at the floor. I asked him what he meant.

"She does whatever she wants to around the house and doesn't have to do anything she doesn't want to do. Plus, she's always in a bad mood and they never do anything about it."

Katy's father jumped to her defense. "Katy's a great girl," he said emphatically. "She has so much potential. But she's just making bad choices."

"What's happened that you and her mom expect so little of her now?" I asked.

"We feel bad for Katy because she seems so unhappy," her dad explained, looking over at her for her acknowledgment of his support. "We don't want to add to her stress."

Katy's father's concern was not unlike that of many parents who are pained by their children's unhappiness, trouble doing well in school, or friendlessness. However, by trying to remove stressors in their children's lives that they actually have some measure of control over, parents can end up over-accommodating their children's needs for extra time, pared-down responsibilities, and kid-glove handling. One down side is that their kids don't get a chance to learn that they can be important, contributing members of the household even while dealing with problems. Their personal struggles and our society's need for them to become good, kind, responsible citizens are two separate things—a message that gets lost in the accommodating. Another down side is the price paid by the family in terms of the resentment that builds toward the over-accommodated child, who, for months or years on end, imposes his or her moodiness, anger, volatility, or, in some instances, physical aggression on everyone.

I told Katy's parents that I understood their reasoning, and that accommodating Katy would appear to be the kind thing to do. "But I actually think that you should be asking Katy for more, not less," I said.

Abruptly, Katy picked her head up to look at me. Perhaps uneasy about where this was going, she joined the discussion. I acknowledged her joining by turning toward her and addressing her directly. I said softly, "You make your dad work very hard."

"Are you sure you want to talk about this with Katy in the room?" Katy's mother asked.

"I wouldn't think of saying it without her here," I responded.

Katy went right back to my initial comment. "Make him work hard for what?" Her eyes narrowed and she bit down hard on the *what.*

I wanted to answer her, but couldn't put my finger on it. **"It's a good question," I said. She watched me think, and then I got it: "For the privilege of parenting you," I said, finally. She held my gaze for a long second before going back to examine the split ends clutched in her left hand.** (*Pearl #1: Establishing credibility with adolescent clients is more important than establishing rapport.*)

This exchange—early in the first session—is an example of how therapists can establish some degree of credibility with a jaded client who doesn't believe that therapy has anything to offer. I didn't get ruffled by the forthrightness of Katy's question, and I gave her an answer she could recognize to be true and operative in the family. It was also something neither of her parents would ever say, given their vigilance not about upsetting their daughter. Ironically, such tentativeness usually has the opposite effect, with children losing faith in their parents' ability to actually help them. I was hoping that Katy was encouraged by the prospect that something different might happen with this therapy.

Katy wasn't done, though. She looked up at her parents with those same narrowed eyes but said to me, bitterly, "Well, they *should* feel lucky. I'm a good kid. I don't get in trouble. I don't do drugs. I'm not into cutting. They have it pretty easy with me, compared to some other kids."

I turned to face Katy more fully and told her that she couldn't decide that for them. "In some ways, Katy, you're right. They do have it easier than a lot of other parents. But in some ways they don't, because they don't know what problems you *do* have. All they know is that you're unhappy, and they don't how to begin to help you. And making it even worse is that they worry that anything they say is going to be the wrong thing."

Katy gave me a look that said I was crazy but that she wanted to know more.

"Your mom and dad are so afraid of adding to your problems that they're second-guessing all their decisions," I obliged. "They've stopped expecting you to contribute to the household. They've stopped asking you to care about other people's feelings. They've stopped asking you to help them help you; they just try to do it all by themselves. **But I'll be honest with you, Katy—the thing that concerns me the most in all this is that you don't seem to feel any need to let them know that you know it's hard on them too.**" (*Pearl #3: Holding teen clients accountable for the impact of their behavior on others, while remaining emotionally warm and available, is a very powerful intervention*) "Why should I be the one worrying about them when I'm the one with problems?!" Katy demanded.

I paused, realizing that Katy's question, left out there to hang in the air for an extra moment, made its own strong statement about her unwillingness to be more sensitive to another's pain while struggling with her own. And then I said, "Because no matter how bad your problems are, you're also part of something bigger—your family, your circle of friends, your community. If you lose sight of how your reaction to the stress in your life affects the people around you, then your world becomes an every-man-for-himself kind of world." I searched for, and caught, her eyes. "Will you really want to live in that kind of world?"

This was an opportunity for me to illustrate to Katy how her way of managing her problems and her moods would ultimately leave her feeling shortchanged, and that even her sense of righteousness wouldn't be able to protect her from that. I wanted to communicate that her ability to get people to back off and treat her gingerly might at first afford her some relief from the stress she experienced, but that it would eventually create even more disconnection and depression. I wanted her to understand that we could help her, but not by giving in to her felt need to be given a pass on holding up her end of things.

I would never have asked Katy to comment on what I said about being a part of something bigger—it would have risked putting too fine a point on something I believed was better left alone, at least for the time being. Talking about it would have made it heavy and ponderous; it would have become an "intervention." I liked it more as a come-hither idea, alluring and a little ethereal. Asking teenagers for direct feedback at times like this, when you are trying to evoke a greater consciousness or wanting them to allow you to affect them, can be counterproductive; they get self-conscious, shake it off. A more economical and graceful way of assessing your effect is by noticing slightly more sustained or less aggressive eye contact or a greater tolerance for silence. Maybe they will let you make them smile. And letting you make them laugh— that's huge.

For the next few sessions, I met with Katy by herself. She was poised to withhold so I asked her only questions I thought she would respect enough to answer: Who was the most tentative around her, what were her parents' blind spots, who in her life would say she took an active interest in them. I learned that the divorce had been nasty, that Katy felt little sense of control over her decisions, and that the pressure in this family to be excellent was oppressive. I also learned that power plays were an integral part of how family members got things done.

Though Katy spoke resentfully about her parents' divorce, she took great umbrage at their insistence that the divorce troubled her. "I really don't care," she said to me. "They think they know everything about me but they don't. The only problem I have is everyone trying to make it seem as if I have a problem."

This comment immediately reminded me of Katy's remark in the first session—"Why should I be the one worrying about them when I'm the one with problems?"—but I didn't bring it up. (*Pearl #2: Teenage clients should not be obligated in future sessions to report on progress, return to a prior conversation, or even show the same degree of concern or commitment regarding a problem they brought up in a prior session.*) Kids feel blindsided when a remark they made in one context is cross-referenced in another context by an adult who is trying to prove a point. Therapists sometimes resort to this when feeling stonewalled by clients, although I think more often it is used out of convenience; they are looking for a shared platform from which to launch the "real" therapy—that is, the part where you talk directly about the kid's problems. But although it may be a convenience for the therapist, to the client it's an ambush.

I don't ever want to give my clients reason to refrain from making a particular remark for fear that I will hold them to it at some later point. This is where I think the issue of trust comes into play most profoundly in adolescent therapy—the question isn't "Can I trust this therapist not to tell anyone what I talk about?" but rather "Can I trust this therapist not to take advantage of something I said earlier, and maybe even meant, but that I no longer want to stand behind? Can I trust this therapist to know what will make me feel patronized or trapped, and refrain from mentioning it, even if it would support a point she's been trying to make?"

I wanted to advocate for Katy but I didn't know what she wanted. I knew she didn't want therapy, and I knew she didn't want to stay behind in school. But from her point of view, she was in a catch-22: "If I start doing well again," she said, "my parents will think that their techniques worked."

I could have reminded Katy of how smart she was and what a shame it would be for her to have to repeat 10th grade or attend summer school, but I didn't. If I *had* done that, I would have been mistaking a symbol of the problem for the problem itself—Katy's inability to maintain her sense of autonomy in a family (and world) that variably lays claim to what was once, but is no longer, theirs.

Instead, I asked, "Is there a way for you to want the same things your parents want for you, without your feeling as if you're losing and they're winning?" Katy stared off at a point just to the side of my head and said with a sigh, "I don't know." I told Katy that I was realizing just how much her autonomy meant to her—enough that she was willing to sacrifice her academics for it, and she nodded in response.

"But it's kind of like when some kid graduates from high school or college and then has to move to the other side of the country in order to feel independent from his parents. You know, he's only really independent when he can do okay on his own living in the very next town." Katy's mouth curved into a wry smile, her first.

I soon figured out what Katy wanted: to sort things out by herself. She'd had counselors and therapists and teachers and parents and grandparents in her face for months, and she had soured on the idea of being counseled. I told Katy's parents that I thought we should respect their daughter's wish to not have to go to therapy. Some things had gotten better anyway: Katy was a little happier with her parents, and they were a little happier with her. Her dad didn't draw her into his conflicts with her mother as much. Her mother had softened a little. Both parents had backed off of the issue of Katy's school performance.

"Doesn't she still need to talk to somebody?" Katy's mom asked.

"Maybe," I responded. "The problem, though, is that for Katy, words have become a form of currency, and as long as others want her to talk more than she wants to talk, whether she does or not will have more to do with being in control than with her wish to engage in dialogue." I suggested that Katy might do better with less involvement by others than with more, at least for right now. I added that was it hard to tell which problems were hers and which belonged to everyone in the family, and that Katy, in need of guidance or not, would brace against anything she felt was being imposed upon her.

"What about school?" the parents asked. I suggested that they leave it to be handled by Katy and the school. "She needs more places where she feels she's in charge, and high school is perfect for that. I think all Katy might need to move forward is a face-saving way out of this situation." I described Katy as somewhat of a scholastic anorexic, and explained that the more they tried to manhandle her education, the less likely she would be to respond favorably. "Your daughter has put her academics up on the block as a message to you both that it is more important to her to feel in control than to feel secure, and that she's willing to scuttle her ship in order to prove it. By letting school be hers and hers alone, you will be disabling the communication function of her academic performance, leaving it as just that—Katy's academic performance."

A year later I heard from Katy's mom. The news was good: Katy was more outwardly happy and engaged with her family than ever before, and she was much more open about herself. In school, she excelled in every class (all honors) except for one in which she didn't like the teacher. Sadly, her relationship with her father had stalled out over what Katy felt was his lack of investment. She and her brother Eric, however, were finally getting along again.

CONCLUDING COMMENTS

Therapists who try very hard to help troubled teenagers can get discouraged if they find themselves losing too many of the very kids who need their help the most. Maybe it's their palpable readiness to assume so much of the responsibility for alleviating their clients' distress without asking enough of their clients. Not only can this feel claustrophobic to kids, but it also ignores the more natural dynamics that guide people when they go to connect no matter what the setting, and it upsets the balance of respect and credibility. I believe it's *this*—not being in therapy specifically—that feels so unnatural to kids. Their instincts tell them it's dangerous; no wonder they spook.

Adolescents should always be able to see how committed their therapists are to their well-being. But how much a therapist cares about a *client* is something separate from how much that therapist cares about the client's *therapy*. With the latter, the client has to care at least as much as the therapist in order to make it work. Many adolescents don't care about their therapy, so we need to take another look at what we're offering them, and make changes. Many theoreticians and clinicians are going about making psychotherapy more teachable, and thus presumably more effective, by reducing it to a collection of sequenced interventions, but that just makes things easier for the therapist, not better for the client. Good psychotherapy is exquisitely difficult to execute and we can't change that fact by distorting the process. The model of therapy I describe in this chapter requires tremendous discipline on the therapist's part, as well as very active mental processing. It's not for everyone, nor is it a panacea. But it is an idea for doing things differently and, I believe, *more respectfully* vis-à-vis the teenagers who come to us for help. Maybe that aspect alone will make it a little easier for them to care.

BIBLIOGRAPHY

Edgette, J. S. (1994). *The handbook of hypnotic phenomena in psychotherapy*. New York: Brunner/Mazel.

Edgette, J. S. (1999, September/October). Getting real: Candor, control and connection with adolescents. *Family Therapy Networker*, 56, 36–41.

Edgette, J. S. (2001). *Candor, connection and enterprise in adolescent therapy.* New York: Norton.

Edgette, J. S. (2002). *Stop negotiating with your teen: Strategies for parenting your angry, manipulative, moody, or depressed adolescent.* New York: Penguin/Peregy.

Edgette, J. S. (2002, January/February). Avoiding the responsibility trap. *Psychotherapy Networker, XX,* 25–26.

Edgette, J. S. (2006). *Adolescent therapy that works: Helping kids who never asked for help in the first place.* New York: Norton. (Reprint of *Candor, connection, and enterprise in adolescent therapy,* 2001, New York: Norton)

BIOGRAPHY

Janet Sasson Edgette, PsyD, practices in the western suburbs of Philadelphia, where for over 20 years she has worked with children, adolescents, young adults, parents, and families. Edgette is the author of five books on psychotherapy and sport psychology, including the popular parenting paperback *Stop Negotiating With Your Teen: Strategies for Parenting Your Angry, Manipulative, Moody, or Depressed Adolescent* and *Adolescent Therapy That Works: Helping Kids Who Never Asked for Help in the First Place* (W. W. Norton, 2006). She frequently speaks at professional conferences and has taught workshops for mental-health professionals, educators, and parents throughout the U.S. as well as in Canada, Mexico, Russia, Croatia, and Germany. More information about Edgette's work can be found at www.janetedgette.com.

Chapter 19

Secure Love:
Working with Adolescents and Families

Martha B. Straus, PhD

In therapy—as in life— we are too often on the search for the quick fix, the one answer that directs us just to "do *this*" and pull straight a tangled web of suffering. We continue to persist even in the face of compelling data that suggest that many forms of treatment are comparably effective, and that specific techniques account for just a tiny fraction of the reason people get better anyway. In our tireless pursuit of something to *do* with adolescent clients, we sometimes forget that people can only grow up whole if they know secure love. The best interventions follow from a frame that holds most centrally this developmental imperative for safety, clarity, and connection.

PEARLS

My three pearls—Gazing with Adoring Eyes, Addressing the Four Questions, and Setting Developmentally-Sound Expectations—are fundamental to effective work with adolescents and families. These ideas aid in case formulation and help shape a compelling course of treatment.

Pearl #1. Gaze with adoring eyes.

"Adoring eyes" describes the way parents might observe a beloved infant in their arms. Good therapists "hold" their adolescent clients through a similar empathic gaze. This intervention is more about therapist demeanor than anything we say or do in a session. But try it—you'll discover that every time you can be mindful and present enough to attend with such warmth, care, and appreciation, you will also be "doing" better therapy.

Securely attached adolescents have every advantage in life: They're more likely to be confident, flexible, empathic, regulated, friendly, and resilient. As babies, they probably had at least one person look upon them repeatedly as though they were perfection personified. Seeing themselves reflected in such delight, they learned that they were loveable; that their very existence brought pleasure to another person. Most of the adolescents we see in treatment aren't this lucky—or they're in desperate need of another dose. In contrast to this emphasis on attachment security, the culture—and traditional therapy—places more of a premium on development of *self*-soothing strategies. It is true that most of our adolescent clients need to learn to become better emotionally regulated. However, they must first know what it feels like to be soothed through the loving containment of relationship. Effective therapy provides the essential experience of *co*regulation of affect; incredibly, our empathic limbic brains are calming and healing for their overwrought ones.

"Adoring eyes" are not some kind of phony or shallow adulation, nor are they conditional upon performing up to someone else's expectations. Rather, they provide a softer space between people, where love and safety can be experienced. When we make ourselves available to an adolescent in this way, we set aside our agendas, goals, treatment plans, and techniques to convey, without words, *I am so glad to see you. You are welcome here. I care about you. You are wonderful. I have nothing more important to do, no one I'd rather be with. Come in and sit down, and I will be able to "hold you" in your struggles.* Although adoring eyes aren't usually considered a technique, they are, nonetheless, foundational—and have a remarkable potential to transform brain and spirit.

Pearl #2. Address the four questions.

I typically map out for adolescents and their families my expectation that we will be exploring some universal and essential themes of adolescence over the course of our work together. I suggest that if we can discover a few answers, the adolescent will feel and behave better. Regardless of diagnosis, effective treatment addresses, to greater or lesser degree, these four concerns:

- *Integrated identity*: How can I start to feel more integrated when I have so many parts and divergent stories about myself?
- *Secure relationships*: Can I depend on you to be here for me when I need you?
- *Bigger meaning*: What really matters? How do I become a part of the larger world?
- *Adult containment*: Who is in charge to help me feel safe and in control of myself?

Outlining these questions serves several useful clinical purposes: normalizing the context of the struggles most adolescents face; helping to identify a range of individual, relational, and systemic strategies for intervention; suggesting possible areas of strength and challenge; and framing content meaningfully.

Pearl #3. Set developmentally sound expectations.

This pearl has become central to my practice over the years, as adolescent clients and their parents struggle to identify a reasonable set of expectations for a given teen. Most therapists I speak to concur that these days we seem to be treating more anxious adolescents and providing greater abundances of psychoeducation and guidance to their overwhelmed and despairing parents. Realistic expectations for independence, monitoring, support, structure, and limits require sufficient knowledge of general—and specific—child development. We are seeing too many organizationally challenged 13-year-olds falling behind in school because they just can't remember which books they need for their homework, too many 16-year-olds making awful decisions while unsupervised for 6 or more hours a day; and too many 19-year-olds unraveling at college before the first semester is over.

The expectations that we now have for adolescent cognitive, social, emotional, and behavioral functioning are too often based primarily upon adult convenience. The typical crowded regional American junior high school, for example, is responsive to economic practicality, not to the actual needs of 12-year-olds to be known, monitored, and supported as their cortexes get remodeled, hormones surge, and social relationships become complicated and absorbing. Working parents need to have kids who can fend for themselves (or be willing to participate in endless activities) after school. Adult narcissism, along with more laudable motives, requires that adolescents behave and produce in pleasing ways; we want them to make life easier for us, and provide us with reflected glory, as well as develop the skills they'll eventually need as adults. In light of the data on adolescent development, it is almost amusing that we expect adolescents to be orderly, appreciative, timely, engaged, organized, motivated, disciplined, respectful, logical, and pleasant.

Without understanding that these qualities come slowly, over time, with neuro-maturation, scaffolding, and patience from us, we're apt to feel angry with them, and bad about ourselves as parents and therapists. We have to set—and reset—the expectations bar based on general and specific developmental understanding in order to provide the external structure and support that enables them to be more successful and safe.

CASE EXAMPLE: EMMA

Emma, age 12, was referred by her beleaguered parents for a myriad of escalating challenges, including school refusal (she was in the sixth grade when we met), noncompliance with medication, self-harming tantrums, poor hygiene, lack of friends, difficulty falling and staying asleep, food hoarding, and compulsive overeating. From the outset, though, I chose not to view Emma in terms of problem behaviors needing modification; rather, I saw her as a whole girl who would benefit most from feeling held in secure love.

Emma had been adopted at the age of 4 after experiencing significant early trauma and disruption. Her adoptive parents were very committed to her and determined to help her overcome her troubled history. They also had three adult biological children who lived outside the home. I worked as part of their team, maintaining contact with them within and between sessions, as needed.

Though Emma had made progress over the years (no longer wetting the bed or requiring supervision in basic self-care, for example), she continued to demonstrate significant emotional, behavioral, learning, and social problems. With the increased expectations and changes of adolescence, she was falling behind more rapidly. Notably, she harbored a growing awareness of her differences and shortcomings. She described this in an early meeting with me, explaining her unwillingness to go to school: "I'm probably the only adopted and learning disabled kid in my school. I'm fat and wear glasses and people say horrible things to me." Any motivation Emma may have had to try to keep up was diminishing as it became harder for her to fit in. Along with a severe reading disability, she was overwhelmed with anxiety and doubt during the school day. She was easily dysregulated by seemingly small changes in routine or the challenges of peer interactions. Emma maintained just one tenuous friendship with a similarly marginalized child; when they had one of their frequent conflicts, she didn't see any reason to go to school at all.

Pearl #1: Gaze with adoring eyes.

I treated Emma for over 4 years, decreasing the frequency of sessions as we progressed. Secure love is slow love; we need to keep returning until we can be held constantly inside the child's heart (and they become special to us, too). Children like Emma, sorting out the sequelae of early attachment trauma, take even longer to develop this object permanence. It's a very big deal: Without it, children cannot develop a coherent identity, enjoy the give and take of relationships, or become a part of their community. All of the interventions I attempted were designed to help Emma develop connections and experience secure love in her life.

From the moment she walked into my office, Emma had my undivided and enthusiastic attention. If she just wanted to sit, we sat. If she wanted to cut out pictures from magazines, listen to music, or play a game, that was the day's agenda. In my office, she could sulk, swear, or snuggle under a blanket. Over the years, we graduated from sitting on the floor to working at a table, from lolling on the couch (often with an iPod bud in one ear) to sitting on chairs and talking, face to face.

During the final 6 months of treatment, I even got a few emails from Emma—she kept me in mind now between sessions—including one saying, "Can't wait to see you. Big surprise." When we met, she shared enthusiastically that her father had taken her for her first driving lesson. She came in and said, "Sorry to keep you guessing. I just had to see your reaction when I told you my news!" By then, she had even come to expect my adoring eyes.

At the beginning of therapy, when it was frequently less gratifying, I also expressed delight and worked to stay right with her no matter how she showed up or where she chose to sit in the room. **She knew, from the beginning, that this was her hour to do with as she wished and that I was there just for her** (*pearl #1*).

We played games for the first couple weeks as she explored my play area the way a younger child might. She began by selecting the simplest games, asking tentatively, "Is it really okay if we play this one? It's not too babyish?" In the third week, she looked up from the Candyland board and inquired, "So, when are you going to ask me some important questions?" I grinned with admiration and told her I was ready when she was. I asked her which important question she thought we should begin with. "Ask me about being adopted," she said.

Maintaining adoring eyes, and the presence that accompanies them, isn't as easy as it sounds. It's astonishingly hard work to be mindful and accepting hour after hour with a moody adolescent. But Emma would let me know when I slipped into a more confrontational or directive mode. She'd cross her arms, glower at me, and say nothing for the rest of the hour, or shut her eyes and fall "asleep," or pretend she hadn't heard me and talk about something else altogether. Once, when I gently tried to explain a simple scaling technique to help her become aware of her anger and manage it better at school, we had a serious rupture. She turned away from me, tight-lipped, and stomped out, telling her parents I was fired. When they eventually got her back in, and I'd apologized, she admonished me, "Don't ever do that again. Don't try to help me like that." No one can be perfectly attuned, so practicing adoring eyes also means repairing and refocusing, heart to heart and mind to mind.

Pearl #2: The four questions.

Throughout our work, Emma and I addressed the four questions through developing coherent identity narratives, strengthening relationships, fostering connections to the larger world, and meeting her profound need for safety and containment.

Identity integration

In early adolescence, the question "who am I?" gets thrown into the cyclotron, as the more unified child self becomes fractured and complex. Young adolescents like Emma, with such a chaotic history, have even more difficulty developing a coherent "story of me." My goal is to invite all of their personas and "selves" into therapy, to help them weave a narrative. One strategy that I used with Emma, making a "life book," is particularly useful for helping with identity integration in adopted and foster teens.

Sometime toward the end of our first year together, Emma came in notably upset. A relative of hers who lived far away was unwell, and she was very worried about him. Her father told me that this seemed strange to him, as Emma had only met this person a couple times, and not for several years. **Thinking of all the losses she had experienced in her short life, I asked Emma if she might tell me about some of the other lost parts of her, too** (*question #1: How can I feel more integrated?*). This was a version of the question "How do I feel more integrated when I have so many parts and divergent stories about myself?" I wondered if this relative also made her think about other people she was missing. She became tearful and said there were so many, she might not be able to name them all. I got out a pad and helped her with the list as she spoke of her birth parents and birth siblings, her adoptive siblings and their partners, and some other relatives, all spread out around the country—some alive but lost to her, some deceased, some unwell, and some just living at a distance. She missed them all as one huge, gaping hole. She began to sob, telling me about her beloved grandmother who had died the year before.

I asked her if she'd like to make a book with me in which we could put pictures and stories of her whole life, so that everyone who mattered could be in one place, and all of her parts could be together.

She was enthusiastic about the idea and tenacious about developing the project. I gave her the option to bring the life book back and forth from home, but she was very clear that she wanted me to keep it in a special drawer in my office. In this way, I began to help her hold her identity story and keep it safe in one place.

Over the next several months, this became a very important piece of work we did together. At first, we attended diligently to the life book. With the help of her mother, Emma brought in copies of her birth and adoption records; photos of her birth family, friends, holidays, pets, and vacations; a piece of fabric from her baby blanket; concert ticket stubs; report cards; and notes about important memories. She narrated to me the story of her life, decorated the pages of the book with stickers, and put captions around the pictures. After many weeks, the intensity surrounding this task subsided and Emma became interested in other projects and conversations. She returned to the life book to add a page from time to time (for example, when the family got a new cat, we added some pet pages, when she had her 15th birthday we made some party pages, and when she made new friends we joyfully added pictures of them, too). She also brought the life book out when she was having a hard time, and would find comfort in combing carefully through it, reading her story, seeing her whole life in one place, with me beside her on the couch. More than 2 years later, when she was feeling much better, Emma came in one day and told me she wanted to bring the life book home. She said she was taking it to school because she was ready for her friends to know all about her, too.

Secure relationships

In some ways, the structure of most therapy helps adolescents experience the consistency, predictability, and security of a stable relationship. We often set up schedules so that clients have their special time in the day and the week, and try our best to show up reliably for them. This routine sets a frame for safe exploration—of the self, others, and the world.

In addition to setting up regular meetings, **I intentionally offered Emma numerous opportunities to know she could rely on me** (*ques-*

tion #2: Can I depend on you when I need you?). In the first year, we completed several sustained projects: Emma left the unfinished puzzles, collages, life book, and stories in my office, perhaps so that she could keep a part of her with me and ensure that she'd have to come back again. I offered to buy a jigsaw puzzle featuring horses, and remembered to bring it. She seemed astonished that I had thought about her between sessions, remembered what I promised, and made space just for her work on a little table in the corner. When I traveled to give talks, I sent her postcards, and if she sent me an email, I'd write her back. I visited her schools, welcomed her friends into the office, listened to her music, and gave her an appointment card "invitation" for the next week, no matter what. I also helped to ensure that Emma had identified adults to whom she could turn in other places, and to strengthen her bonds with her parents and adult siblings. By the end of our work together, Emma felt held in secure relationships and was therefore much less angry and depressed.

Bigger meaning

When we first met, Emma was buried under a massive problem list, and her sources of pleasure, connection, and purpose were too few. She didn't experience herself as competent, and she expected failure, disappointment, and rejection as a matter of course. Her oppositional behavior and tantrums helped to make this a self-fulfilling prophecy, and they kept her isolated and unable to learn new ways of being in relationships and in the community. Her retreat into fantasy and television further disconnected her from people and purpose.

Emma's parents knew that participation and contribution would help her, but they had pretty much conceded the epic struggle to get her to agree to try anything new. She refused to do chores and was utterly uninterested in after-school activities or sports. External incentives and rewards were not motivating because she so feared the unknown and failing. **Nevertheless, in the first couple years of our work, we gradually made three changes in Emma's life to help her feel she belonged in her larger community** (*question #3: How do I become a part of the larger world?*). Reluctant at first, she eventually engaged more fully, with notable improvement in her functioning.

First, we advocated successfully for her to attend a small, special-ized alternative junior high school, beginning in seventh grade, where she could know and be known by everyone in the school quickly, and get plenty of individual support. Second, Emma began to attend an activity group for adopted girls (while her mother went to the parents' support group), and there she found connection to several kids who brought in their own difficulties and horrible histories. She was one of the higher-functioning girls in the group and took pleasure in being helpful to her peers. She even eventually told me, "I am so lucky to have been adopted by my parents. You should hear how crazy some of those other families are." Third, we found a horse stable that offered therapeutic riding. Slowly, Emma developed the courage to take lessons with a wonderful, patient instructor. She also agreed, the summer before she began high school, to "pay" for some of her lessons by mucking the stalls and feeding the horses (and the beloved barn cats) on the weekends. Over time, with these interventions on board, Emma developed skills and maturity, became less isolated, and partic-ipated more enthusiastically and confidently in life outside of the safety of her house.

Adult containment

Emma usually won power struggles. She had an impressive array of strategies for controlling people and situations; her no-fail default option was to just stop speaking or moving. In the face of pressure, she could turn into the Great Sphinx of Giza and there was nothing anyone could do about it. Although many adults thought she'd benefit from redoubled efforts at domination and consequences, her wise parents had long since discovered that frontal approaches seldom worked. They understood, even before I came on board, that Emma needed empathy, not coercion.

We changed her school environment so she could feel safe and learn to control herself instead of others. **Using collaborative problem-solving strategies along with humor, love, and patience, Emma's parents also figured out better ways to keep her on track, developing her ability to stay regulated, to negotiate, to laugh, and to behave competently** (*question #4: Who is in charge to help me feel safe and in* *control of myself?*). Emma learned to ask for help, to describe her internal states, and to solve problems. Safely contained by a caring and consistent adult presence, Emma's anxiety diminished notably.

Pearl #3: Setting developmentally sound expectations.

From the moment of the referral, I wondered about the mismatch between Emma's level of functioning and the demands being placed on her. I reviewed what we knew of her developmental history closely, and over the next few months, I arranged for additional psychological, educational, and social-emotional testing, played with Emma, and spoke with her parents at length, adding my own opinions to the mix. **I considered Emma's progress overall, but I also explored her specific cognitive, social, emotional, and behavioral trajectories. I informed my thinking by comparing Emma's development to more typical development, and I helped Emma's parents sort out and absorb the nature of her delays and derailments** (*pearl #3*). They had left their other kids unsupervised at age 12, but Emma would get into trouble (turning on the stove, eating a pound of cheese, clogging the toilet, locking the dog in the basement) when they tried to leave her alone for even a couple of hours. Most kids her age went to the homes of other children, but Emma didn't like leaving hers. She needed to be told to shower or she'd forget; if they left scissors around, she cut up magazines and newspapers before anyone had a chance to read them. Behaviorally speaking, when we first met, Emma acted more like a preschooler than an early adolescent. Although it pained her parents to accept this fact, for a time it was not safe or reasonable to expect much more of her. Like a toddler, Emma had to be in places with adults nearby, available to her when she needed to check in, attending to her if she became distressed.

When Emma struggled, I asked first how we could change the environment and our approach—adults had to do the work to set the stage for success for her. At least initially, she was mostly in survival mode anyway; it wasn't reasonable to expect her to step up her own efforts even more. Emma needed to have more confidence in us. We had to accept her for who she was, and scaffold on the new learning, staying available nearby and ready to help as needed. Gradually, Emma began to look and act more like a young adolescent. As she developed over time, held in secure love, she also rose to life's challenges with increasing confidence, compassion, and initiative.

CONCLUDING COMMENTS

Through our years together, Emma began to gain more traction in her life. She was mainstreamed back into high school (with lots of support), had her first boyfriend, went to dances, got herself up in the morning (showered, dressed, and packed in time for an early bus), managed at home on her own when her parents were out, texted and emailed, learned how to cook, began to drive, and met friends in town for coffee. Although less anxious and more competent than when we started, Emma still lagged behind: The developmental legacy of early attachment trauma will probably have lifelong implications. But she made real gains, along her own trajectory, and was living a happier life.

If Emma needs to return to therapy, I'll be glad to see her again, but I'm not sitting by the phone. I recently received a great email from her saying she was on her way to the beach for a family vacation. Recalling the mail I had sent her from my travels, she wrote, "I'm gonna send YOU a postcard this time. LOL." We are still thinking about each other, even though we don't meet anymore. But my work is done: We now live forever in each other's hearts.

BIBLIOGRAPHY

Brooks, R. (1994). Children at risk: Fostering resilience and hope. *American Journal of Orthopsychiatry, 64,* 545-553.

Dallos, R. (2006). *Attachment narrative therapy.* NY: Open University Press.

Hughes, D. (2007). *Attachment-focused family therapy.* NY: Norton.

James, B. (1994). *Handbook for treatment of attachment-trauma problems in children.* Lexington, MA: Lexington Books.

Kagan, R. (2004). *Rebuilding attachments with traumatized children.* NY: Haworth.

Lewis, T., Amini, F., & Lannon, R. (2001). *A general theory of love.* NY: Random House.

Perry, B.D. (2006). Applying principles of neurodevelopment to clinical work with maltreated and traumatized children. In N. Webb (Ed.) *Working with traumatized youth in child welfare* (pp 27-52). NY: Guilford.

Solomon, M., & Siegel, D. (Eds.) (2003). *Healing trauma: Attachment, mind, body, and brain*. NY: Norton.

Stien, P., & Kendall, J. (2004). *Psychological trauma and the developing brain*. NY: Haworth.

Straus, M (1994). *Violence in the lives of adolescents*. NY: Norton.

Straus, M. (1998). *No-talk therapy for children and adolescents*. NY: Norton.

Straus, M. (2007). *Adolescent girls in crisis: Intervention and hope*. NY: Norton.

Taffel, R. (2005). *Breaking through to teens: A new psychotherapy for the new adolescence*. NY: Guilford.

BIOGRAPHY

Martha B. Straus, Ph.D., is a professor in the Department of Clinical Psychology at Antioch University New England Graduate School in Keene, New Hampshire, and adjunct instructor in psychiatry at Dartmouth Medical School. She maintains a private practice in Brattleboro, Vermont, provides clinical supervision and community consultation, and lectures internationally for groups and conferences. Dr. Straus is the author of numerous articles and four books, including most recently, *Adolescent Girls in Crisis: Intervention and Hope* (W. W. Norton, 2007), and the highly acclaimed *No-Talk Therapy for Children and Adolescents* (W. W. Norton, 1998).

Chapter 20
Repairing Broken Mirrors: Working With Adolescents Through the Parents

David B. Wexler, PhD

I do my best therapy with teens by doing therapy with parents. Although I have developed great relationships over the years with the adolescents I have worked with, the greatest leverage and greatest satisfaction level comes from helping the parents "get" their kid in a new and more productive way.

Parents matter. Not only because of the decisions they make or the strategies they use, but also because of the way in which the adolescent's sense of self is shaped by the mirroring of parents. Teens who claim that they are autonomous and don't care what their parents think or how they are being viewed by them are lying through their teeth.

PEARLS
In working with parents as way to get through to teens, I have found the following three guidelines—mantras for parents—to be clinical pearls.

Pearl #1. It's not your child's job to make you feel good about yourself.
Every parent is a sucker for this. Self psychology theory highlights how the *mirroring selfobject* plays a primary role in developing and maintaining a cohesive sense of self. The response from the other, the

"object," serves as a mirror reflecting back a picture of the individual—positive or negative, worthy or unworthy, valuable or degraded.

We usually think of this process in terms of how children are affected by parents or how clients are affected by therapists. But this particular pearl identifies the way it happens in reverse. Parents, too, rely on their kids to make them feel good about themselves. They shouldn't, but they do. The child is selfobject mirror to the adult. The dysfunctionality of this mirroring process from child to parent leads parents to overreact to the behaviors, achievements, mood states, and even core personalities of their kids. It's as if the parent is constantly scanning the behavior of the child and secretly asking the question: *What does this say about me?* And thus the parent is extremely vulnerable to narcissistic injuries when the child fails at a task, acts shy at a birthday party, doesn't keep his or her room clean, or simply voices autonomous opinions. The conclusion of this sequence, far too often, is that the parent aggressively turns against the child or teen for making the parent feel ineffective or anxious.

I remember the story of a second-grade teacher who felt chronically ineffective in his work. Furthermore, his 5-year-old daughter was clearly a handful, as 5-year-old daughters tend to be. One day he came home and her toys were scattered throughout the house. He told her to pick them up, and she ignored him. He raised his voice and told her again, and she had a 5-year-old smartass answer. Then he picked her up and sat her on her bed, screaming at her that she had better listen to him, *now*!

His next words, in relating this story in his marital therapy session, have always stuck with me: "I let these second-grade kids run all over me all day long, but I'll be damned if I'll let that happen in my own home!" It was all about him. When he heard himself say these words out loud, in front of his concerned wife and me, he started to cry. He told us that it just sounded so pathetic.

The message for parents, of course, is that this psychological process is normal and human—and quite dangerous. The more that parents can recognize (with full emotional honesty) how they are overreacting to their kids as mirrors to themselves, the greater capacity they have to keep it in check.

Pearl #2. *The story you tell yourself about your teen makes all the difference.*

As humans, we are hardwired to form coherent narratives about the events in our lives, and parents are always telling themselves a story about their kids. Like all stories, they are merely subjective versions of the facts. These narratives are based on a thousand historical factors and years of social conditioning, sometimes extremely valuable and sometimes extremely distorted.

When a teenager withdraws, the parents have to develop a story to explain this. *Is he clinically depressed? Is he purposely being disrespectful and ungrateful? Is this normal teenage behavior? Is he on drugs? Is this a healthy sign of separation, setting the stage for individuation? Is there something wrong with us?!*

Family therapist Jane Nelsen has advised parents this way: "Count on teenagers to be obnoxious. Step back and try to see it as cute" (Nelsen, J., & Lott, L., 1994, p. 149). That requires a new narrative, and it makes a difference. As any cognitive therapist or narrative therapist will tell you (or, for that matter, any analyst who focuses on cognitions), a new story has a profound impact on the emotional reaction of the parent and on the decisions the parent makes in choosing how to respond—or whether to respond at all.

Furthermore, teens can sense how their parents perceive them. Some parents don't quite believe this, but it can have a profound effect when the parent visualizes the teen in a positive way, with a positive aura and with a positive vision of the future for this young person. Maybe it's psychological, maybe it's cosmic, maybe it's just a way of calming the parent. But I know that when I assign parents the task of writing 10 things they are grateful for about their son or daughter, things often improve.

Pearl #3. *Nothing works always.*

The most important rule about parenting is that there are no true rules. There are guidelines, which in general seem to work reasonably well most of the time with many kids and many families. But that's about as definitive as we can be, and when parents rigidly adhere to a parenting strategy they often stifle their own creativity and fail at the task.

This reminds me of a story I once heard from the mother of a son. She had learned, from reading all the best books, that the preferred way to help build true self-esteem in kids was to say "Wow, you should feel really proud of yourself!" instead of "I feel so proud of you!" One day, when her son was 14, she said this preferred sentence to him and he looked at her, vulnerable and stricken, and said, "How come you never tell me that *you're* proud of me?" She explained her philosophy, reassured him of her pride in him—and was reminded that no advice about raising kids is always right.

CASE EXAMPLE: STUART

Stuart was the father in a family I was treating in family therapy because of ongoing conflicts between the parents and their 13-year-old daughter, Megan. At the time of the incident I am about to describe, I had been seeing them in one combination or another (a couple of times all together, one time with just Megan alone, but most of the time with just Stuart and his wife) for about 3 months, maybe eight sessions total. The most powerful sessions were those with the parents. Family-systems models inform us that change anywhere generates change (or at least disequilibrium) elsewhere. In this case, the parents' issues (particularly Stuart's) were the lever.

Stuart felt powerless—not only in managing his two kids, 13 and 11, but throughout the rest of his life as well. He came by these feelings honestly. Injured in Vietnam, he had lost a leg. He had spent many of the subsequent 30 years fighting with various VA clinics about problems with his prosthetic leg. He felt frustrated and helpless. In his job, he felt insignificant: He was low on the totem pole, not earning the respect that a man of his age and experience should have.

One day he came home from work to the wailing of Megan. Apparently, Megan's "best friend" had been spreading rumors accusing her of some sort of promiscuous sexuality. Stuart listened to his wife as she told him what had triggered all this. And he came up with a plan, in the spirit of being a good father who feels the pain of his kids and wants to do everything he can to come through for them when they are hurting.

Stuart announced his plan: "Okay, here's what we're going to do. We're going to call your friend's mother and insist that she get her daughter to apologize. *And* she needs to go back to the kids that she told this to and tell them that she made it up and that she is sorry!'"

Megan's response to this plan was to wail "*Nooooo!*" even louder than before, the way only a 13-year-old girl can wail. Stuart's wife turned to him and quietly stated the obvious. "I don't think she wants us to do that."

Stuart's response was to stand up and lay down the law: "I know what I'm doing here. It's time that you all listened to me for once! If you don't go along with my plan, it's a sign that you don't respect me—and I'm outta here!"

Neither wife nor daughter said anything. Stuart stormed out of the house and actually spent the night in a hotel. He came back the next morning rather sheepishly, realizing that he had thrown an adult version of a temper tantrum.

When he had blown up, he didn't know how to recognize what he was going through, or how to name it or express it. He just felt compelled to escape it through a grandiose attempt to feel powerful. He lost his perspective; suddenly the unfolding drama had turned into a drama only about himself.

His daughter's distress (and his family's rejection of his plan) had become a broken mirror, and her drama had become merely a reflection on him. He had not been capable of recognizing that this was actually a potential *twinship* (another form of selfobject) and bonding experience. In reality, they were all feeling powerless together.

To his credit, Stuart—a good man behaving badly if there ever was one—understood soon afterward what had happened. **This was the most important issue for Stuart to come to grips with: His daughter's unhappiness and his family's reluctance to adopt his plan was not a referendum on him** (*Pearl #1. It's not your child's job to make you feel good about yourself.*). He came to realize how vulnerable he was to feeling ineffective; he had simply become unbearably overwhelmed with feelings of powerlessness.

I approached Stuart in this situation utilizing the fundamental principles of "pacing and leading" as originally developed by Milton Erickson. I needed to demonstrate my profound respect of the broken-mirror experience (the "pacing" part) and still help guide him toward a more productive way of viewing himself, his family, and his life story (the "leading" part). I said to Stuart: "I can only imagine how painful it must have been for you to see Megan hurting so much—because I know you love your daughter very much. And you are a good man, with good values, and you really want to be the type of man who can protect his family and the people he loves. You must have felt so damn helpless seeing her in such distress and not knowing how to make it better. And you have had plenty of experience with feeling helpless in your life."

"And this is a time when it makes sense to remember that no man can always fix his family's problems—that this is not a reflection on your manhood or your worth as a father. This is a time to pull out of your hat the parenting response that fits the situation. This situation called for simple empathy and simple patience. Those are the manly responses sometimes. I know you can do that."

When Stuart realized how many of his own issues and needs he was bringing to the table in these everyday family dramas, he developed one of the most valuable skills in parenting. He was able to access his observing ego and watch what was happening to him and others, then generate a response based on these observations.

Stuart had panicked when he told himself the wrong story about this incident. His initial narrative, computed in milliseconds as narratives generally are (although the blueprint takes a lifetime to develop), told him not only that his self-worth as a father was at stake, but also that his daughter was at great risk and could not recover from this trauma without his active intervention. In reality, she was over it 24 hours later and proved, again, to be considerably more resilient than this worried father realized.

Stuart's wife coached him on this: "You need to trust Megan more. I know she seems so wild and so emotional a lot, but it all blows over really quickly. Half the time, when we do nothing in response to all her drama, she does just fine. It's really better that way."

I couldn't have said it better myself. **Stuart was projecting his own insecurity and pessimism onto his daughter. Much of his life overwhelmed him; he couldn't imagine that his daughter was much different, and he thus felt anxiety about her dysphoric emotional** states. **But her story was different from his, which his wife and I continued to remind him of.** (*Pearl #2. The story you tell yourself about your teen makes all the difference.*)

In this family drama, Stuart was operating on principles he had learned from parenting classes and magazine articles: A good parent should be prepared to take action to help his child. He wanted, understandably, to make sure that his daughter knew that he cared about her enough not just to use active listening but also to take charge of a threat to her well-being.

Good parental values are based on sound generalizations like taking decisive action to protect your children. But nothing works always. **In Stuart's case, this was a time to reflect and collaborate rather than boldly take intervening action** (*pearl #3*). It turned out that this was a time to trust his daughter's resiliency rather than to panic because of her immediate (and, as it turned out, temporary) despair and distress.

One thing to be aware of in this case and in working with parents of teens in general: Helping Stuart recognize his own issues and helping him respond more constructively had a significant ripple effect on the family system and on the teen in particular. And no small credit for the eventual success in this case was due to Stuart's ability to take responsibility for his "misbehavior" and directly communicate this to his daughter. This allowed her to be compassionate toward him and see him as a flawed but well-meaning "good man behaving badly"—not just a clueless and controlling father. This change was worth more than a lot of individual therapy sessions with her could ever have been.

I continued to see this family for several years, and I watched Megan grow and mature. Her father's increasing self-acceptance and clarity about his daughter, and about his role in her development, helped pave the way.

CONCLUDING COMMENTS

For the past 25 years, I have been working on ways to integrate central principles from self psychology with more practical interventions from cognitive-behavioral therapy and solution-oriented psychotherapy. What I know now, more clearly than ever before, is how crucial the experience of a cohesive, confident, and integrated self is to human well-being and to human relationships. Self psychology theory teaches us that the range of selfobject relationships and experiences is central to maintaining this cohesive self. And most powerful of all is the *mirroring selfobject*, the breakdown of which I refer to as the "broken mirror." Other selfobject relationships, such as the *idealized selfobject*, the *twinship selfobject*, the *adversarial selfoject*, the *efficacy selfobject*, and so on, enhance this state of self-cohesion. Therapists' awareness of the power of these selfobject relationships, ability to help clients identify them, and ability to foster them in the therapeutic relationship and in family relationships are crucial.

To my everlasting satisfaction and delight, I have discovered that many previously defended people are surprisingly receptive to identifying and taking responsibility for their own broken mirrors—and to moving forward into a more mature level of functioning as a result. I have seen many parents learn this concept and remind themselves of pearl #1 *(It's not my child's job to make me feel good about myself)* with great results.

Integrated into this approach is a deep appreciation of the profound effect that cognitions (story, narrative, beliefs, perspective) have on subsequent emotions and subsequent behaviors. When a parent reframes narratives in a positive (or at least more productive) way, lots of other things fall into place. The bratty child becomes the child who is in a bad mood. The teen who refuses to try harder at anything becomes the teen who is terrified of feeling incompetent or ashamed. The middle-school girl who plays social games is trying to learn about the world of relationships. And the teenager whose room is a mess is meeting his job description—not necessarily predicting a life of sloth.

When the parent thinks like this, he or she is less susceptible to the demons generated by the broken mirror. Better parenting results.

But insight and therapeutic relationships are not the only way to foster self-cohesion. Any experience that enhances these selfobject needs does this job. When it comes to helping parents offer their best possible selves to the teens that need the best from them, it often astonishes me that some of the simplest principles from cognitive-behavioral interventions can have such a powerful effect: active listening, respectful and assertive communication, making "I statements," positive reinforcement. When their personal issues are interfering less, parents are able to utilize many of these interpersonal behaviors with very rewarding results. Practically anyone can use these—except when broken mirrors or excessive anxieties are getting in the way.

Finally, the third pearl of wisdom comes from years of personal and professional experience, especially personal and professional failures. I have been a parent of two kids, now grown, and there were many times that the well-researched approach recommended by parenting books completely backfired and only a counterintuitive approach got us anywhere. My wife taught me this. Sometimes, when everyone around us would have screamed for discipline and consequences, a simple conversation worked better. At other times, going for soothing, affectively attuned responses to these kids only made things worse. For all of us working with the complexities of helping teens and families, rigid orthodoxy is determined to fail. Respecting the personal experiences and intuitions of both parents and kids, and negotiating creative strategies, should always trump what the rules say—or at least carry a lot of weight.

BIBLIOGRAPHY

Nelsen, J., & Lott, L. (1994). *Positive discipline for teenagers*. Rocklin, CA: Prima Publishing.

Wexler, D. B. (1991). *The adolescent self: Strategies for self-management, self-soothing, & self-esteem in adolescents*. New York: Norton.

Wexler, D. B. (2004). *When good men behave badly: Change your behavior, change your relationship*. Oakland, CA: New Harbinger.

Wexler, D. B. (2005). *Is he depressed or what? What to do when the man you love is irritable, moody, and withdrawn*. Oakland, CA: New Harbinger.

Wexler, D. B. (2006). *STOP domestic violence: Innovative skills, techniques, options and plans for better relationships*. New York: W.W. Norton.

Wexler, D. B. (2009). *Men in therapy: New approaches for effective treatment*. New York: W.W. Norton.

BIOGRAPHY

David B. Wexler, PhD, is a clinical psychologist in San Diego and the executive director of the nonprofit Relationship Training Institute. He has received the Distinguished Contribution to Psychology award from the California Psychological Association and the Practitioner of the Year award from the Society for the Psychological Study of Men and Masculinity, a division of the American Psychological Association. Wexler is the author of many books and has appeared on hundreds of radio and television programs throughout North America to help educate the public about relationships in conflict and how to resolve them. He can be contacted through www.RTIprojects.org.

Section Eight:
Conclusion

Chapter 21

From the Inside Out:
The Therapist's Attachment Patterns
as Sources of Insight and Impasse

David Wallin, PhD

For the last 10 years or so, my work—practicing, teaching, and writing about psychotherapy—has been inspired by, and organized around, my interest in the clinical applications of attachment theory research. The culmination of that labor is a book, *Attachment in Psychotherapy* (2007), in which I identified three findings that appeared to have the most profound and fertile implications for treatment: first, that co-created *relationships of attachment* are the key context for development; second, that *preverbal experience* makes up the core of the developing self; and third, that *the stance of the self toward experience* predicts attachment security better than the facts of personal history themselves. Accordingly, my approach as a clinician has focused on the therapeutic relationship as a developmental crucible, the centrality of the nonverbal dimension, and the transformative influence of reflection and mindfulness. This way of working leads directly to the three "clinical pearls of wisdom" I'll briefly introduce and elaborate upon in the next few pages, and then illustrate with clinical material.

PEARLS

Pearl #1. Know your own attachment patterns.
Despite the reality that "we are the tools of our trade" (Pearlman &

Saakvitne, 1995), the impact of the therapist's own psychology upon his or her clinical effectiveness is a topic the psychotherapy literature has largely ignored. From the attachment perspective within which I work, this omission appears very problematic. At the heart of the matter is my assumption that, in childhood and psychotherapy alike, the relationship is where the developmental action is. Just as the child's original attachment relationships make development possible, it is ultimately the new relationship of attachment with the therapist that allows the patient to change. But development, of course, takes two. For this reason, the finding of attachment research that *the parent's security, insecurity, or trauma is regularly transmitted to the child* must surely catch our attention. For it suggests that not only as parents but also perhaps as therapists, our ability to generate a secure attachment relationship will be profoundly affected by the legacy of our own attachment relationships—a legacy that is, for many of us who choose this work, marked by trauma. Regardless of our theoretical orientation, then, our own attachment patterns may well be the single most influential factor in shaping—that is, enhancing but also constraining—our capacity to create with the patient a genuinely therapeutic relationship.

Let me be more specific. Attachment history is "engraved" in the psyche. It takes the form of internal representations and rules for processing information that derive from our experiences of what has and has not "worked" in relation to particular attachment figures. These "rules of attachment" are quite literally rules to live by, given that they initially emerge from interactions with caregivers upon whom we depend for our very survival. The key issue here is what has been ruled in and what has been ruled out in the relationship with our original attachment figures. Put differently, the question is: What have we been able to *integrate* (because it elicited an attuned response from attachment figures) and what have we needed to defensively *dissociate* (because it threatened the survival-critical attachment bond)? The answers to this question shape our attachment patterns, determining not only how we *relate* to ourselves and to others, but also what we allow ourselves to *know*. For what in infancy began as behavioral "strategies" for optimizing the relationship to attachment figures soon become emotional, cognitive, and attentional strategies that determine how freely we can feel, think, sense, and remember. As therapists, then, our own (more or less troubled) attachment history—marked by the dissociations it has imposed and the integration we have managed to achieve, often with the help of personal therapy—is always both an asset and a liability.

On the one hand, we know others most profoundly on the basis of what we know about ourselves. Such self-knowledge can be a therapeutic resource to the extent that we have been able to recognize, tolerate, and make meaningful sense of the painful aspects of our own history—that is, to *integrate* them. Then our personal experience may confer a heightened capacity for empathic understanding grounded in our partial identification with the patient's own difficult experience. Moreover, the freedom we have won to think deeply and feel fully can equip us well to kindle or strengthen the patient's capacities for reflection and emotion regulation. Finally—because of the mutual reciprocal influence therapists and patients inevitably exert upon one another—our real-time awareness of the ways *our* attachment patterns are presently being enacted with the patient can help to illuminate the patient's *own* attachment patterns.

On the other hand, the impact of the therapist's history—particularly experiences that have yet to be integrated—can have adverse effects on treatment. To begin with, our view of the patient can be clouded by what we're unable or unwilling to know about ourselves. Additionally, our own attachment-derived skew toward thinking at the expense of feeling—or vice versa—can undermine our ability to upgrade the patient's ability to think and feel in an integrated fashion. Most problematically, impasses in treatment can arise out of the need to keep at bay our own unbearable, and hence dissociated, experiences of self or other. These impasses can take the form of *collusions* or *collisions*. In keeping with our own attachment rules and patterns, we may find ourselves colluding with the patient to avoid experiences that are troubling to us and, not infrequently, to the patient as well. Alternatively, disowned aspects of ourselves—not only our dissociated experiences and our dread of them, but also our wish to work them through—can be defensively "relocated" in the patient. Then we may find ourselves caught in collisions with patients who evoke reactions in us that initially arose (but often had to be suppressed) in response to our original attachment figures. Or we may find ourselves embroiled in conflict when we unconsciously push our *patients* to take on developmental challenges that we have only ambivalently or incompletely addressed ourselves. As therapists, in short, we need to be aware of the ambiguous relationship between what we recognize in the patient on the basis of overlapping experience and what we project onto the patient on the basis of what we've yet to fully integrate in ourselves.

Pearl #2. Ask, "What am I actually doing with this particular patient?"

From an attachment perspective, therapy heals when the quality of the therapist's presence and interventions can help patients both to deconstruct the attachment patterns of the past and to construct fresh ones in the present. From a slightly different angle, the therapist aims to create a relationship within which the patient may be able to integrate experiences that have previously had to remain dissociated. But our deliberate efforts to offer the patient a new and healing attachment relationship are invariably complicated, if not undermined outright, by the hidden pressures and constraints of our *own* attachment patterns. Hence the necessity of the question: "What am I actually *doing* with this particular patient?" Scrupulously examining what in fact we're doing as we relate to the patient can help us to access the nonverbal subtext of the therapeutic conversation, which may in turn illuminate the impact of our own attachment patterns as they are enacted in the relationship with the patient. Such self-scrutiny also has the invaluable potential to reveal the perceptible edge of dissociated experience in *both* partners in the therapeutic couple—which is vital because accessing dissociated experience is a precondition for its eventual integration. To make all this clearer requires a brief turn to the realm of nonverbal experience.

All of us are profoundly affected by experiences that are difficult to put into words. Such experiences can be hard to articulate for different reasons: Their origins may be preverbal, they may be defensively dissociated, or they may have occurred in the shadow of trauma that disabled the brain structures that underpin speech and autobiographical memory. Though unspoken or unspeakable, these implicit experiences—Bollas (1987) called them the "unthought known"—are nonetheless communicated. How so? In treatment, therapists and patients regularly *evoke in each other* and *enact with each other* aspects of themselves (memories, feelings, conflicts, internalized images of self and other) that they are unable to put into words. Both for better and for worse, these nonverbal communications generate the web of transference-countertransference *enactments* that arises as the attachment patterns of therapist and patient interlock. And given the inescapable reciprocal influence that helps shape such enactments, the therapist's attachment patterns are nearly always manifest in ways that are meaningfully, rather than adventitiously, related to those of the patient.

Repeatedly asking ourselves what we're actually doing with the patient can thus help us both to identify our role in these ongoing enactments and to access the dissociated experience that psychotherapy aims to integrate. To be most effective, the self-inquiry I advocate should pose not only the key question—"What am I actually *doing* with this patient?"—but also two others aimed at deepening our understanding: "What is the *implicit relational meaning* of what I'm doing?" and "What might be my *motivation* for doing what I'm doing?" As I'll explain shortly, the first question can best be answered when the therapist mobilizes a *mindful* stance, the next two when the therapist mobilizes a reflective or *mentalizing* stance.

Pearl #3. Mobilize first a mindful stance, then a reflective or "mentalizing" stance.

Recognizing our role in enactments can be a considerable challenge because we're never altogether transparent to ourselves. We remain ignorant of much of what we do, partly because it is simply an automatic, unreflective expression of who we are, and partly because we tend to *suppress* awareness of what might trouble or unsettle us. The latter can be a particular problem for therapists whose history of trauma has imposed dissociations, including—almost universally—dissociated feelings of shame.

Adopting a stance of *mindfulness*—the centerpiece of a 2,500-year-old Buddhist tradition—can help to overcome these barriers, because it breaks the trance of conducting treatment as if we were on autopilot. When we aim to be mindful, it's as if we "snap out of it" by deliberately choosing to pay attention to our here-and-now experience with the patient as, moment by moment, this experience unfolds— neither judging nor evaluating it, but simply pausing to notice what we're doing while we're doing it. Moreover, cultivating mindfulness promotes acceptance, so mindfulness can function as an antidote to the shame that constricts self-awareness. Finally, a mindful stance not only facilitates the recognition of our role in enactments, but may also help to loosen their grip.

Simply asking ourselves what we're doing with the patient is a kind of "mindfulness in action" (Safran & Muran, 2003) that allows us to grasp—at a literal, explicit, "facts of the case" level—the details of our participation in the ongoing enactment. Then, having explicitly identified the nature of our action (empathizing, interpreting, offering advice, making a joke), we need to understand its implicit meaning— particularly in light of the relationship between our own psychology and that of the patient. For again, the clinician's attachment patterns as played out in the therapeutic interaction are nearly always meaningfully related to the attachment patterns of the patient. In trying to understand our conduct both in terms of its implicit relational meaning and in terms of our motivation, our key resource is our ability to *mentalize*—that is, to make sense of behavior by inferring the mental states (feelings, beliefs, desires) that underlie it.

With one rather prickly patient, for example, my initial self-inquiry—mindfulness in action—allowed me to see that what I was actually doing early in the session was . . . nothing. At the explicit behavioral level, I was making room for the free flow of the patient's spoken thoughts by making sure to share none of my own. Privately exploring the implicit relational meaning of my silence, I recognized my fear that whatever words I spoke, my patient would experience them as intrusive and hurtful—and would probably become angry. Yet I felt that I was in a bind, for if I couldn't speak, I couldn't help. And as for the question of my motivation? I realized that with this particular patient (and no doubt with others as well), I was bending over backwards to avoid experiencing myself as *destructive*.

Eventually I broke my silence by sharing my dilemma about speaking—wanting to say something useful, but fearing his anger in response to words of mine he was likely to experience as disruptive incursions on his own thoughts. This disclosure allowed him to share with me a related dilemma of his own: Should he risk "letting me in" when his history had proven that his only safety lay in mobilizing an off-putting "force field" of ever-ready anger? As he went on to describe the "three-headed monster" (narcissistic father, seductive mother, sadistic brother) against which his force field had originally been deployed, it suddenly occurred to me that the fear of destructiveness that had shut me up was linked with another kind of monster: a dreaded, shame-ridden facet of myself that I had recently come to call the "Bug."

CASE EXAMPLE: JACOB, THE "BUG," AND I

To begin at the middle of this story, I'll say that one memorable day I was sitting with a patient who, despite a history replete with horrific trauma, seemed to bear no visible scars. Apart from some discontent with the quality of his intimate relationships, Jacob was apparently a very happy man who lived a charmed life. Yet he lived, I felt, on the surface. To keep safely distant from the neglect, loss, and abuse of his traumatic past, he was distant from himself while letting no one fully know him. To offset this distance and compensate for what (I felt) was missing in his life—the experience of being known and deeply cared for as a whole person—he indulged in various forms of "acting out" that put him at considerable risk.

On the day in question, Jacob was telling me with pleasure about still another stroke of good fortune that had recently come his way; he followed this with some uncurious words about his risky behavior, a little as if he were confessing. Such communications from Jacob were all too familiar to me, as were my responses to them. To today's good news, I responded as if I shared in his pleasure; to the confession, as if his conduct were worth exploring in an effort to better understand its meaning and allure. Then, rather suddenly, it struck me that the words

I was speaking to Jacob had begun to have a hollow sound and that his face in response to them was unexpressive. Plainly something was off. **Deliberately attempting now to land in the present moment, I paused to silently inquire of myself, *What was it that I was actually* doing *as I related to Jacob?* (*Pearl #2.*)** I became aware of the effort I was expending in order to be there for him, for it certainly wasn't coming naturally. **I realized that I had been operating as if on autopilot, without thoughtful intention, almost compulsively offering Jacob what amounted to a kind of pseudo-therapy. If I were to talk about what was really going on inside myself, I would have to say something about my anger and my envy that Jacob seemed to be able to do whatever he wanted whenever he wanted to do it—with no repercussions or even pangs of conscience! I was extremely distressed at the intensity of what I was feeling and tried, silently and privately, with little success, to make sense of what I was experiencing. (*Pearl #3: Mobilize first a mindful stance, then a reflective or "mentalizing" stance.*)** I felt immobilized and realized that, in fact, I'd been effectively immobilized for some time. I recognized that my patient and I were at an impasse.

Taking a step back for a moment, I'd say that sometimes as therapists we're capable—having recognized the impasses in which we're lodged—of understanding and resolving those impasses through diligent self-analysis and dialogue, negotiation, and exploration with the patient. On the other hand, there's often truth to the old joke that the problem with self-analysis is the countertransference. As I've mentioned, we're never completely transparent to ourselves, in part because we're compelled to remain blind to sights that deeply trouble us. Moreover, our capacity for useful reflection is always compromised when we find ourselves gripped by intensely disturbing feelings. Hence the necessity at times for the "two-person mentalizing" available in the form of consultation and the therapist's own therapy, both of which I made use of in attempting to resolve the impasse with Jacob.

In a small group consultation with colleagues Susan Sands and David Shaddock, I talked about my experiences with Jacob—and specifically the problem of doing therapy with someone who communicates as if *he* has no problems. With an obvious surplus of emotion I discussed the anger and envy I had recently become aware I felt in the presence of this man who seemed to possess the psychological and practical wherewithal to live with nearly perfect freedom. I also discussed the repetitious and frustrating sequence of the work with Jacob's high-risk behavior: how we would approach it, seem to get somewhere, then find it slipping off the radar screen, only to have it reappear again—and again. The patient I sketched seemed large and strong, capable of being intimidating—though I wasn't aware of feeling intimidated. What I *did* often feel with Jacob was a sense of *lack*, as if I had much less to offer than I usually feel I do. Sometimes it was hard to think clearly or feel fully in his presence. At worst I could feel deadened or invisible. Rarely did I feel needed.

About all this my colleagues had many useful things to say. But what opened my eyes and my heart was Susan's saying, "We now know about what it's like for you to be with him, but can you tell us something about how he got to be the way he is? Something about his childhood?" I literally felt stunned to realize that I hadn't said a single word about Jacob's experiences growing up, which were largely experiences of coping with trauma. As I began to describe this lonely story of constant squalor and intermittent horror, I had two nearly simultaneous images so vivid that they were like living presences: The first was of Jacob as a helpless and humiliated little boy; the second was of myself as a similar kind of little boy. And what felt like the superimposition of our related—though certainly not identical—experiences, one upon the other, brought me to tears. As I sobbed, the meaning of the impasse with Jacob crystallized for me, virtually in an instant.

In my own therapy I had recently been struggling with a profound and disturbing set of feelings that I had come to refer to as the "Bug" (think Kafka's *Metamorphosis*). I initially experienced these utterly excruciating emotional sensations as nearly impossible to bear and no easier to name, though the visceral sense they carried was that I was disgusting, destructive, dangerous. Because they were inside me, or because I felt at some primal level that they simply *were* me, there seemed no escape from them save through self-destruction. Perhaps needless to say, I never believed that the Bug was all of me, so I could feel the self-destructive impulses without feeling compelled to act on them. What I have come to believe is that the Bug is a residue of my preverbal experiences with a mother who found her baby's needs (and undoubtedly her own needs) disgusting and dangerous.

The emotional response to being treated as a bug is probably best summed up with the word *shame*—the nearly intolerable pain of feeling not just that one has *done* something bad, but that one *is* bad. In my own therapy I had stumbled upon this dissociated pain and I was apparently averse to dragging Jacob—who I "knew" intuitively was as vulnerable to it as I—into that particular torture chamber. Nor evidently did I wish to spend any more time there myself, even vicariously, if I could somehow avoid it.

And so I had avoided it—by colluding with Jacob in living out a relationship between the two of us in a safer realm where need, vulnerability, and shame were relegated to the sidelines. At center stage in that psychological Green Zone were variations on the theme of omnipotence (and, perhaps, impotence). **Rather than experience the danger of seeing or feeling in Jacob the shamed and fearful boy (or baby) with whom I might painfully identify, I had been focused self-protectively—if angrily, enviously, and somewhat impotently—on the man who could do anything.** (*Pearl #1. Know your own attachment patterns.*)

Perhaps unremarkably, when I next met with Jacob our relationship had a profoundly different and deeper "feel"—I presume because, through Jacob in a sense, I had further integrated a disowned part of myself. This allowed me both to *be* more of a whole person when I was with him and to experience *him* as more of a whole person. Of course, there was no "miracle cure." But shortly after the session we agreed to meet more frequently and to address in a more deliberate and head-on fashion the "acting out" with which we had previously grappled superficially, only to let it slip away. In the sessions following that pivotal meeting, Jacob also began to talk—often pointing with his hand in the direction of his belly—about his vague, shameful sense of inferiority and its origin in the troubling experience of his early years.

CONCLUDING COMMENTS

My choice to concentrate in these pages on the impact of the therapist's *own* troubling origins and attachment patterns has to do, in part, with the fact that this important matter tends to be slighted in most of the clinical literature—as it does, I suspect, in much of our clinical practice—despite the fact that the primary creative instrument of the therapist is a *self* whose resources and liabilities are originally forged in the crucible of personal history. And as I have mentioned, the therapist's personal history is liable to be one that bears the scars of trauma. Strikingly in this connection, attachment research shows that many infants classified at 12 months as "disorganized" (presumably as the result of growing up with attachment figures whose *own* unresolved trauma made them frightening to their babies) have by age 6 developed a "controlling-caregiving" strategy. It may well be, then, that early on many of us were groomed to be therapists as we learned to take control of our own frightening attachment figures by taking care of them.

In suggesting that the therapist's attachment patterns are often shaped by trauma, I am departing from a conventional view that patients and therapists alike may be tempted to embrace—namely, that the vulnerabilities in the therapeutic couple reside primarily if not exclusively in the patient. This view is a fiction that may serve the hopes of the patient and the self-protective needs of the therapist. But it is a fiction that diverts attention from the important reality that it is actually the interaction of the attachment patterns of *both* partners— their strengths and vulnerabilities, their integrations and dissociations—that ultimately determines the extent to which a new and healing attachment relationship will develop in psychotherapy

I'm proposing that we regard the therapist's vulnerabilities, like those of the patient, as integral and inevitable facts of life in psychotherapy. They are not necessarily best understood as psychopathological. Instead they may be seen as evidence of human imperfection. These vulnerabilities—in interaction with those of the patient—can generate difficulties in therapy that present obstacles, but also opportunities. When enactments engage the core vulnerabilities of the patient *and* the therapist, there is a risk of rupture, to be sure, but there is also the potential to provide the patient with a corrective relational experience and the therapist with a chance to further his or her own ever-unfinished psychological work.

BIBLIOGRAPHY

Bollas, C. (1987). *The shadow of the object: Psychoanalysis of the unthought known.* New York: Columbia University Press.

Goldbart, S., & Wallin, D. J. (1998). *Mapping the terrain of the heart: Passion, tenderness, and the capacity to love.* Lanham, MD: Jason Aronson.

Pearlman, L. A., & Saakvitne, K. W. (1995). *Trauma and the therapist: Countertransference and vicarious traumatization in psychotherapy with incest survivors.* New York: Norton.

Safran, J., & Muran, C. (2003). *Negotiating the therapeutic alliance: A relational treatment guide.* New York: Guilford.

Wallin, D. J. (2007). *Attachment in psychotherapy.* New York: Guilford.

BIOGRAPHY

David Wallin, PhD, is a clinical psychologist and author in private practice in Albany and Mill Valley, California. A graduate of Harvard who received his doctorate from the Wright Institute in Berkeley, he has been practicing, teaching, and writing about psychotherapy for nearly three decades. His recent book, *Attachment in Psychotherapy*, is presently being translated into seven languages. He is the coauthor (with Stephen Goldbart) of *Mapping the Terrain of the Heart: Passion, Tenderness, and the Capacity to Love.* He has lectured on attachment and psychotherapy in Europe, Canada, and throughout the U.S. For more information, please see www.davidjwallin.com/index.cfm.

Index

In this index, *f* denotes *figure*.

12-step meetings, 38, 40, 42

AAI, *see* Adult Attachment Inventory
    (AAI)
abandonment, 135–36
abreaction, 182–83, 187
abuse, *see* trauma and therapy
accelerated experiential-dynamic
    psychotherapy (AEDP), 43, 44, 45
access, to mature parts of self, 145–46,
    150–51
accountability, with adolescents, 209–10,
    213–14
addictions
    of behavior and thinking, 36–37, 39, 40
    case example, 37–41
    stories of self as, 25, 29, 30
adolescents and therapy
    accountability, 209–10, 213–14
    affect regulation, 219–20
    autonomy, 215–16, 220–21, 227–29
    case examples, 210–17, 222–30, 235–38
    content control, 208–9, 214–15
    credibility, 208, 212
    developmentally sound expectations,
        221–22, 229–30
    empathy, 219–20, 223–24

four questions, addressed, 220–21,
    225–29
goals of, 209
identity, 220–21, 225–26
mirroring selfobject, 232–33, 236–37, 239
nothing works always, 234–35, 238, 240
parental involvement, 232–40
principle of "least want", 207
rigidity, 234–35, 240
themes of, 220–21, 225–29
treatment effectiveness, 209, 217
adoption, *see* attachment trauma
"adoring eyes", 219–20, 223–24
Adult Attachment Inventory (AAI), 44
AEDP, *see* accelerated experiential-
    dynamic psychotherapy (AEDP)
affect
    array, 3, 4, 4*f*, 5, 8, 9
    expression of, matching or leading,
        170–71, 175, 179
    see also nonverbal expression
    transformance and, 44–45, 49–50, 53
affect regulation
    in adolescent therapy, 219–20
    in attachment trauma, 43, 45–46, 48, 51
    in children's therapy, 170–71, 172, 173
    in couples therapy, 144–54
affirmation rituals, 97
aggression case example, 174–78